History and National Destiny
Ethnosymbolism and its

History and National Destiny:
Ethnosymbolism and its Critics

Edited by

Montserrat Guibernau and John Hutchinson

Blackwell
Publishing

9600 Garsington Road, Oxford OX4 2DQ, UK
350 Main Street, Malden, MA 02148-5018, USA
550 Swanston Street, Carlton South, Melbourne, Victoria 3053, Australia

First published 2004 as Nations and Nationalism Special issue 10(1&2) by
Blackwell Publishing Ltd

Library of Congress Cataloging-in-Publication Data has been Applied for

A catalogue record for this title is available from the British Library.

ISBN 1-4051-2391-5 (paperback)

Set in India
by Macmillan
Printed and bound in the United Kingdom
by Page Brothers

The publisher's policy is to use permanent paper from mills that operate a
sustainable forestry policy, and which has been manufactured from pulp
processed using acid-free and elementary chlorine-free practices. Furthermore,
the publisher ensures that the text paper and cover board used have met
acceptable environmental accreditation standards.

For further information on
Blackwell Publishing, visit our website:
http://www.blackwellpublishing.com

Contents

Contributors

JOHN A. ARMSTRONG has been Emeritus Professor of Political Science of the University of Wisconsin, Madison, residing in his native city of St. Augustine since his retirement from the active faculty, where he taught from 1954 to 1986. Among his many works, *Nations before Nationalism* (1982) has been particularly influential. At present he is exploring the role of world civilizations, especially in relation to nation-states and religions.

BRUCE CAUTHEN is Lecturer in the Department of Political Science, Emory University, Atlanta, Georgia. He has written extensively on Afrikaner and Confederate nationalism.

WALKER CONNOR is currently Distinguished Visiting Professor at Middlebury College. Over the past four decades, he has published numerous articles and books dealing with national identity and nationalism including his seminar work, *Ethno-nationalism: the Quest for Understanding* (1994). He is currently completing a monograph on national self-determination to be published by Cambridge University Press.

MIROSLAV HROCH, studied History and Literature at the Charles University Prague 1951/56 (PhD 1962). He became Professor of General History in 1989, and has been Professor in History in the Faculty of Humanities since 2000. His main fields of research are trade and politics in the seventeenth century; comparative studies of revolutions; and nation-forming processes in Europe.

THOMAS HYLLAND ERIKSEN is Professor of Social Anthropology at the University of Oslo. His main research interests are identity politics, globalization and the history of anthropology. His most recent books in English are *Tyranny of the Moment* (2001), *A History of Anthropology* (with F. S. Nielsen, 2001) and *Globalisation: Studies in Anthropology* (2003).

JOSHUA A. FISHMAN is Distinguished University Research Professor, Social Sciences, Emeritus, at Yeshiva University (NY) and Visiting Professor of Linguistics and Education at Stanford University (CA) and at New York University (NY). He has been at work on language and ethnic identity since before 1972 when his *Language and Nationalism* first appeared. His *Handbook and Ethnic Identity* (1999) and *Can Threatened Languages be Saved?* (2001) are his most recent books in this area.

MONTSERRAT GUIBERNAU, PhD University of Cambridge, is Reader in Politics at the Open University. Her main publications include: *Catalan Nationalism: francoism, transition and democracy* (Routledge, 2004) *Nations without States* (Polity Press, 1999); and *Nationalisms: the nation-state and nationalism in the twentieth century* (Polity Press, 1996). She is the editor of *Governing European Diversity* (Sage-OU, 2001) and *Nationalism: debates and dilemmas for a new millennium* (Proa Press-CETC, 2000). She has co-edited *The Ethnicity Reader: nationalism, multiculturalism and migration* (Polity Press, 1997), *Understanding Nationalism* (Polity Press, 2001), and *The Conditions of Diversity in Multinational Democracies* (IRPP-MacGill University Press, 2003). She is currently preparing the book *National Identity and its Future* (Polity Press, 2004).

JOHN HUTCHINSON is Senior Lecturer in Nationalism in the Government Department at the London School of Economics. He is the author of *The Dynamics of Cultural Nationalism* (Allen & Unwin, 1987) and *Modern Nationalism* (Fontana, 1994) and has completed a third monograph *Nations as Zones of Conflict* (Sage). He has co-edited with Anthony Smith *Nationalism* (Oxford University Press, 1994), *Ethnicity* (Oxford University Press, 1996), and *Nationalism* (Routledge, 2000), and with Montserrat Guibernau, *Understanding Nationalism* (Polity, 2001).

MARY KALDOR is Professor in the Government Department at the London School of Economics. She has written on global civil society, new wars especially in the Balkans, and humanitarian intervention. Her most recent book is *Global Civil Society: An Answer to War* (Polity, 2003).

ERIC KAUFMANN is Lecturer in Politics and Sociology at Birkbeck College, University of London, UK and holds a PhD from the London School of Economics. He is the author of *The Rise and Fall of Anglo-America: The Decline of Dominant Ethnicity in the United States* (Harvard University Press, forthcoming, spring 2004) and editor of *The Challenge of Ethnicity: Majority Groups and Dominant Minorities* (Routledge, forthcoming, fall 2004). Most recently, his work has appeared in *Ethnic & Racial Studies* (23 June 2001), *Historical Sociology* (14 January 2001) and *Geopolitics* (7 February 2002).

ATHENA S. LEOUSSI (PhD) is Lecturer in Sociology and European Studies and Associate Member of the Department of History at the University of Reading, UK. She is also Curator of the Archive of National Visual Symbols. Her publications include, *Nationalism and Classicism: the Classical Body as National Symbol in Nineteenth-Century England and France* (1998), *Circles of Light: the Making of the Ionides Art Collection in the Victoria and Albert Museum* (2001), and the *Encyclopaedia of Nationalism* (2001).

ANTHONY D. SMITH is Professor of Ethnicity and Nationalism in the Government Department at the London School of Economics. His previous publications include *Theories of Nationalism* (1971, 1983), *The Ethnic Origins of Nations* (1986), *National Identity* (1991), *Nationalism and Modernism* (1998), *The Nation in History* (2000) and *Nationalism* (2001). His most recent book, *Chosen Peoples*, was published at the end of 2003.

STEIN TØNNESSON is a historian specialising in global and Asian history. Before coming to the International Peace Research Institute (PRIO) as Director in 2001, he led a research project at the University of Oslo on disputes concerning sovereignty to islands and maritime delimitation in the South China Sea. During the 1992–98 period, he led a project at the Nordic Institute of Asian Affairs (NIAS) in Copenhagen on Southeast Asian nation-building in the 1940s. He has published books on war and revolution in Vietnam, Norwegian sports history, and national identity in Asia.

OLIVER ZIMMER is Lecturer in Modern European History at the University of Durham. He is the author of *A Contested Nation: History, Memory* and *Nationalism in Switzerland 1761–1891* (Cambridge University Press, 2003) and *Nationalism in Europe 1890–1940* (Palgrave/Macmillan, 2003).

Preface

For over thirty years Anthony D. Smith has been one of the most original and productive explorers of the origins and characteristics of ethnic and national identities. In 2004 he retires as the first Professor of Nationalism and Ethnicity at the London School of Economics and Political Science, having established the LSE, through the vigorous postgraduate culture he has inspired, as one of the world centres for research into nationalism. To honour his intellectual achievement we have assembled a mix of established and younger scholars in order to examine some of the central problems that he has addressed during his long career and to assess how far his distinctive ethnosymbolic framework has furthered research in the field. As readers will discover, the problems he has helped define remain live and contested, and we expect him to illuminate debates on these issues for many years to come. This is very much an assessment of work-in-progress.

In organising this collection of articles, we have incurred many debts. We would like to thank the Executive of the Association for the Study of Ethnicity and Nationalism (ASEN), which inspired the idea of the book, our fellow editors of the journal, *Nations and Nationalism*, and, of course, our contributors (including Anthony Smith himself) who worked hard to meet tight deadlines. We are very grateful to Blackwell for undertaking publication of this work, and, in particular, to Sarah Phibbs for her encouragement from the very beginning and to Lena Hawkswood who has overseen so efficiently the production process. We would also like to express our gratitude to Seeta Persaud, the managing editor of *Nations and Nationalism*, for her strong administrative support, and to Esra Bulut for her careful proof-reading. Finally, we thank Dr Gordana Uzelac for her help with the cover design of the accompanying book.

Montserrat Guibernau and John Hutchinson

the association for the study
of ethnicity and nationalism

History and National Destiny

MONTSERRAT GUIBERNAU and JOHN HUTCHINSON

Introduction

This volume celebrates Anthony D. Smith's path-breaking contribution to the study of nations and nationalism. Its objective is to assess and debate various issues concerning the ethno-symbolic approach propounded by him.

Ethnosymbolism stands in opposition to the modernist approach underpinning constructivist and instrumentalist theories of nations and nationalism. It argues that such theories fail 'to accord any weight to the pre-existing cultures and ethnic ties of the nations that emerged in the modern epoch' (Smith 1999: 9). In Smith's words: 'For ethno-symbolists, what gives nationalism its power are the myths, memories, traditions, and symbols of ethnic heritages and the ways in which a popular *living past* has been, and can be, rediscovered and reinterpreted by modern nationalist intelligentsias. It is from these elements of myth, memory, symbol and tradition that modern national identities are reconstituted in each generation, as the nation becomes more inclusive and as its members cope with new challenges' (Smith 1999: 9).

According to Anthony D. Smith, the basic themes or motifs derived from the claims made by ethno-symbolism are:

1. *La longue durée.* The origins and formation of nations as well as their possible future course should be traced over long periods of time, and we should not 'tie their existence and formation to a particular period of history or to the processes of modernization' (Smith 1999: 10). Nations are historical phenomena.
2. *National past, present, and future.* This is a major theme examined under three headings: recurrence, continuity, and reappropriation. Smith argues that the majority of nations and nationalism emerged in the modern world while admitting that some nations pre-dated modernity. In his view, 'the rubric of continuity points to the persistence of cultural components of particular nations' (Smith 1999: 11), while reappropriation represents a 'reaching back into the ethnic past to obtain the *authentic* materials, and ethos for a distinct modern nation' (Smith 1999: 12).
3. *The ethnic basis of nations.* Most nations, modern and pre-modern, were based on ethnic ties and sentiments and on popular ethnic traditions, which have provided the cultural sources for later nation-formation (Smith 1999: 13).

4. *The cultural components of ethnies.* The pre-existing components and long-term continuities of ethnic communities and nations are cultural and symbolic rather than demographic.
5. *Ethnic myths and symbols.* Myths of ethnic origin and election, and symbols of territory and community are key components of ethnicity.
6. *Ethno-history.* This denotes the ethnic members' memories and understanding of their communal past or pasts, rather than more *objective* and dispassionate analysis by professional historians (Smith 1999: 16).
7. *Routes to nationhood.* It refers to the various processes leading to the construction of modern nations.
8. *The longevity of nationalism.* It concerns the power and durability of nations and nationalism encompassing 'nationalism as a modern ideological movement, but also the expression of aspirations by various social groups to create, defend or maintain *nations* – their autonomy, unity and identity-by drawing on the cultural resources of pre-existing ethnic communities and categories' (Smith 1999: 18).

This volume aims to explore the implications of this framework by bringing together scholars from different perspectives to address some of the major issues in the field. Anthony Smith in setting out a prospectus for the contributors laid down a challenge which he framed in these terms:

Of the many issues that have engrossed, and divided, scholars in the study of nationalism, none has been so critical as the problem of the origins of nations. All other issues have in the end revolved around this question: should we regard nations as perennial in history, perhaps even primordial to the human condition, or are they a product of very specific, modern conditions, and hence qualitatively novel? Unlike the fashionable question as to whether nations are 'real' or 'constructed' (since in a sense all human categories and associations are 'constructed', but for the participants they are all too 'real'), this seems to me to be a genuine problem, and one which has a strong bearing on the persistence or erosion of a sense of national identity in a 'post-modern' world.

Of course, the question of the modernity or antiquity of nations depends in part on our definitions of the concept of 'nation'; but it also reflects a view about the relations between nations and 'nationalism'. Broadly speaking, those who believe that nationalism (the movement and ideology) was instrumental in creating nations also subscribe to a modernist belief in the post-Revolutionary advent of nations. Conversely, those who hold that the rise of a nationalism depends on the prior existence of a corresponding nation (or *ethnie*) tend to regard nations as neither so recent nor so novel, but rather as phenomena that reflect continuity and recurrence across the pre-modern/modern divide.

A further perspective argues that, even if nations and nationalism are temporally and qualitatively modern, they draw much of their content and strength from pre-existing *ethnies*. Though most nations have been created out of ethnically heterogenous populations, those that can point to a dominant *ethnie* as the fulcrum of their community and state, have been historically among the most influential and sociologically among the most 'successful' in terms of longevity, consciousness and distinctiveness, if not always of power. Hence, the study of the components of *ethnies* (myths of descent and election, attachment to homelands, shared memories of ethno-history, various symbols of identity, etc.) has become an important focus for illuminating the origins and persistence of nations.

These manifold debates have created several clearly discernible 'positions' on the basic issues in the field. Thus we can speak of a modernist, a primordialist, a perennialist and an ethnosymbolic approach – as well as a variety of less well defined 'post-modern' (not necessarily 'post-modernist') approaches. This is not to say that all scholars subscribe to one or other of these approaches; various combinations are possible, and have been effected. But as a heuristic tool (and pedagogic aid), these approaches serve as a useful point of departure for further research and analysis.

Out of these conflicting paradigmatic approaches, a number of more specific debates and issues have engaged, and divided, the scholarly community. They include:

1. Problems of definition and nomenclature: more specifically, how we are to distinguish 'nations' from ethnic communities (or *ethnies*) and national states, and how the phenomena described by these concepts are related, historically and sociologically;
2. The problem of 'pre-modern nations': in what sense, and to what degree, we may legitimately speak of 'nations' (if not 'nationalism') in pre-modern epochs in different parts of the world; and how far back in time we can trace the components of modern nations;
3. The problem of participation: whether we can speak of 'elite nations' and 'middle class nations', or only of nations that in which the majority of the population participates, i.e. 'mass nations'; and if the latter, what proportion of the designated population counts for this purpose;
4. The related problem of 'citizenship': whether nationhood always requires 'citizenship' in a polity, or how far non-political membership (e.g. of a religious community) may act as a functional equivalent; and hence whether the concepts of both 'nation' and 'nationalism' are predominantly political or mainly cultural;
5. The problem of 'ideology': to what extent we should regard 'national*ism*' as a political ideology on a par with other such ideologies, or as a form of culture and a secular or political 'religion';
6. The question of 'typology': whether there can be a single 'core doctrine' of nationalism, or, whether the term 'nationalism' is a shorthand for a variety of discourses and ideologies, some of them more 'voluntarist' and others more 'organic';
7. The issue of 'chosenness': the relationship between earlier concepts of ethnic election and modern nationalism, and the degree to which a sense of national identity is continuous with, influenced by or radically different from religious beliefs in chosen people;
8. The problem of 'memory': how far ethnic history should be regarded as a construct of present (nationalist) elites or whether, as shared memories of 'golden ages', it can exert an inspirational influence on the creation of modern national cultures and a sense of national destiny;
9. The problem of 'homelands': how far popular attachments to 'historic homelands' are the product of modern states and elites strategies, or are grounded in primordial cultural beliefs, ethnic history and memories of wars and sacrifice;

10. The problem of popular 'resonance': how far elites can mobilise populations by creating and channelling mass sentiments through rituals and traditions, or are constrained by pre-existing popular myths, symbols and traditions;
11. The problem of 'representation': how far images of the nation disseminated in literature and art should be regarded as cultural artefacts of elites in the creation and diffusion of the national idea, or, whether they can be seen as expressions and crystallisations of a pre-existing ethnicity or sense of national identity, with artists and writers articulating the 'voice' of the nation, or its major myths, memories and symbols;
12. The problem of 'passion' or 'mass sacrifice': how far nationalist fervour and sacrifice can be understood as strategic choice and calculation, or more in terms of familial bond and religious commitment;
13. The problem of 'ethnicity': the extent to which modern nations and nationalism are still permeated by ethnic attachments and exclusiveness, and how far the 'ethnic-civic' dichotomy of nations and nationalisms is a valid distinction and a useful heuristic tool;
14. The problem of 'transcendence': how far nations, as well as nationalism, as products of modernity, are likely to be superseded by 'post-modern' continental networks or global associations, or whether nations and their members' sense of national destiny, if not nationalism, are in a sense 'transhistorical', or are reinvigorated by globalism, and hence likely to persist.

Content and structure

We asked the scholars represented here to engage with one or more of these questions in their contributions.

John Armstrong is with Anthony Smith the scholar most associated with the study of the nation in *la longue durée*. Here he considers the questions of definition and periodisation. He argues that viewing the nation as an ideal type has limited Smith's nuanced conceptualization of historical development of identity communities; a feature which Smith has managed to overcome with his vigorous defence of the ethnie as a usual preparatory stage for the nation. He highlights Smith's rejection of both rigid periodization and fixed ideology in defining the emergence of nations. A recurrent question concerning some scholars of nationalism refers to the difficulty in distinguishing between ethnie and nation chronologically. Armstrong states that greater research into regions outside Europe will probably support the conclusion that the ethnie is a highly appropriate term for the modern European heirs of Hellenism. In his view, however, this may not be appropriate for Far Eastern peoples or Africans who had to endure colonial struggles for self-determination. In addition, Armstrong emphasizes that the legacy of myths and symbols, crucial to Anthony D. Smith's ethnosymbolic approach, has derived to a great extent from the Jewish and the Christian traditions. He stresses existing differences within these religions and moves on to consider the broader influence of religion on nations and nationalism. In particular he wonders whether a consideration of how African religions with their novel, but far from unprecedented, pantheon may contribute to ethnic formation will revise our current understanding of the role of religious structures.

Bruce Cauthen explores the theme of 'Chosen peoples', the subject of Anthony Smith's most recent book. He focuses on the relevance attributed by Smith to the myth of divine election for modern nationalist movements. Cauthen, as well as Armstrong and Smith, highlights the significance of religion for the study of nations and nationalism and signals its recent political resurgence after 9/11. He analyses Smith's account of the ways in which myths of ethnic election serve as a mechanism for socio-cultural survival and a stimulus for ethno-political mobilization, paying particular attention to how the concept of chosen people intensifies the identification of a community with its homeland. He argues, following Smith, that religious chosenness continues to inspire the United States of America's sense of national mission and has exerted an enduring influence in its foreign policy even throughout the 1980s. He considers how such a sense of mission inspired the USA in its struggle against communism, the Vietnam War and the end of the Cold War. In his view, after 9/11, Americans have seemed to rediscover a sense of national mission against insidious threats seeking to undermine its democracy and prosperity.

Anthony Smith is frequently criticised (see Eriksen contribution) for overstressing the ethnic component of nations. In Walker Connor's essay, part of a long running debate with Anthony Smith concerning the antiquity of nations, he is taken to task for his confusion of state and nation, and for his attempt to deny that nations must be mass social formations. He questions Smith's assertion that some nations existed in pre-modern times. In Connor's view, the nation is the largest group that can command a person's loyalty because of felt kinship ties; it is, from this perspective, the fully extended family. However, the sense of unique descent need not and, in nearly all cases, will not accord with factual history, since nearly all nations originate from the mixing of peoples from various ethnic origins. For this reason, what matters is not chronological or factual history but sentient or felt history. Connor maintains that elites have made general claims about the existence of national consciousness within their countries when until quite recent times it is doubtful whether ostensibly nationalistic elites even considered the masses to be part of their nation.

Thomas Hylland Eriksen seeks to overcome the divide between constructivism and primordialism. He agrees with the latter in claiming that community and shared memories are crucial for the formation of national sentiment, while he accepts the former's emphasis on creativity in conjuring nations into existence since, in his view, national solidarity can emerge from diverse seedlings. It is his contention that there is no logical reason why the mythomoteur often referred to by Smith should necessarily generate an ethnic group rather than another kind of corporate entity based on ascription. Following this line of argument, Eriksen wonders whether one is a member of a nation by virtue of a shared ethnic identity/origin, or by virtue of living in the same place. Eriksen considers territorial and kinship forms of identification and concludes that the crucial question to be answered is: under which circumstances do metaphoric kinship and metaphoric place of the national kind function? In his view, there are some empirically functioning alternatives to the ethnic nation, which are limited by both human experience and human nature.

Eric Kaufmann and Oliver Zimmer consider Smith's contribution to the study of the role of dominant ethnicity within contemporary nations. They argue that Smith acknowledges the current interplay between dominant ethnies and the nation. In their view, while Smith offers an accurate analysis of how dominant ethnic come to form the core of modern nations, he fails to consider evidence questioning the tenacity of dominant ethnies within post-industrial Western nations. Kaufmann and Zimmer argue that Smith partly evades discussing the future of dominant ethnicity because his primary concern is to consider the viability of nations in relation to supranationalism and globalization as new forms of cultural-political organization which are currently being developed. It is their contention that greater emphasis should be given to the possibility of trans-national 'life-style' enclaves and subcultures usurping ethnic-national identity.

Joshua A. Fishman has long been associated with a primordialist approach to the role of language in national identifications. Here he examines the relationship between corpus planning (how the language morphologies are constructed) and status planning (the domains, public and private, in which languages are used) as two necessarily co-present aspects of any total language planning effort. One-post Klossian assumption to which he subscribes is that (successful) status planning is the real stimulus to subsequent corpus planning. In the light of data collected by the author he constructs a more complex model in contrast with the unidirectional nature of his earlier theory. He argues that regardless of where our account of language planning begins, one state feeds into the next in an ongoing feedback sequence. He identifies four dimensions of corpus planning: purity versus vernacularism, uniqueness versus internationalization, classicization versus *Sprachbund* dimension and *Ausbau* versus *Einbau* as directions of corpus planning. He stresses that various novel additional factors possess the potential to bring about a redirection and re-balancing of previous emphases in corpus planning. It is his contention that changes in the ethnocultural and political orientation of particular societies impact upon corpus planning in order to adjust it to the objectives of the new authorities leading their respective speech-and-writing communities.

In many contexts, particularly the stateless nations of Central and Eastern Europe, national identities arise first among tiny groups of intellectuals, and one of Smith's enduring interests is in what he calls vernacular mobilization, namely the construction of the nation via communitarian rather than state-led strategies. Miroslav Hroch's work on the phases of nationalism has made a deep impact on the field. Here, he considers the origins of the Czech nation (Bohemian nation): in particular he analyses the processes leading to the transition from Phase A dominated by nationally 'neutral' scholars to Phase B defined by their national engagement. He describes the political and cultural environment within which nationalism arose and explains the reasons that convinced some intellectuals to construct a new Bohemian national identity which managed to permeate the masses. Hroch mentions the influence of the secularization of higher education together with the liberalization of intellectual and scientific life in the emergence of a new intelligentsia of professional individuals partially independent from state and religious control. He stresses the impact of the French revolution, the military billeting during the Napoleonic wars, and the various civic celebrations, which took place in the 1790s, in fostering a sense of community. He then considers various factors and events resulting in the construction of a distinctive national identity around 1800.

Montserrat Guibernau argues that Anthony D. Smith's classical theory of nations and national identity fails to establish a clear-cut distinction between the concepts of nation and state. In her view, by including 'legal rights and duties for all members' Smith is attributing to the nation one of the fundamental characteristics of the state. Guibernau offers a critique of Smith's classical definition of the nation and moves on to consider Smith's recent changes to it while considering the reasons which might have motivated them. Drawing on some key aspects of Smith's theory she advances an alternative definition of national identity in the twenty-first century. She considers some new challenges posed by globalization to classical strategies in national identity construction and, in particular, she examines the political dimension of national identity. Guibernau locates the emergence of the nation-state, nationalism and national identity in late eighteenth century Europe.

The question of the transition between premodern ethnic and modern national identities remains underexplored. John Hutchinson examines how an emphasis on the persistence of ethnic identities is compatible with the innovative, even revolutionary, character of nationalism and the rise of the territorially extensive, socially mobile, and mass political units that we call nations. He considers the impact of neo-classical and romantic ideas upon the national revivalists' construction of a dynamic view of the role of ethnic communities in history. He refers to romantic revivalists as moral innovators, providing novel directions at times of social crisis and able to generate change by a 'regeneration' rather than an eradication of collective traditions. Hutchinson stands against theories, which portray the nation as invented, instead he speaks of an *overlaying* of tradition.

Athena S. Leoussi considers the problem of the representation of the nation in the visual arts. Drawing on Anthony D. Smith's work, Leoussi examines how from the eighteenth-century onwards, demotic, historical and ethno-cultural themes became a constant source of inspiration for artists both inside and outside Europe. She illustrates her assertion by specific references to the presence of national art in a wide range of countries. She argues that the participation of artists in the formulation, crystallization and celebration of ethno-cultural roots and identities succeeded in transforming modern societies. In her view, the development of national art has been closely connected with the rise of modern art. It is her contention that visual arts have acted as crucial vehicles of cultural nationalism, have been accepted as 'national' and have become totemic symbols of the nation.

Stein Tønnesson examines the future of national states in a global world. He challenges classical assumptions about how to measure the 'success' of states. In his view, at present, the success of states is measured by their ability to adapt to regional and global trends, promote exports, attract investments and skilled labour, promote research, wield political influence at a regional and global level and 'brand' the nation culturally. He examines Anthony D. Smith's typology of routes to nationhood and argues that a further route based on the idea of 'class', emerging within some Asian countries, should be included. He examines China, Singapore, Russia and Vietnam as case studies. Tønnesson moves on to consider which of the four types of state (ethnic, civic, plural and class) are better equipped to survive and flourish in the global age. He concludes that the most successful national states may be those whose populations engage not just individually, but nationally, in global issues.

Mary Kaldor considers nationalism to be a political process, a subjective affirmation and re-affirmation that will not necessarily disappear in an era of globalization. In contrast with Smith, she argues that nationalism is a modern phenomenon, inextricably linked to the rise of the modern state and to industrialization. She establishes a distinction between 'spectacle nationalism', as an evolution from the more militant nationalism of the first half of the twentieth century employed to legitimize existing states, and what she refers to as 'new nationalism'. The latter is anti-modern, exclusive, backward looking, bred in conditions of insecurity and violence, and has much in common with religious fundamentalism. She examines the role of violence within new nationalisms and illustrates it with references to various recent conflicts emerging in various parts of the world. Kaldor considers the role of war in generating nationalism and analyses the ideology of global Islam promulgated by Osama Bin Laden and Al Qaeda as a new variant of the new nationalism which emerged in the late 1990s. She stands for cosmopolitanism as an ideology combining humanism with a celebration of human diversity.

Reference

Smith, Anthony D. (1999). *Myths and Memories of the Nation.* Oxford University Press: Oxford.

1

Definitions, periodization, and prospects for the *longue durée*

JOHN A. ARMSTRONG

Defining nation and ethnie

Any social science approach to a historical problem demands careful development of definitions, with full awareness that these definitions will, to a great extent, determine the response scholars will bring to the issues posed. The examination of the phenomenon defined as nations is no exception, although at the start of many research projects students do not recognize this. In some studies the problem, or at least certain aspects of it, have already been carefully examined; in effect the parameters of the approach have been set in advance, as in many studies of economic development. To be sure, problems of nationhood and ethnicity in specific regions have attracted close scrutiny. At the turn of the twenty-first century, however, it should be evident that generalizations concerning the characteristics of nations over centuries are just beginning.

The social science approach, especially concerning Europe, has been to assume that the unit of study should be the nation-state whose boundaries have been, with minor changes, represented on twentieth-century maps. For example, during the earlier decades of that century Carlton J. H. Hayes' textbook provided a handy framework for numerous treatments of individual countries, but by 1933 he had published a probing collection on the origins and diffusion of nationalism. In 1935 he published the revised edition of his textbook of which part four, treating the nineteenth century, was entitled *Democracy and Nationalism*. Whereas earlier editions of the textbook had taken the nation-state (especially in Europe) as the natural unit of study, the 1935 edition and his 1933 collection became major models for students during the interwar years and for some time thereafter. Hans Kohn (1944) provided a similar emphasis on diffusion of the nationalist ideology to other European countries during the post Versailles years.

With the revival of interest in nationalism during the l960s, scholars began to wonder whether diffusion could account for the rapid growth and fervor of nationalism (see especially Waldron, 1985). Some turned to economic explanations, including Marxist explanations derived from nationalist movements outside Europe. Anthony D. Smith (1984: 299–300), on the other hand, questioned whether even in England the obvious widespread consciousness of class distinctions was so marked by a 'lack of cultural depth' as to be incapable of sustaining a protracted struggle for social transformation. Crawford Young (1993: 22–23) suggested none of the modern diffused ideologies could exert sufficient affective attraction in many developing countries to overcome 'primordial' religious and family loyalties.

The issue is a critical one, going back to the French Revolution as the widely acclaimed beginning of forcible modernization. As the renowned American historian Lynn Hunt concludes a very recent article, the doctrines and practice of revolutionaries 'made possible not only the Terror, but also the authoritarian police state of Napoleon, socialism, communism, fascism, and, of course, representative government'. But these same revolutionaries had discovered how difficult it was to preach the social contract while forced to engage in 'the more mundane daily life with political institutions' (Hunt 2003: 19). In fact, Maurice Agulhon (1979) has vividly shown how conscious these revolutionaries were of the need to replace the images and symbols of the former religious, political and social order. Whatever the validity of these symbols of Marianne in combat, their affective appeal to dissatisfied radicals was strong enough to dominate such radical movements for a half-century. Smith notes that Auguste Comte as well as John Stuart Mill agreed that the Revolution had performed a vital requirement by replacing status quo forces (Smith 1991: 145). Marx more than agreed; his ideology supported the achievement of the bourgeoisie in sweeping away clerics, kings, and nobles themselves, as well as their traditions, in considerable measure by substituting a nationalist ideology and its symbols. Once that was accomplished, the bourgeoisie had fulfilled, in Marx's worldview, its historic function and (as Lenin insisted more thoroughly) should be swept away in its turn by a proletarian consciousness.

Like many others, Anthony Smith was quite aware of the tendentious nature of such rhetoric. Like most social scientists, he recognized the importance of economic modernization. Again, like most social scientists, Smith accepted the concept of social construction of received institutions and ideologies. In contrast to Marxist and marxisant analysts, however, he decisively rejected the assertion that classes (a category itself subject to social construction) must play a dominant role in the history of modernization. The process of elite intervention in that history was far more complicated and contingent. For Smith, this insight opens up a realm of historical contingencies, including inherited national myths, symbols and other durable aspects of nationalism.

Periodization

The issues just treated and references to 'primordialism' suggest that forces operating to produce nationalism (some would add 'and all recent nations') are intimately related to historic periods. Smith advanced (1989: 107) a working definition of the nation, 'a named community of history and culture, possessing a unified territory, mass educational system, and common legal rights'. Admitting (Smith 1989:107) that such a definition contained a large portion of the modernist position, he added 'I take the definition from the ideals and blueprints of a generation of nationalists and their followers'. But he recognizes that one or more definitional categories may be missing in a concrete case.

Even so, the characteristics of a nation viewed as an ideal type severely limited Smith's nuanced conceptualization of historical development of identity communities, his major field of study. His vigorous defense of the ethnie as a usual preparatory stage for the nation overcame this restriction. Previously this term, originating in Greek, had been widely adopted in France and elsewhere on the Continent to refer to an ethnic group that had not attained independence.[1] Soviet Russian scholarship, however, tended to refer to national groups not recognized as union-republics (sometimes with UN membership) as 'nationalities', a common term for ethnic groups in the USA and some other English-language publications. Smith (1989: 110–113) points out that an ethnie that became a nation usually retained the name it had held – sometimes as far back as the medieval period, and occasionally dating back in the case of the Jews even to ancient times : 'A multitude of ethnies in the ancient and medieval worlds ... at first sight resemble but are not nations'. These resemblances occasionally included similar myths, symbols, and histories and cultures.

In fact, the resemblances were so strong that theorists of national development, especially in the 1980s and later, found it impossible to distinguish between ethnie and nation chronologically. In English, the most elaborate rejection of the distinction, especially for Britain, has been Liah Greenfeld (1992). She ascribed nation status to the USA, a thoroughly modern civic nation with recognized boundaries but lacking many of the historic traditions and cultures attributed to civic nations by Smith (1986: 113). Several settler nations on attaining nineteenth or early twentieth-century independence without a preparatory period as ethnie also seemed to put in question the historical role of the ethnie.

Historiographical developments, such as the considerable recent literature arguing that France was not even linguistically unified until Napoleon III's compulsory military service, followed a few decades later by mass public education, appear to demonstrate that even the paradigm state for modernization theory emerged very unevenly. Scholars of modernization could defer their examination of national achievement of modernity by ascribing earlier manifestations to the ethnie. While gradually recognizing that civic nations emerged at a far earlier stage by adopting the affect characteristics of the ethnies preceding them, Smith (2000: 39) has rejected both rigid periodization and fixed ideology in defining the emergence of nations. Further data on a unified economy was attained by Greenfeld who has advocated the end of the sixteenth century with mercantile capitalism under Elizabeth I as the start of the modern English nation.

On the other hand, Andreas Kappeler, the most distinguished German historian of ethnies and nationalities in Russia, after systematic investigation concludes that no nationalism could exist in the eighteenth century there because the embryonic propagator of such concepts was not usually the political authority (Tsarism) but the religious force of Orthodoxy (Kappeler 1986: 83–99). Montserrat Guibernau and John Hutchinson (2001: 3) have recently pointed out that the relation between religion and nationality is one of the most under-researched topics in the entire field of nation and ethnic studies. This is, it seems to me, entirely correct. In the final section of this paper I shall endeavor to show, through two non-European examples, why this is, and why Smith (1994; 1996) and his two colleagues so candidly urge making up for the scarcity of research on the nationalism-religion connection. Here this urgency can be at least partially inferred from Smith's earlier work (1984: 283).

Not only are the postwar ethnic autonomy movements simply a recent variation of a wider ethnic and national revival going back to the late eighteenth century in Europe; this latter revival is but the latest of a series of such resurgence, some of them purely local and others widely diffused. In pre-Roman antiquity, just as in the early European Middle Ages, and in the Far East and Africa more recently, that ancient and widespread social formation, the ethnie, has occupied a variable but important position in the hierarchy of human allegiance and has, on occasion, served as a focus for political movements and organizations.

It is fairly evident that in this remarkable appreciation, nearly two decades before his editorial group expressed the need for more research on relations of nationalism and religion, Smith was pointing to eras before those that most of us can handle historically to suggest the influence of religion on political allegiances resembling nationalism. More recently, this inference has been supported by Kappeler's suggestion that it was often Orthodoxy rather than the Tsarist regime that instigated political moves in the early modern period.

At the same time that he was probing these ancient political motivations, Anthony Smith was moving during the 1970s from the dichotomy between primordialism and modernism to a triple distinction between primordialism (generally considered a questionable classification), perennialism, and modernism. In reference to my own work (Armstrong 1973; 1982; 1992; 1995) he saw both acceptance of very old ethnies (Jews, Armenians, etc.) that had periods of evident nationhood a millennium ago, and other ethnies that were completely subjected politically, but evolved culturally – a historic pattern which one may consider (as Smith does) perennial nationhood. At the same time, my work occasionally identified discrete periods when general national assertiveness was clearly evident. Usually such periods alternated with periods when national and ethnic factors were far from the forefront of political consciousness. Examples might be the *Voelkerwanderung* between the Roman Empire and Charlemagne's partial restoration; the struggle between popes and anti-popes; or between Reformers and Counter-Reformers, when appeal to national consciousness (especially linguistic) was strong. But the religious conflicts were followed by the age of absolutism until the French Revolution. One may term such alternations, usually involving a multitude of ethnic groups, 'cyclical perennials'; but pending much more searching historical investigation, one cannot predict that sufficient regularities were present to be confident in using the adjective 'cyclical'. I am sure Anthony Smith has such questions in mind, and will employ his extraordinary skill to clarify the issues.

Clearly the issues involving perennialism are closely involved with periodization as well. Although some scholars may prefer substitutes like proto-nation, retention of ethnie has good arguments. Whether these will stand up to deeper historic understanding of phenomena preceding the age of industrialization and the sharper turn of the French Revolution remains to be seen. It is at least possible that sweeping extension of research to regions outside Europe will support a conclusion that the ethnie is a highly appropriate term for the modern European heirs of Hellenism. This may not, however, be appropriate for Far Eastern peoples or Africans who have attained quasi-dominance in some Western Hemisphere regions after cruel struggles unarmed with the political and philosophic skills inherited by their European masters.

In contrast to Frederik Barth, Smith does not concentrate on symbols used as border guards. He does, however, stress the importance of symbols originating well before the modern era, along with the myths which articulated them. Even taken alone, this insight has given him a remarkable position as a theorist of the 'legacy of the distant past' and as an interpretor of modern investigations by specialized classicists and medievalists (Smith 1984: 291). This is feasible only because Anthony Smith has an extensive historical background, especially in humanities like art history, rare among social scientists. This circumstance points clearly to the long research path that needs to be trodden to understand how nations emerged, what the turning points and essential transformation of characteristics were, and how changes were linked to the essential requirements of modern nationalist movements.

Prospects

Because the legacy of myths and symbols has derived to such a great extent from the Jewish and the Christian traditions, the center of investigation of ethnies (or whatever the perennialist may eventually employ for the *longue durée* preceding modern nationalism) will revive investigation of the religious sphere. Understandably, many scholars will prefer to limit their scope to Europe, or to Europe and parts of the globe (possibly fewer than they imagine) where European religious patterns have been firmly implanted. However, even European Christianity has varied so much over time and place that the subjects that can be examined comparatively and in comparison to national subjects are inexhaustible. This applies not only to the familiar – and lamentable – divisions between Orthodoxy and the West, including the former's intervals of iconoclasm. It also applies to the West's Reformation and Counter-Reformation, echoing sharply still in parts of Europe, America, and southern Africa within separate churches, even before the impact of symbolic variations such as those in the pre-Tridentine and post-Tridentine Roman Catholic

Churches. Corresponding changes following the Second Vatican Council, or accompanying medieval Renovatio of classic symbols, will require research extending far beyond the customary ecclesiastical or social science intellectual subjects.

Along with Steven Grosby, Anthony Smith has already been a pioneer of such investigations. It may seem to be an unwarranted imposition even to suggest that he might extend his study to new geographical regions. However, although it is over 50 years since I heard Arnold Toynbee lecture, and considerably longer since I intently studied his great volumes, I have not met a more profound prescription for grasping the nature (and lessons) of history than his advice to acquire a fresher and probably more valid perspective by thorough study of other civilizations. To Toynbee the classicist this prescription initially, and no doubt essentially, applied to the classic Greco-Roman civilization. But he offered as well the array of civilizations, long dead or uncomfortably alive, that rested on a different religious, and an enduring cultural basis from Western Christendom to a degree to which the latter civilization, variable as it was, could not offer.

Oriented (it is strange how one reverts to this curious verb, so familiar in military and civil life during the years around World War II) pragmatically while getting a belated higher education, I could scarcely acquire the full acquaintance with our classic heritage that Toynbee so superlatively demonstrated. I am convinced that Anthony Smith has an advantage there that will become evident as he works at his projects of explaining the myth-symbol complex that so often is related to the classics. Be that as it may, I chose Russia as my area study, which implied learning two languages of the region plus graduate courses in five disciplines directly related to it. As a third area specialization (for years I had qualified by the same criteria just mentioned for the Western European area) I chose the Middle East on the idea (in 1947) that, with drastically reduced requirements, it would be as important for Russian foreign and domestic policy as any region other than the Far East. From the perspective of civilizations the Middle East is more distinctive than Russia, which (in contrast to Toynbee) I have long had difficulty in conceiving as a separate Christian civilization. By studying and observing the Middle East, one does obtain a very special perspective on modern as well as earlier history.

The published response of the comparatively few scholars who have fully specialized on the Middle East testifies to the deep and lasting impression they have gained. This is especially true of the young Quaker scholar at the University of Chicago, Marshall G. S. Hodgson. Before his premature death in 1968 he had prepared (but not entirely published) the massive work on Islam's history that, in my opinion, constitutes the masterpiece of area studies. Essentially it is a history of ideas and movements rather than of the externals of politics and economics, and for that reason is the more amazing. Consequently Hodgson begins the study with a discussion of Islamic civilization, skillfully and objectively comparing it to Western civilization while thoroughly establishing Islam's claim to be a co-heir of Persian, Greek, and Jewish cultures. In his introduction, that has been compared in scholarly profundity to Toynbee's work, Hodgson provides numerous practical suggestions valuable for any one undertaking a complex study of any civilization. Some readers will remain unconvinced that Iranian civilization and Arabic civilization remained distinct under the many centuries of Islamic influence; but, he writes 'if we make it a single civilization, we must give some reason why' (Hodgson 1974: 32).

For Xavier de Planhol, 'The nations of the Prophet' were rather different (1993: 22–26). 'The major languages, Arab, Persian, and Turkish possessed numerous words to designate ethnic groups, but it is significant that none of these ever furnished the vocabulary for incipient nationalism' (1993: 22). However, the concept of territorial patriotism arose well before nationalism in a distinctive country like Egypt, where the invader of this Ottoman possession, Bonaparte, tried to utilize the sentiment. 'Even today in the Muslim world, nationalism arises not from a positive affirmation, but as in the nineteenth-century Central European and Balkan nations from a feeling of oppression' (1993: 26). The anti-peasant sentiment in many areas undermines solidarity. 'The nation (omma) is only an intermediary, a stopping point along the road to a superior stage' – unity of Muslims (1993: 30). In the final analysis, de Planhol can only term Turkey a complete nation, whereas Iran remains partly an empire, Afghanistan an anti-nation, the Maghreb rather stable royal states, those of Arabia unstable. Surely (to me) this is partly because where there are only temporary stopping points as states, no ruler, king or dictator, has legitimacy compared to that of the religious spokesmen.

For the time being these hints (which seem moderate to me) concerning the factors differentiating Islamic nations from contemporary European nations must suffice. But bear in mind that even a century ago modernizing nations of European origin confronted interventions by militant religious organizations only somewhat milder than those now prevalent in much, but not all of the Islamic sphere. One must hope that belligerent passions will subside enough to permit thorough exploration in the near future. Lacking personal observation or protracted study of eastern and southern Asia, any comments I might make about prospects there for really deepening our understanding of the evolution of nations would be of little value.

There is one other sphere, often dismissed or even ridiculed, that could present serious difficulties for a major new nation-state. Brazil, with a population of nearly 200 million is the fifth largest country in the world, and next to the USA the largest in the Western Hemisphere. Brazil's area and natural resources also place it in the front rank for future prospects. It has recently conducted a genuine presidential election, and is unified linguistically by the Portuguese language. At a recent meeting of the Council on Foreign Relations' new Miami branch (consisting mainly of ex-diplomats and businessmen) suggestions were made that the USA give Brazil priority over Spanish American countries in the near future.

Nevertheless, a sharp religious division, accompanied by cultural cleavages, appears to threaten the country's unity. Protestant missionaries work unhampered in this nominally Roman Catholic population, but pressure to return to non-Christian faiths is growing. In several Spanish-American countries such pressure has arisen mainly among native American Indians; in Brazil the population of non-European origin is predominantly African by descent, and close to a majority if one (somewhat questionably) combines 'blacks' and 'pardos' (brown). By far the greatest authority on the ancestral and reviving religions of this population is sociologist Roger Bastide. His book on African religions appeared in 1980; both the original French and the English translation attracted wide interest. Fifteen years later a second French edition appeared (Bastide 1995). While generally updated, the new edition was most remarkable for its brief preface by one of Bastide's colleagues, who informs us that Bastide has become not only a Brazilian, but an initiate of the principal African religion in Brazil, *candomblé*.

My own brief observations suggest that *candomblé* has coexisted for centuries with Catholicism, as in the Bomfeim church of Salvador da Bahia, where many of the adornments and motions of the worshippers suggest *candomblé* influences. Apart from Brazil, manifestations of clandestine takeover of Catholic churches by devotees of African religions have even appeared in the USA. The pantheist cult known in the Caribbean as santeria was brought by Cuban immigrants to the south Florida church worshippers of Our Lady of Charity, popularly known as Our Lady of Exile (Tweed 1997: 79). In Bahia followers of European appearance predominate, whereas at Our Lady of Exile, Cuban blacks are more prominent. Elsewhere (New Orleans, Savannah) in the southeastern USA, where the African worship is known as voodoo, adherents are almost all from a tiny minority (generally politically inactive) of the African-American communities.

Bastide describes the formation of the pantheon (with somewhat varying names) of these religions as the coalescing, under forcible abduction of slaves from scattered African homelands, of regional or tribal deities, with each assigned to a special protective role perceived as helpful by the god's devotees. Bastide's description almost precisely fits the pantheons composed of Greek gods with differing attributes commemorated in the Homeric epics and subsequent Hellenist dramas. In turn, the Romans adapted their pantheism to the Greek model, usually retaining different names; e.g. Athena became Minerva, but remained goddess of wisdom. Even the barbarian Germanic pantheon was similarly reworked on the Roman and Greek models. Incidentally, all three religions were of Aryan origin, thus ethnically and geographically remote from the African cults (Borkenau 1981). Since the Brazilian experience, although centuries old, is still unfolding, following Bastide's careful, yet sympathetic analysis may provide the serendipitous advantage of improved understanding of very remote ethnoreligious experiences in Europe. Nevertheless, the chief motive for carefully following the evolution of *candomblé*, santeria, and voodoo will probably remain the recognition that cults, which include features abhorrent and possibly dangerous for non-believing neighbors, require vigilance, restrained by tolerance for unusual beliefs, especially when they are the product of striving for solace during centuries of oppression. Years before *candomblé* was carefully scrutinized, a politically popular slogan in Brazil was creating a new tropical civilization. If this project is serious, results will inevitably look different from the civilizations of Europe, North America, and of the Muslim world.

I cannot anticipate completing systematically any of the various areas of research that Anthony Smith has so trenchantly identified. It is, however, a matter of great satisfaction for me to find, inspired by and often taught by Anthony Smith and his colleague John Hutchinson, such a devoted group intent on making consideration of nations and ethnies a major subject of research. I believe that in future decades their work will revolutionize the application of sociological models to history. My own suggestions on the broader influence of religion on nations and nationalism leads to consideration of how African religions with their novel, but far from unprecedented pantheon, may help in a needed reconsideration of the religious structures known to the nineteenth century. Perhaps this reappraisal will extend as far as the sociological pantheons (Marx, Durkheim, Weber) of that century or even to sociologist-theologian Peter Berger's contention that all pantheons are to satisfy the human need for secure identification when confronting the inevitability of death.

Note

1   Roland Breton's little book on the subject in German translation was published in Vienna in the *Ethnos* Series (Breton, 1983).

References

Agulhon, Maurice. 1979. *Marianne au Combat: l'imagérie et la symbole républicaine*. Paris: Flammarion.

Armstrong, John A. 1973. *The European Administrative Elite*. Princeton, NJ: Princeton University Press.

Armstrong, John A. 1982. *Nations before Nationalism*. Chapel Hill, NC: University of North Carolina Press.

Armstrong, John A. 1992. 'The autonomy of ethnic identity: historic cleavages and nationality relations in the USSR' in Alexander J. Motyl (ed.), *Thinking Theoretically about Soviet Nationalities*. New York: Columbia University Press, 23–43.

Armstrong, John A. 1995. 'Towards a theory of nationalism: consensus and dissensus' in Sukumar Periwal (ed.), *Notions of Nationalism*. Budapest: Central European University Press, 34–43.

Bastide, Roger. 1995. *Les religions africaines au Brésil: contribution à une sociologie des interpénétrations de civilization*. 2nd ed. Paris: Presses Universitaires.

Breton, Roland. 1981 [1983]. *Lob der Verschiedenheit: die Ethnie: Volk und Volksgruppe in der Gesellschaft der Gegenwart: Ethnos*, Vol. 5, Trans. from the French *Les ethnies* Vienna: Wilhelm Braumuller, 1983.

Borkenau, Franz. 1981. *End and a Beginning*. New York: Columbia University Press.

Greenfeld, Liah. 1992. *Nationalism: Five Roads to Modernity*. Cambridge, MA: Harvard University Press.

Guibernau, Montserrat and John Hutchinson (eds.) 2001. *Understanding Nationalism*. Cambridge: Polity.

Hayes, Carlton J. H. 1933. *Essays on Nationalism*. New York: Macmillan.

Hayes, Carlton J. H. 1935. *A Political and Social History of Europe*, vol. 2. New York: Macmillan.

Hodgson, Marshall G. S. 1974. *The Venture of Islam: Conscience and History in a World Civilization*, vol. 1. Chicago, IL: University of Chicago Press.

Hunt, Lynn. 2003. 'The world we have gained: the future of the French Revolution', *American Historical Review*, 108: 1–19.

Kappeler, Andreas 1986. 'Nationalismus im Völkerreich Russland' in Otto Dann (ed.), *Nationalismus im vorindustrieller Zeit*. Munich: Oldenburg.

Kohn, Hans. 1944. *The Idea of Nationalism*. New York: Macmillan.

Planhol, Xavier de. 1993. *Les nations du Prophète: Manuel géographique de politique musulmane*. Paris: Fayard.

Smith, Anthony D. 1971. *Theories of Nationalism*. London: Duckworth.

Smith, Anthony D. 1981. *The Ethnic Revival*. Cambridge: Cambridge University Press.

Smith, Anthony D. 1984. 'Ethnic myths and ethnic revivals', *European Journal of Sociology*, 25: 283–305.

Smith, Anthony D. 1986. 'History and liberty: dilemmas of loyalty in Western democracies', *Ethnic and Racial Studies*, 9: 43–65.

Smith, Anthony D. 1989. 'The origins of nations,' *Ethnic and Racial Studies*, 12: 340–67, republished in Geoff Eley and Ronald G. Suny (eds.). 1996. *Becoming National*. Oxford: Oxford University Press.

Smith, Anthony D. 1991. *National Identity*. London: Penguin.

Smith, Anthony D. 1992. 'Ethnic identity and territorial nationalism in comparative perspective' in Alexander J. Motyl (ed.), *Thinking Theoretically about Soviet Nationalities*. New York: Columbia University Press.

Smith, Anthony D. 1994. 'The crisis of dual legitimation' in John Hutchinson and Anthony Smith, *Nationalism*. Oxford: Oxford University Press, 113–29.

Smith, Anthony D. 1996. 'Ethnicity, religion, and language' in John Hutchinson and Anthony D. Smith (eds), *Ethnicity*. Oxford: Oxford University Press, 189–97.

Smith, Anthony D. 2000. *Nations in History: Historical Debates about Ethnicity and Nationalism*. Hanover: University Press of New England.

Smith, Anthony D. 2001. 'Nations and history' in Montserrat Guibernau and John Hutchinson (eds) *Understanding Nationalism*. Oxford: Polity, 9–31.

Tweed, Thomas A. 1997. *Our Lady of Charity: Diasporic Religion at a Cuban Catholic Shrine*. New York: Oxford University Press.

Waldron, Arthur N. 1985. 'Theories of nationalism and historical explanation', *World Politics*, 37: 416–33.

Young M. Crawford (ed.) 1993. *The Rising Tide of Cultural Pluralism: the Nation-State at Bay?* Madison, WI: University of Wisconsin Press.

2

Covenant and continuity: ethno-symbolism and the myth of divine election

BRUCE CAUTHEN

Religion and politics

The tragic events of September 11, 2001 have caused many analysts to reconsider the influence of religion on politics. Indeed, in the words of Karen Armstrong, 'In the middle of the twentieth century, it was generally assumed by pundits and commentators that secularism was the coming ideology and that religion would never again become a force in international affairs. But the fundamentalists have reversed this trend and gradually, in both the United States and the Muslim world, religion has become a force that every government has been forced to take seriously' (Armstrong 2001: vii–viii). Yet, although the devastating assault on New York and Washington horrifically drove home this reality, countless and varied events, including the rise of the Taliban in Afghanistan and the BJP in India, the continuing failure to reach a peace settlement in the Israeli–Palestinian conflict due to the growing influence of religious revivalist rejectionists on each side, numerous episodes of ethno-confessional violence in Africa and Asia, controversies concerning the teaching of evolution and creationism in US public schools, and, of course, the preliminary terrorist attacks orchestrated by *al-Qaeda* during the preceding decade, must have surely signaled the political resurgence of religion – if indeed it had actually ever completely retreated from the public sphere. In any event, especially after 9/11, it is impossible to dismiss religion's profound imprint on world politics. Indeed, after contemplating the disorder of the global system following the attacks, Christopher Catherwood, correctly concludes, 'one thing can perhaps be said for certain: religion will be a major player in international affairs. The religious dimension of questions cannot now be safely ignored' (Catherwood 2002: 165).

The myth of divine election

However, it remains to be seen if this renewed analytical awareness of the role of religion in politics will also extend to a concept which has been at the core of many modern nationalists movements – the myth of divine election. Indeed, the concept of *chosenness*, that is of a particular people especially anointed by the Deity to discharge a providentially-ordained mission, to fulfill a holy and cosmologically-determined destiny, or who collectively possess a divine warrant to subdue, and propagate the faith in, a heathen land, has been throughout history a uniquely potent catalyst for social mobilization and national coherence.[1] When the cause of a people is conceived to be the very will of God, the collectivity is infused with a powerful sense of purpose which transcends the more mundane considerations of socio-political organization. Theirs is a charge which defies human contemplation and a calling to which all members of the community must respond. Failure to promote and realize the collective vocation may incur the wrath of the Creator, lead to the dismemberment of the people, and – for its individual members – the prospect of eternal damnation.

The classic example of a chosen people is, of course, the ancient Hebrews whose epic narrative of election, exodus, exile in the wilderness and ultimate redemption has been related to successive generations through the Old Testament.[2] Although myths of ethnic election are hardly confined within the Judeo-Christian tradition, many Christian communities have seen themselves as successors to biblical Israel as collective recipients of divine favor and therefore as the new Chosen People (O'Brien 1988, chs 1–2). Adrian Hastings argues that the first proto-typical nation, England, originated during the Middle Ages and arose from the biblical model of the ancient Hebrews. Hastings reveals that Bede, an eminent authority on the Bible, recognized parallels between his English nation – with its single language and collective allegiance to God – and the Israelites of the Old Testament (Hastings 1997: ch. 2). Although there are other examples of pre-Reformation collectivities who were self-assured of a distinct and sublime communion with the Almighty, Conor Cruise O'Brien shows that Protestant communities – which interpreted the Scriptures, especially, the Old Testament literally – were particularly susceptible to self-conceptions of chosenness as an increasingly powerful identification with the ancient Israelites produced an irresistible and infinitely formidable fusion of religion and nationalism (O'Brien 1988: 19–25). Hartmut Lehmann and William R. Hutchinson reveal: 'Nothing inspired this symbiosis of nationalism and Christianity more than the chosen people model as it was derived, accurately or not, from the Hebrew scriptures. Indeed, without such symbols as the "Old Testament" account of a chosen people, a people united under God, the frequently powerful union of nationalism and Christianity might have been less feasible in nations like Great Britain, Germany, or the United States' (Lehmann and Hutchinson 1994: 288). Certainly it seems difficult to adequately comprehend nationalism as an ideology without acknowledging its religious concomitant from which it so often draws its fervor. Indeed, Anthony D. Smith claims that even the first use of the term 'nationalism' – interestingly not until 1836 – in English 'appears to be theological, the doctrine that some nations are divinely elected' (Smith 2001: 5).

Although there have been contemporary studies which have examined the identification with the ancient Hebrews of various communities and the ways in which this self-conception as a latter day Israel shaped their socio-political development,[3] considering the profound influence of the myth of divine election on so many modern nationalists projects, the subject has hardly attracted pervasive scholarly attention. Clifford Longley explains, 'At first glance (at least to my modern eye) the concept sounds utterly outdated, or something confined to fundamentalist extremists. That is doubtless one reason why researchers have left it alone' (Longley 2002: x). Moreover, much of the contemporary research has been of a decidedly deconstructionist approach which attempts to analytically dissect and ultimately dismiss the historical myth of divine election – as it relates to a particular people – as slightly more than a quasi-religious subterfuge, fabricated and manipulated by a nationalist elite, and imposed on the masses as a vehicle for political mobilization. In this regard, the concept of chosenness is often interpreted as merely a sanctimoniously-contrived ideology – retroactively interjected into history – to justify a dubious record of ethnocentrism, racism, colonialism, warfare, enslavement or worse.[4]

And, to be sure there has been a rather conspicuous lack of analysis of the myth of divine election from a comparative perspective.[5] Furthermore, with the exception of Smith, the subject has been largely neglected by many of the most prominent theorists of nationalism. Smith points out that myths of ethnic election are often overlooked by other scholars of nationalism who subscribe to the 'modernist' paradigm with its emphasis on more recent variables in the creation of nations such as the state, economic determinants, and the intelligentsia (Smith 1992: 440; 1993: 9; 1998).

Smith's ethno-symbolic approach

Smith's interest in the myth of divine election is multi-faceted and his extensive research in this regard has shed very valuable light on the concept.[6] Smith's ethno-symbolic approach which contemplates the subjective scope of the myths, symbols, and memories which in themselves constitute ethno-national identity has proven a most instructive perspective from which to analyze the communal conviction of chosenness.[7] Smith assesses the ways in which myths of ethnic election serve as a mechanism for socio-cultural survival and a stimulus for ethno-political mobilization. He also indicates how the concept of the chosen people intensifies the identification of the community with its homeland. Moreover, Smith seeks to demonstrate the extent to which the properties of modern secular nationalism are analogous to the characteristics of antecedent myths of ethnic election and how the persistent power of this underlying idea of chosenness continues to influence communities even today.

Two Types of Election

Walbert Bühlmann argues, 'Most peoples, on all continents, nourish and foster a marked ethnocentrism, generally accentuated and supported by religion ....

They see themselves as an altogether special people – as the people of God, and hence explicitly or implicitly, a chosen people' (Bühlmann 1982: 187). However Smith cautions:

A myth of divine election should not be equated with mere ethnocentrism. Ethnic communities have quite commonly regarded themselves as the moral centre of the universe and as far as possible affected to ignore or despise those around them. A myth of ethnic election is more demanding. To be chosen is to be placed under moral obligations. One is chosen on condition that one observes certain moral, ritual, and legal codes, and only for as long as one continues to do so. The privilege of election is accorded only to those who are sanctified, whose life-style is an expression of sacred values. The benefits of election are reserved for those who fulfill the required observances. (Smith 1992: 441)

Yet, Smith does distinguish between two different types of ethnic election which he describes as 'missionary' and 'covenantal'. Smith relates, 'missionary election myths exalt their ethnie by assigning them god-given tasks or missions of warfare or conversion or overlordship...' (Smith 1999b: 15). In the 'missionary' myth the community believes itself to be divinely anointed to preserve and promote the true faith and to champion the ecclesiastical establishment which sustains it. Moreover the community feels itself compelled to assiduously deliver new congregants to the religion through a vigorous campaign of proselytism which may often entail conquest. Smith argues that this is the most common variety of chosenness and that myths of this sort of ethnic election infused Armenians, the Franks, the Orthodox Byzantines and Russians, Catalans, medieval Magyars who resisted the Ottoman expansion, and Catholic Poles. And, according to Smith, non-Christian peoples such as the Arabs during and after the time of the Prophet and Shi'ite Persians during the Safavid period were also inspired by the myth of missionary election (Smith 2000a: 67; 2000b: 804).

However, the covenantal form of divine election is far more demanding. Like that of biblical Israel which provides the model for this kind of chosenness, the election of the people which subscribes to this contractual myth is conditional upon the strict compliance with divine, moral commandments, the scrupulous adherence to the holy ordinances, the faithful commemoration of sacred rituals, and the conscientious discharge of the consecrated and collective vocation – to dutifully fulfill that which is seen to be the will of God. Smith notes that the covenantal myth has been less evident historically and primarily attached to certain Protestant communities which have seen themselves as the theological heirs and trans-historical successors of the ancient Israelites such as the Puritan settlers of New England, the Ulster Scots, and Afrikaners (Smith 2000a: 67; 2000b: 804–805). Smith observes:

To see oneself as potentially 'an holy nation' is to link chosenness indissolubly with collective sanctification. Salvation is accessible only through redemption which in turn requires a return to former ways and beliefs, which are the means of sanctification. Hence the recurrent note of 'return' in many ethno-religious traditions which inspire movements of both religious reform and cultural restoration. Given the ineluctable subjectivity of ethnic identification, this moral summons to re-sanctify the potential elect provides a powerful mechanism for ethnic self-renewal and long-term ethnic survival (Smith 1991: 37).

Indeed, Smith emphasizes that the myth of divine election sustains the continuity of cultural identity, and, in that regard, has enabled certain pre-modern communities such as the Jews, Armenians, and Greeks to survive and persist over centuries and millennia (Smith 1993: 15–20). Moreover, myths of divine election have empowered a number of *ethnies* even to prevail against patently catastrophic corporate reversals as the loss of political independence and exile from the ancestral homeland (Smith 1992: 440).

'Patterns of Ethnic Survival'

Chosenness is the supreme guarantor of ethnic durability and Smith links myths of divine election to four different 'patterns of ethnic survival' which he describes as *imperial-dynastic*, *communal-demotic*, *emigrant colonist*, and *diaspora-restoration* (Smith 1992: 446–448).

As Smith points out, in the *imperial-dynastic* pattern, it is the monarch or royal family which espouses the myth of election. Yet, the conception of chosenness is eventually transmitted to their subjects as well through the people's identification with the regnal emblems and customs. Ultimately the election myth is sustained by this formidable 'conjunction of dynasty, land and people'. And, with the recession of royal supremacy, the myth of election is even more intimately invested in the people who now become the principal locus of corporate sanctification (Smith 1992: 446–447). Yet it is the people itself which provides the repository for the election myth in the *communal-demotic* pattern – particularly an *ethnie* which attempts to maintain its traditional culture in the midst of alien invasion and occupation in a homeland which is thought to retain a sacred character (Smith 1992: 447). As is suggested by the name of the third pattern, the *emigrant-colonist*, the myth of divine election is invested in an immigrant community which seeks to establish a new moral order in the wilderness, or at least in an unfamiliar territory, to which they believe they have been delivered by the deity (Smith 1992: 447–448). And, finally, it is the reclamation – or the emotive corporate longing to do so – of an abandoned homeland from which the community originated in the distant past which vehiculates the myth in the final model of ethnic survival which Smith calls the *diaspora-restoration* pattern. He explains, 'The return of the community to its ancestral home from which it had been exiled became the precondition of collective redemption' (Smith 1992: 448). And, historically, such myths have provided an irresistible stimulus for territorial aggrandizement, mass insurrection, collective translocation, and struggles for the communal recovery of the lost homeland (Smith 1992: 448).

The Sacred Homeland

The idea of the homeland is central to the four configurations of ethnic persistence which Smith describes. And, indeed, Smith has consistently maintained that a collective identification with a particular territory is an essential foundation of ethnic identity (see Smith 1986: 28–29; 1995: 56). Yet the homeland is far more than simply the site of physical habitation, it is invested with a psychological dimension of symbiotic belonging. Smith clarifies, 'we find many groups of people endowing with a particular collective emotion a specific terrain which they occupy, whether it be a local district, a region or a wider ethnic territory. What is at stake is the idea of an historic and poetic landscape, one imbued with the culture and history of a group, and vice versa, a group part of whose character is felt by themselves and outsiders to derive from the particular landscape they inhabit, and commemorated as such in song and verse' (Smith 1997: 11).

Smith employs the term, *ethnoscape*, to describe the mystical affinity of the people for *its* homeland; and, as might be expected, the dynamic is especially coherent in a community which is infused by a collective self-concept of divine election. Indeed, Smith observes, 'Myths of ethnic chosenness not only underpin peoples and cultures; they also provide charters and title deeds of sacred homelands' (Smith 1992: 450). And, indeed, what impetus could more profoundly unite the consecrated community with its homeland than the belief that it was ceded to them by the deity as a sacred parcel signifying the people's election? For a ' "holy people" adhering to a single sacred life-style, repeated performance of sacred acts in fulfillment of the mission with which the community is entrusted sanctifies the land and turns it into a reward for faithful observance of a "covenant" ' (Smith 1997: 14). Yet, the homeland is also consecrated as it encompasses the terrain on which heroic ethnic forebears led the community in the collective realization of its providential destiny and contains the soil in which they now rest. Smith relates, 'These legendary or historical figures are venerated by the people for the benefits, material and spiritual, that they bestow on the community, and for the divine blessings they bring on the people. So the places where holy men and heroes walked and taught, fought and judged, prayed and died, are felt to be holy themselves; their tombs and monuments become places of veneration and pilgrimage, testifying to the glorious and sacred past of the ethnic community' (Smith 1997: 14).

And, even if modernity and rationalism should ultimately dilute the collective religious conviction of the elect community, the homeland will likely retain its sacred character. Smith explains:

Indeed, as secularization becomes more common, ancestral homelands acquire greater sanctity. This is partly the result of displacement of effect: the transfer of awe and reverence from the deity and his or her 'church' to the location of the shrine and its worshippers, for here all of the members participate equally by virtue of being ancestrally related to the territory in question. In this case, to *have been* hallowed suffices; once blessed, the land becomes even more sacred, because it attracts to itself much of the exaltation and holy love that was formerly accorded the deity. Thus 'religion', or in this case religious sentiments, permeates the secular forms and hence penetrates the realm of worldly politics (Smith 2000b: 807).

Yet, Smith is skeptical about the extent to which the present-day forces of rationalism and materialism have succeeded in consigning the myths of ethnic election to the pre-modern past, and he observes that traditional religion remains a pervasive influence in the modern world (Smith 1992: 449). Moreover, according to Smith, the secular ideology of modern nationalism itself appropriates the sacred character of religious antecedents. Indeed, Smith asserts, 'Nationalism is the secular, modern equivalent of the pre-modern, sacred myth of ethnic election' (Smith 1991: 84).

Ethnic election and modern nationalism

Smith explains 'that nationalism, as an ideological movement that seeks autonomy, unity and identity for a population deemed to be a nation, draws much of its passion, conviction and intensity from the belief in a national mission and destiny; and this belief in turn owes much to a powerful religious myth of ethnic election. Modern nationalism can be seen in part as deriving from powerful, external and pre-modern traditions, symbols and myths which are then taken up and recast in the nationalist ideologies of national mission and destiny as these emerge in the crucible of modernization' (Smith 1999a: 332). Yet, this does not necessarily mean that the myth of divine election has been entirely supplanted by modern nationalism. It is a durable collective mind-set and Smith reminds, 'The profound consequences of the concept of a chosen people, the passionate attachment to sacred lands and centers ... proved to be an enduring legacy for many peoples from late antiquity to modern times, sustaining their sense of uniqueness and nurturing their hopes of regeneration' (Smith 1991: 50). And, consequently, Smith clarifies that even today, 'We sometimes find examples of a symbiosis and even a fusion between the earlier religious myths and the nationalist ideal. Here the old religious myths, particularly where they are associated with the idea of a "covenant" between a people and its god, have survived intact, and are more or less consciously fused with a modern ethno-political nationalism' (Smith 1999a: 332).

Smith maintains that there is an affinity and indeed an 'ideological kinship between religious myths of ethnic election and nationalist ideals of mission and destiny' (Smith 1999a: 335). Just as a myth of ethnic election infused the elect people with a sense of moral ascendancy over outsiders, the ideology of nationalism also morally elevates the members of the nation above those who are not a part of the ethno-national community. Nationalism also entails the promise of the eventual triumph of the nation in a similar manner to which the myth of chosenness assured an ultimate providential rescue from degradation and oppression. The myth of divine election erected a formidable barrier between the sanctified community and others whom the deity did not favor. Nationalism too establishes socio-cultural criteria which distinguishes members from non-members in the demarcation of an exclusive ethno-national boundary. And, as all members of the elect ethnie were expected to faithfully discharge the duties required to maintain their collective election, nationalism also commands of its adherents a common responsibility of popular participation in the various national tasks which ensure the survival and success of the nation (Smith 1999a: 334–339).

Smith also advises that in some cases there is a covariance between an intense nationalist project and the ethnic myth of election which preceded it. He states, 'in both Holland and England in the late sixteenth and seventeenth centuries, there was a strong affirmation of both religious and national chosenness. In these cases, the two were inseparable: their nationalist ideals and sense of mission were a consequence of their belief in the divine election of their ethnies, and that belief was reinforced by their territorial national ideals' (Smith 1999a: 340).

The Example of the USA

According to Smith, this same covariance between ethnic chosenness and intense nationalism is also evident in the example of the USA 'despite the fact that religious fervor had declined, even in New England, by the end of the eighteenth century. Nevertheless, a strong case can be made that early Puritan beliefs in divine Providence and ethno-religious election helped to shape the central national myths of mission and destiny in the War of Independence and the foundation of the Republic' (Smith 1999a: 340). And, as Smith also points out, it was this same collective conception of religious and national chosenness which incubated the transcendent and irresistible article of America's sanctified national mission – manifest destiny.

Much has been written on the self-conception of the USA as a latter-day Israel and how the myth of chosenness defined the character of an American ethos, mandated the establishment of a just and upright nation, infused the citizens of a fledgling republic with an overarching sense of purpose, and prescribed the promotion of republican institutions through territorial expansion (Hudson 1970: ch. 1; Johnson 1986: 6; Tuveson 1968; Grosby 2002: ch. 9). Furthermore, the myth of divine election encouraged Americans to interpret their history through a religious prism and, in this regard, provided a stimulus for socio-political mobilization (Cherry 1997: 19). Ernest Lee Tuveson argues, 'confidence in the ideal of America as the new chosen people reached a peak of enthusiasm in the years immediately preceding 1860' (Tuveson 1968: 187). Certainly both antagonists in the Civil War were utterly convinced that the conflict was the fulfillment of biblical prophecy and that the Almighty was certainly on their side (see Beringer *et al.* 1986: ch. 5). And, although James Moorhead advises that there were often contradictory visions of American destiny, he demonstrates that the myth of election continued to influence the public debate surrounding such events as the acquisition of colonial possessions in 1898, the entry of the USA into the First

World War, and the passage of the anti-immigration National Origins Act of 1924 (Moorhead 1994). Yet, Winthrop S. Hudson suggests that the 'theological language, religious metaphors, and biblical allusions' which so powerfully informed the political dialogue of the USA declined after the First World War with the collective national confidence 'in a living God (judging, correcting, disciplining, guiding, and directing the American people) being slowly eroded and reduced to the pale affirmations of twentieth century "civil religion"' (Hudson 1970: xi). And, to be sure, only a very few studies have examined how the American myth of divine election has functioned in the more contemporary period.

However Smith argues that the older myth of religious chosenness continues to inspire contemporary America's sense of national mission and has exerted an enduring influence on US foreign policy even throughout the 1980s (Smith 1999a: 348). Indeed, in his impressive study of US global interventionism during the early days of the Cold War, John Fousek persuasively argues that the 'traditional nationalist ideologies of American chosenness, mission, and destiny' created a powerful anticommunist consensus which electrified Washington's determination to confront Soviet expansionism (Fousek 2000: 7). Conrad Cherry notes that the influence of the Protestant religious revival in the USA during the 1950s could be felt in even the highest offices of the land and patriotic Americans believed it to be their religious duty to defend democracy from the scourge of atheistic communism (Cherry 1998: 303–305). This concept of a providential mission to combat communism was very clearly articulated in Barry Goldwater's historic and controversial speech in 1964 in which he accepted the nomination of the Republican Party for President. Disillusioned by what he saw as the failure of the Kennedy and Johnson administrations to beat back the communist advance in Southeast Asia and elsewhere, the redoubtable Senator from Arizona declared: 'The good Lord raised this mighty Republic to be a home for the brave to flourish as the land of the free – not to stagnate in the swampland of collectivism, not to cringe before the bully of communism'.

William W. Cobb points out that the Puritan myth of Americans as a chosen people indeed figured prominently in the formulation of US policy toward Vietnam. However, Cobb recognizes an inherent tension in terms of the historical interpretation of the foundation myth among those who believe that America's elect status and national mission compels the active promotion of its lofty ideals of democracy and freedom abroad and those who feel that the providential destiny of the USA should only provide the model which other nations should seek to follow. Cobb demonstrates that the first interpretation often influenced policymakers to escalate American involvement in the conflict while the latter version of the myth sometimes reinforced the apprehension of critics of the war. In any event, despite the traumatic failure of the USA to accomplish its 'mission' in Vietnam, Cobb concludes that the myth of a providential destiny so deeply ingrained in the national consciousness survived the defeat in Southeast Asia and would subsequently continue to provide a justification for American interventionism abroad (Cobb 1998). Cherry, however, is not nearly so certain and argues that following the US reversal in Vietnam, 'the rhetoric of an aggressively pursued national destiny abroad seemed to connect less and less with the American experience. The failure of that long and costly war to deliver on several presidential administrations' promises to preserve democratic interests in the world rendered the rhetoric suspect' (Cherry 1998: 307).

Yet, the 'rhetoric' would return in a most robust, unalloyed, and unapologetic manner when Ronald Reagan entered the White House in 1981 and it seemed to strike a responsive chord among an American people which had again been aroused by the spirit of religious revivalism.[8] At his inauguration Reagan read aloud from II Chronicles 7:14: 'If my people, which are called by my name, shall humble themselves, pray and seek my face, and turn from their wicked ways; then will I hear from heaven, and will forgive their sin, and will heal their land' (cited in Schweizer 2002: 129). As if the messenger of the Almighty, Reagan indeed reminded his countrymen that they were an elect nation and that the covenant sealed by their Puritan forebears was still in force and that Americans must fulfill their providential destiny. Professing a vision of national renewal and collective redemption, Reagan promoted a project which was both political and religious to recover the golden age of American stability and prosperity and to reclaim the national greatness of the USA which was the holy birthright of the American people. And, amplifying Goldwater's cosmic summons, Reagan preached that a vigilant prosecution of the campaign against the godless communist menace was inextricably linked to America's providential mission (Edel 1987: ch. 9; Erickson 1985: ch. 5; Combs 1993, ch. 4). According to a recent biographer, following the assassination attempt in 1981, the un-reconstructed Cold Warrior became firmly convinced that God had rescued him so that he as president could combat the fiendish nemesis which he would ultimately denounce as the 'evil empire' (Schweizer 2002: 133–137). As Wilbur Edel reiterates, 'more than any other aspect of the Reagan program, the battle against Soviet communism took on the character of a crusade of good against evil' (Edel 1987: 149). And, of course, Reagan's vice-president and successor, George Bush was quick to invoke a divine blessing when he triumphantly heralded the end of the Cold War and he also employed the language of religious election to justify the intervention in Somalia and Desert Storm (Cobb 1998: 197–8; Cherry 1998: 307; Lehmann and Hutchinson 1994: 285–286). And, his son, the current President George W. Bush reminded Americans that theirs remained a special destiny when, in his inaugural address, he proclaimed 'an angel still rides in the whirlwind and directs' the progress of the nation (Longley 2002: 9–10).[9]

But, does the idea of a providential destiny continue to resonate in the American people in a world made more complicated and less secure by the events of 9/11? Conrad Cherry remains skeptical. Writing in the late 1990s, he emphasizes the lack of stability in the post-Cold War era and concludes, 'The new disordered situation would mute considerably any bold, self-confident claims about American destiny under God in the world at large' (Cherry 1998: 308). However, Longley argues that the attacks on New York and Washington have actually reinforced both an American sense of destiny and chosenness (Longley 2002: 69). There is much to substantiate Longley's assertion and, in a way, his claim should come as no surprise. Indeed, O'Brien reminds us that notions of chosenness – although they may remain dormant for years – usually reappear during times of crisis (O'Brien 1994: 144). It should be remembered that shortly after the planes crashed into the World Trade Center and the Pentagon, Pat Robertson and Jerry Falwell warned their countrymen that God was chastising an increasingly apostate American nation for permitting abortion and homosexuality. Although most Americans would hardly subscribe to this view of extreme covenantal logic – and, indeed both conservative churchmen ultimately retracted their callous and insensitive commentary, it does seem that Longley's observation is correct. Americans have certainly seemed to rediscover a sense of national mission to preserve their 'city on the hill' against the insidious threats which seek to undermine American democracy and prosperity. And, did not President Bush – at least initially and, in this case, most unwisely – employ the term 'crusade' to describe the War on Terror which his administration announced that it would vigorously prosecute against the enemies of freedom? And, even though the Bush White House has scrupulously reiterated its stance that the military campaign is in no way directed against Muslims *per se*, a number of prominent evangelical Protestant leaders – some of whom with close political connections – have made extremely offensive and provocative denunciations of Islam and its founder which inevitably suggests that the American people are engaged in a holy war against the infidel. Yet, in any event, the official rhetoric which has trumpeted the strike on Afghanistan and the invasion of Iraq is hardly devoid of religious fervor and emphasizes the righteous cause of a civilized, moral, and democratic society against the forces of evil and darkness.

It is also interesting to note that a number of polls conducted after 9/11 indicated that many Americans were re-embracing organized religion. Certainly evangelical Protestantism seems to be flourishing as evidenced by the commercial success of contemporary Christian music, the rapid growth of religious movements such as Young Life, and the vigorous expansion of foreign missions – especially it seems into Muslim lands. Writing after the upheaval of the World War I, Edward Frank Humphrey observed that Americans were reevaluating 'the elements of our nationalism; we are asking ourselves, "What is Americanism?"' (Humphrey 1924: 8). Humphrey seemed to suggest that religion, which had been such an integral determinant of US history might well exert a remedial and restorative influence. And, today, it seems that religion is equally readily available to fill the void. As the recent controversy surrounding the removal of a monument to the Ten Command-ments from an Alabama courthouse illustrates, religion in the USA has never completely retreated from the public square and – particularly in these uncertain times – it surely seems to resonate in the national consciousness and to remind Americans of a sense of providential destiny. Smith is indeed quite correct to emphasize the continuity of the myth of national election in the American experience.

Clash of the Elect?

And there is yet another intellectually intriguing observation in Smith's research which may also shed light on another aspect of international politics in the post 9/11 period. Smith notes that a politically powerful 'sense of national mission and destiny' is not only characteristic of the USA but also of contemporary France. Smith reveals, 'The Gaullist belief in France's national civilizing mission and her separate cultural destiny has had profound consequences for both the creation of European unity *vis-à-vis* the Anglo-Saxons and for France's leadership of her former colonies in Africa' (Smith: 1999a: 348). Could it be that the current atmosphere of estrangement in Franco-American relations represents far more than merely a disagreement over intervention in Iraq and the attendant issues relating to oil and reconstruction contracts? Might it be that the dispute between Washington and Paris is symptomatic of an increasing collision of the competing national missions of two nations which are powerfully infused with a sense of providential mission? It is a question which certainly warrants further attention. And, surely no one could provide a more compelling analysis in this regard than Anthony D. Smith.

Notes

1   This passage is taken from Cauthen (1999: 17).
2   There are a number of studies of the concept of election as it applied to biblical Israel from historical, theological, and philosophical perspectives. See Booth (1959); Pythian-Adams (1934); Rowley (1950); Danell (1953); Jocz (1958); Heller [n.d.]; Sohn (1991); Wells (2000); Novak (1995); and Eisen (1995).
3   For studies of the English and British, see Hastings (1997); Greenfeld (1992), ch. 2; McLeod (1999). For the Welsh, see Llywelyn (1999) and Davies (2002). For the Afrikaners, see Templin (1984) and Cauthen (1997). And, for antebellum Southerners and Confederates, see Peterson (1978) and Faust (1988).
4   This passage is taken from Cauthen (1999: 18). This deconstructionist attitude is clearly reflected in du Toit (1983, 1984, 1985, 1994) who argues that the Afrikaner myth of election was a fabrication of a nationalist elite which ultimately reinterpreted Afrikaner history through this sublime prism. Akenson (1992: 56–59) offers a critical appraisal of du Toit's approach. However, Zangwill (1918: 52–53), also argues 'that the British imperial project had already reached the stage of maturity before intellectuals attempted to invest it with religious significance'. And, Marstin (1979: 75–78) relates that even though Americans genuinely subscribed to the idea of a divine covenant during the days of the early republic, the election myth eventually degenerated into a cynical justification for imperial expansion.
5   Akenson (1992), Hutchinson and Lehman (1994), Cauthen (1999), Jospe, Madsen, and Ward (2001) and Longley (2002) do however provide comparative studies. See also Elazar (1996).
6   It is indeed unfortunate that the submission deadline for this chapter precedes the publication date of, and thus prevents comment on, Smith's most recent work on ethnic election which is

entitled *Chosen Peoples: Sacred Sources of National Identity* and is forthcoming from Oxford University Press in November 2003.

7   For a detailed discussion of ethno-symbolism, see Smith (1998: ch. 8).

8   Although Cherry (1998: 307) acknowledges that Reagan appropriated religious themes, he provides only minimal commentary in this regard. See Combs (1993: 105) and Johnson (1986: 12–13) for discussions of Reagan's emergence on the heels of the religious revival.

9   Longley (2002) offers an extremely interesting appraisal of how the myth of divine election has functioned in the USA and persuasively argues that a sense of chosenness continues to infuse American identity.

References

Akenson, Donald Harman. 1992. *God's Peoples: Covenant and Land in South Africa, Israel, and Ulster*. Ithaca, NY: Cornell University Press.

Armstrong, Karen. 2001. *The Battle for God: a History of Fundamentalism*. New York: Ballantine.

Beringer, Richard E. *et al.* 1986. *Why the South Lost the Civil War*. Athens, GA: University of Georgia Press.

Booth, Osborne. 1959. *The Chosen People: a Narrative History of the Israelites*. St. Louis, MO: Bethany.

Buhlmann, Walbert. 1982. *God's Chosen Peoples.* [trans.: Robert R. Barr] Maryknoll, NY: Orbis.

Catherwood, Christopher. 2002. *Why the Nations Rage: Killing in the Name of God*. Lanham, MD: Rowman & Littlefield.

Cauthen, Bruce. 1997. 'The myth of divine election and Afrikaner ethnogenesis' in Geoffrey Hosking and George Schöpflin (eds.), *Myth and Nationhood*. London: Macmillan.

Cauthen, Bruce. 1999. *Confederate and Afrikaner nationalism: myth, identity and gender in comparative perspective*, unpublished PhD thesis, University of London.

Cherry, Conrad. (ed.) 1997 [1971]. *God's New Israel: Religious Interpretations of American Destiny*. Chapel Hill, NC: University of North Carolina Press.

Cobb, William W. 1998. *The American Foundation Myth in Vietnam: Reigning Paradigms and Raining Bombs*. Lanham, MD: University Press of America.

Combs, James. 1993. *The Reagan Range: the Nostalgic Myth in American Politics*. Bowling Green, OH: Bowling Green State University Popular Press.

Danell, G. A. 1953. 'The idea of God's people in the Bible' in Anton Fridrichsen *et al.* (eds.), *The Root of the Vine: Essays in Biblical Theology*. Westminster: Dacre.

Davies, Grahame (ed.). 2002. *The Chosen People: Wales and the Jews*. Bridgend UK: Seren.

Du Toit, Andre. 1983. 'No chosen people: the myth of the Calvinist origin of Afrikaner nationalism and racial ideology', *American Historical Review* 88: 920–52.

Du Toit, Andre. 1984. 'Captive to the nationalist paradigm: Professor F. A. van Jaarsfeld and the historical evidence for the Afrikaner's ideas on his calling and mission', *South African Historical Journal* 16: 49–82.

Du Toit, Andre. 1985. ' 'Puritans in Africa?' Afrikaner Calvinism and neo-Kuyperian Calvinism in late nineteenth century South Africa', *Comparative Studies in Society and History* 27: 209–40.

Du Toit, Andre. 1994. 'The construction of Afrikaner chosenness' in William R. Hutchinson and Hartmut Lehmann (eds.), *Many Are Chosen: Divine Election and Western Nationalism*. Minneapolis, MN: Fortress.

Edel, Wilbur. 1987. *Defenders of the Faith: Religion and Politics from the Pilgrim Fathers to Ronald Reagan*. Westport, CN: Praeger.

Eisen, Robert. 1995. *Gersonides on Providence, Covenant, and the Chosen People: a Study in Medieval Jewish Philosophy and Biblical Commentary*. Albany, NY: State University of New York Press.

Elazar, Daniel J. 1996. *Covenant and Commonwealth: From Christian Separation through the Protestant Reformation*. London: Transaction.

Erickson, Paul D. 1985. *Reagan Speaks: the Making of an American Myth*. New York: New York University Press.

Faust, Drew Gilpin. 1988. *The Creation of Confederate Nationalism: Identity and Ideology in the Civil War South*. Baton Rouge, LA: Louisiana State University Press.

Fousek, John. 2000. *To Lead the Free World: American Nationalism and the Cultural Roots of the Cold War*. Chapel Hill, NC: University of North Carolina Press.

Greenfeld, Liah. 1992. *Nationalism: Five Roads to Modernity*. Cambridge, MA: Harvard University Press.

Grosby, Steven. 2002. *Biblical Ideas of Nationality: Ancient and Modern*. Winona Lake, IN: Eisenbrauns.

Hastings, Adrian. 1997. *The Construction of Nationhood: Ethnicity, Religion and Nationalism*. Cambridge: Cambridge University Press.

Heller, Bernard. (n.d.). *The Jewish Concept of the Chosen People*. Cincinnati, OH: Tract Commission.

Hudson, Winthrop S. (ed.) 1970. *Nationalism and Religion in America: Concepts of American Identity and Mission*. Evanston, IL: Harper & Row.

Humphrey, Edward Frank. 1924. *Nationalism and Religion in America 1774–1789*. Boston, MA: Chipman Law.

Hutchinson, William R. 1994. 'Introduction' in William R. Hutchinson and Hartmut Lehmann (eds.), *Many Are Chosen: Divine Election and Western Nationalism*. Minneapolis, MN: Fortress.

Hutchinson, William R. and Hartmut Lehmann (eds.). 1994. *Many Are Chosen: Divine Election and Western Nationalism*. Minneapolis, MN: Fortress.

Jocz, Jakob. 1958. *A Theology of Election: Israel and the Church*. New York: Macmillan.

Johnson, Paul. 1986. 'The almost chosen people: why America is different' in Richard John Neuhaus (ed.), *Unsecular America*. Grand Rapids, MI: William B. Eerdmans.

Jospe, Raphael, Truman J. Madsen and Seth Ward (eds.). 2001. *Covenant and Chosenness in Judaism and Mormonism*. Teaneck, NJ: Fairleigh Dickinson University Press.

Juergensmeyer, Mark. 1993. *The New Cold War: Religious Nationalism Confronts the Secular State*. Berkeley, CA: University of California Press.

Kepel, Gilles. 1994. *The Revenge of God: the Resurgence of Islam, Christianity, and Judaism in the Modern World* [trans. Alan Braley]. Cambridge: Polity.

Lehmann, Hartmut and William R. Hutchinson. 1994. 'Concluding reflections – and a glance forward' in William R. Hutchinson and Hartmut Lehmann (eds.), *Many Are Chosen: Divine Election and Western Nationalism*. Minneapolis, MN: Fortress.

Longley, Clifford. 2002. *Chosen People: the Big Idea that Shaped England and America*. London: Hodder & Stoughton.

Llywelyn, Dorian. 1991. *Sacred Place: Chosen People: Land and National Identity in Welsh Spirituality*. Cardiff: University of Wales Press.

Marstin, Ronald. 1979. *Beyond Our Tribal Gods: The Maturing of Faith*. Maryknoll, NY: Orbis.

McLeod, Hugh. 1999. 'Protestantism and British national identity, 1815–1945' in Peter van der Veer and Hartmut Lehmann (eds.), *Nation and Religion: Perspectives on Europe and Asia*. Princeton, NJ: Princeton University Press.

Moorhead, James H. 1994. 'The American Israel: protestant tribalism and universal mission' in William R. Hutchinson and Hartmut Lehmann (eds.), *Many Are Chosen: Divine Election and Western Nationalism*. Minneapolis, MN: Fortress.

Novak, David. 1995. *The Election of Israel: the Idea of the Chosen People*. Cambridge: Cambridge University Press.

O'Brien, Conor Cruise. 1988. *God-land: Reflections on Religion and Nationalism*. Cambridge, MA: Harvard University Press.

O'Brien, Conor Cruise. 1994. 'Response' in William R. Hutchinson and Hartmut Lehmann (eds.), *Many Are Chosen: Divine Election and Western Nationalism*. Minneapolis, MN: Fortress.

Peterson, Thomas Virgil. 1978. *Ham and Japeth: the Mythic World of Whites in the Antebellum South*. Metuchen, NJ: Scarecrow.

Pythian-Adams, W. J. 1934. *The Call of Israel: An Introduction to the Study of Divine Election.* London: Oxford University Press.

Rowley, H. H. 1950. *The Biblical Doctrine of Election.* London: Lutterworth.

Schweizer, Peter. 2002. *Reagan's War: the Epic Story of His Forty-Year Struggle and Final Triumph Over Communism.* New York: Doubleday.

Smith, Anthony D. 1986. *The Ethnic Origins of Nations.* Oxford: Basil Blackwell.

Smith, Anthony D. 1991. *National Identity.* London: Penguin.

Smith, Anthony D. 1992. 'Chosen peoples: why ethnic groups survive', *Ethnic and Racial Studies* 15(3): 436–56.

Smith, Anthony D. 1993. 'Ethnic election and cultural identity', *Ethnic Groups: an International Periodical of Ethnic Studies* 10(1–3): 9–25.

Smith, Anthony D. 1995. *Nations and Nationalism in a Global Era.* Cambridge: Polity.

Smith, Anthony D. 1997. 'Nation and ethnoscapes', *Oxford International Review* 8(2): 11–18.

Smith, Anthony D. 1998. *Nationalism and Modernism: a Critical Survey of Recent Theories of Nations and Nationalism.* London: Routledge.

Smith, Anthony D. 1999a. 'Ethnic election and national destiny: some religious origins of nationalist ideals', *Nations and Nationalism* 5(3): 331–55.

Smith, Anthony D. 1999b. *Myths and Memories of the Nation.* Oxford: Oxford University Press.

Smith, Anthony D. 2000a. *The Nation in History: Historiographical Debates about Ethnicity and Nationalism.* Hanover, NH: University Press of New England.

Smith, Anthony D. 2000b. 'The "sacred" dimension of nationalism', *Millennium: Journal of International Studies* 29(3): 791–814.

Smith, Anthony D. 2001. *Nationalism: Theory, Ideology, History.* Cambridge: Polity.

Sohn, Seock-Tae. 1991. *The Divine Election of Israel.* Grand Rapids, MI: William B. Eerdmans.

Templin, J. Alton. 1984. *Ideology on a Frontier: the Theological Foundations of Afrikaner Nationalism, 1652–1910.* Westport, CN: Greenwood.

Tuveson, Ernest Lee. 1968. *Redeemer Nation: the Idea of America's Millennial Role.* Chicago, IL: University of Chicago Press.

Wells, Jo Bailey. 2000. *God's Holy People: a Theme in Biblical Theology.* Sheffield: Sheffield Academic Press.

Zangwill, Israel. 1918. *Chosen Peoples: the Hebraic Ideal Versus the Teutonic.* London: George Allen & Unwin.

3

The timelessness of nations

WALKER CONNOR

Preamble

In 1989, I presented a paper entitled 'When is a nation?' at a conference in London.[1] Anthony Smith, who attended the conference, subsequently requested that I allow it to appear in *Ethnic and Racial Studies* (Connor 1990). The article appears to have elicited a surprising amount of interest in LSE circles. John Hutchinson and Anthony Smith were good enough to include it (in abbreviated form) in their Oxford collection on nationalism (Hutchinson and Smith 1995: 154–159). Smith, who (as any serious student of nationalism is aware) has written voluminously and eruditely on the evolution of national identity, graciously credited me with 'bringing [the issue of dating a nation] into the open as an issue in its own right and in revealing its importance for an understanding of the place of the nation in history and in the contemporary world' (Smith 2002: 68). The Fourteenth Annual Conference of the Association for the Study of Ethnicity and Nationalism (ASEN) to be held at LSE during 2004 is entitled 'When is the nation?', and my participation was solicited, according to an ASEN officer, because it was I who had raised the issue.

Now this is all very flattering but, at the risk of impersonating Dickens' deceitfully self-deprecating Uriah Heep, my piece does not merit such attention. The article in question was a modest, ten-page effort, little more than a few ruminations omitted from a just completed piece entitled 'From tribe to nation?' (Connor 1991). The title of the earlier work, absent the question mark, had been assigned; my addition was to indicate that the progression, assumed by some anthropologists, from family, to band, to clan, to tribe, to nation has certainly not proved to be an iron law of group evolution. Cases were offered of peoples who once appeared to many to be destined to form a nation (e.g., a Slavic 'nation') but which in fact produced several nations, as well as cases in which nations evolved from highly unlikely multiethnic materials (e.g., the English, French, or German nations). Toward its end, the article addressed the question of when did national consciousness become a reality among those European peoples – Dutch, English, German, Russian, Swedish, etc. – who have unquestionably evolved into nations. After acknowledging the inspiration for raising the question to Eugen Weber's *Peasants into Frenchmen: the Modernization of Rural France, 1870–1914* (Weber 1976) and examining other data, the article concluded that today's nations came into being much more recently than has been generally acknowledged.

As implied by its title, 'When is a nation?' focalized to a greater degree upon the issue of when did various nations emerge. Smith's piece in 2002, which was alluded to earlier, was essentially a critique of this article. His principal concern was that it was too modernistic, not permitting sufficient allowance for the possibility of nations existing prior to the nineteenth century. He attributed this to my insistence that nationalism is a mass – not an elite – phenomenon. This is indeed fundamental. If one person accepts as conclusive early historical references to the existence of a nation on the part of an aristocrat, cleric, or scribe, while another discounts such claims in the absence of evidence of national consciousness among the putative nation, sharp disagreement concerning the time of the nation's emergence is to be anticipated.

Smith also maintained that our disagreement was rooted in different perceptions or definitions of the nation, and, in the course of reviewing some of his work for this response, I was indeed surprised to learn that our perceptions of the nation are at far greater variance than I had realized. As will be noted below, my own definition of the nation is tied inextricably to ethnicity: a belief in or an intuitive conviction of common descent. In a very early work, Smith explicitly denied any significant role to ethnic considerations and emphasized common citizenship as an essential element (Smith 1971: 180, 171, 186, 187). However, after reading what I consider to be his magnum opus – *The Ethnic Origins of Nations* (Smith 1986) – which contained statements such as 'not only must nations be founded upon ethnic cores if they are to endure' (p. 207) – I thought our perceptions were compatible.[2] However, as will be noted below, Smith's use of *nation* is far more inclusive than my own. Indeed, I fear so much more inclusive that intellectual dialogue may be impossible.

What follows, nonetheless, is essentially a response to Smith's concerns beginning with the matter of definitions. Perhaps it is worth noting that this is the first time that I have ever responded to a critique of my work. I do so in acknowledgment of my respect for Smith's scholarship.

What is a Nation?

Smith finds my definition of the nation inadequate in that it amounts to a purely psychological explanation at the expense of more objective components. Here is my definition and a corollary:

Definition: The nation is the largest group that shares a sense of common ancestry.
Corollary: The nation is the largest group that can be influenced/aroused/motivated/mobilized by appeals to common kinship.

Each of these definitions differentiates the nation from all other groups. Is there a Basque, Polish, or Welsh nation? Yes. Is there an American, British, or Indian nation? No.

Each of these definitions is complete in itself. Are there elements that contribute to the feeling of common ancestry? Of course! The major students of nationalism before World War II customarily investigated factors that often accompany national consciousness: common language, religion, and the like. But as stated 30 years ago, when investigation is concentrated on the essence of the nation, such tangibles are 'significant only to the degree that they contribute to the sense of uniqueness' (Connor 1972: 337). They are the commonly encountered accompaniment, the accoutrement, of the nation, and their impact upon national identity should be studied through a comparative lens.[3] That impact will vary both among nations and over time.

The definition employed by Smith in his 'Dating the nation' is quite different. The nation, he wrote, is 'a named human population occupying an historic territory, and sharing myths, memories, a single public culture and common rights and duties for all members' (Smith 2002: 65). This is not a definition that succeeds in categorizing nations according to their essence. It would not, for example, differentiate the notion of British from that of Welsh. Or Belgian from Fleming. Or Spanish from Basque.

It is evident that Smith's 'nation' is much more supple than my own. A very succinct yet comprehensive statement of his overall approach to the nation attests to this (Smith 2001: 86–87):

[T]here have emerged two symbolic conceptions of the modern nation. On the one hand, there is a more 'civic-territorial' ideal of the nation, one which emphasizes the importance of long-term residence in a clearly demarcated territory, of the part played by unified law codes and legal institutions over the whole territory, of the equal and common rights and duties of citizenship in the territorial nation, and of the central role of a public, civic culture for all citizens which embodies the myths, memories and symbols of the nation. On the other hand, there is a more 'ethnic-genealogical' conception of the nation, which stresses the importance of presumed ancestry ties and kin relatedness for citizenship, the crucial role of popular mobilization and a participant populace, the centrality of vernacular language, customs and culture, and the binding force of authentic, native historical memories of and in the homeland. ... [T]here is considerable overlap between these two conceptions of the nation. Actual instances of the nation have both civic and ethnic components, and there is a constant oscillation and flux between the preponderance of civic or ethnic myths and symbols. The notions of a unified national identity, a homeland and citizenship play vital roles in both conceptions, and both insist on the importance of possessing a common and distinctive mass culture.

Smith's first 'nation' is therefore synonymous with citizenship in a state regardless of that state's ethnic composition. Although Smith's second conception of 'the nation' is concerned more with kinship and ancestry, it also ties the nation solidly to citizenry in a state. This association with the state is also evident in his earlier cited definition with its references to 'a single public culture and common rights and duties'.[4] And in a still earlier definition (Smith 1991: 14), Smith included as essential 'a common economy', which, of course, could be experienced (if at all) only within a single state. According to Smith's criteria, then, the Germans of West and East Germany were not a single nation between 1945 and the reunification of 1990, nor currently are the Basques, Catalans, and the many other national peoples divided by state borders.

The use of the word nation to refer to a state or to the citizenry of the state regardless of its ethnic composition, as well as the corresponding tendency to use nationalism to refer to loyalty to the state (which should be termed patriotism) rather than to the nation as I have defined it, is very common in the literature,[5] and has been the principal cause of the ambiguity and confusion plaguing the study of nationalism (Connor 1978).[6]

The current vogue among writers on nationalism is to refer to loyalty to the state as civic nationalism and loyalty to the nation as ethnic nationalism. But this only tends to propagate the misconception that we are dealing with two variants of the same phenomenon. If Smith and others prefer to use civic identity or civic loyalty in preference to patriotism – fine. But the fundamental dissimilarities between state loyalty and nationalism should not be glossed over by employing the noun nationalism to refer to two quite different phenomena.

There is much more involved here than mere semantics. The two loyalties are of two different orders of things (kinship versus civic), and while in the case of a people clearly dominant within a state (for example, the ethnically Turkish or Castilian peoples) the two may reinforce one another, in the case of minorities (such as the Kurds of Turkey or the Basques of Spain) the two identities may clash. Indeed, the political history of the world since the Napoleonic Wars has been largely a tale of tension between the two identities, each possessing its own irrefragable and exclusive claim to political legitimacy. I therefore recommend the following glossary:

Glossary

Ethnic – derived from *ethnos*, the ancient Greek word for a nation in the latter's pristine sense of a group characterized by common descent; the prefix *ethno* therefore means national.

Ethnonationalism – a redundancy, coined in response to the general tendency to *misuse* the word nationalism to convey loyalty to the state rather than to one's national group; it is designed to leave no doubt in the reader's mind that the author is discussing loyalty to the nation.

Ethnocracy – an ethnically homogeneous political unit; it can vary in size from a small village to a modern state.

Gemeinschaft – an association resting upon a sense of kinship, real or imagined; gemeinshaft groupings include the family, band, tribe, and nation.

Gessellschaft – an association of individuals resting upon the conviction that their personal self-interest can be best promoted through membership in the group; whereas a gemeinschaft society is based upon sentiment, the gessellschaft society is in large part a product of rational self-interest (in political philosophy, the case for the political legitimacy of the gessellschaft state has been closely tied to the notion of the social contract).

Nation – a group of people sharing a myth of common ancestry; it is the largest grouping that can be mobilized by appeals to common blood (nation is often *improperly* employed as a synonym for state, as in the League of Nations or the United Nations, or as a synonym for the citizenry of a state regardless of its ethnic complexity, as in references to 'the American nation').

Nationalism – identity with and loyalty to one's nation in the pristine sense of that word (see above); nationalism is often *incorrectly* used to refer to loyalty to the state.

Nation-state – that relatively rare situation in which the borders of a state and a nation closely coincide; a state with an ethnically homogeneous population.

Patriotism – devotion to one's state and its institutions (*civic nationalism* is the currently fashionable, but confusing, substitute for patriotism; *civic loyalty* or *civic identity* would better convey this type of devotion, without misrepresenting it as a form of nationalism).

State – the major political unit in world politics; country.

The dating of nations

Some of Smith's criticisms of 'When is a nation?' appear to be due to a misunderstanding. The article did not rule out the possibility of ancient and/or medieval nations. It did not address the issue. What it did address, as noted at its outset, was the time of the emergence of national consciousness among those European peoples who are 'currently recognized nations'. Moreover, the article did not deny historical roots to nations (the existence of which Ernest Gellner and Smith once debated under the rubric of whether nations have navels). Again, it did not address the issue, but it did acknowledge the evolutionary character of the nation in the opening sentence of the abstract: 'Although numerous authorities have addressed the question, "What is a nation?", far less attention has been paid to the question, "At what point *in its development* does a nation come into being?"' (Emphasis added.)

Ethnic identity and ethnic conflict have been fixtures throughout history, but today's special foci of ethnic identity, which we call (or should call) nations, are relatively recent creations, very few antedating the late nineteenth century. As noted, Eugen Weber deserves credit as the pathfinder. He documented that most people within France in 1870 lived in culturally isolated rural villages and were devoid of French consciousness. Awareness of being French expanded in subsequent decades as more intensive communication and transportation networks developed and centralized administration (particularly over the schools) improved, but the process was still incomplete by World War I. A survey of group identities on the part of European migrants to the USA during the nineteenth and early twentieth centuries confirmed that the French example was not unique. Concepts of Croatian, Italian, Norwegian, Polish, Lithuanian and the like were largely absent. People regularly identified themselves in terms of village, clan, district, region, or a local ethnic identity such as Kashube.

Settlement patterns in the host country, as well as the names and membership of social organizations, reflected these divisions. Relations between small collectivities who ostensibly formed a single national group were often conflictual, and intermarriage was extremely rare.

The Dutch who came to the USA in the 1840s and 50s represent a particularly fascinating case because (1) they came from a small country that posed no barriers to transportation and communication and (2) had long been treated by historians as a people sharing a common identity. But upon arrival in the USA, they proved to be a remarkably diverse people whose local identities obscured any common Dutch consciousness.

Immigrants carried this localism to America and frequently tried to create segregated enclaves within larger Dutch communities. The pattern was particularly evident in the colony of Holland, Michigan. The central town, called simply *de stad*, was founded in 1847 largely by people from Geldeland and Overijssel provinces. Within two years, new arrivals founded villages within a 10-mile radius bearing the provincial names of Zeeland, Vriesland, Groningen, Overisel, North Holland, Drenthe, and Geldersche Buurt (Gelderland Neighborhood), or the municipal names Zutphen, Nordeloos, Hellendoorn, Harderwijk, and Staphorst. There was even a settlement called Graafschap, consisting of Dutch-speaking, Reformed Church Germans from Bentheim in Hanover. The majority of settlers in these villages originated in the place bearing the village name; they spoke the local dialect and perpetuated local customs of food and dress. The entire Michigan settlement was known as *de Kolonie*, but it required the passing of the first generation before the colony became a common community. The Pella, Iowa, and Chicago settlements, also founded in 1847, similarly had particular regional origins (Thernstrom 1980: 287).

Recent scholarship conducted by specialists on the history of one or another European people does not challenge the validity of the American example. There is a consensus that a broad scale national consciousness cannot be detected among the Baltic, Germanic and Slavic peoples prior to the nineteenth century. We have already noted Eugen Weber's concurrence with regard to most people living within France. Even the remarkable case of the Dutch in the USA is replicated by the Danes at home. Again, despite their limited number and a small country offering no physical barriers to integration (as well as a lengthy history as a kingdom), Danish national consciousness was a surprisingly recent, nineteenth century development (Ostergard 1992).

The literature on the English represents a partial exception. There has been a recent spate of monographs and articles, variously assigning the emergence of nationalism among the English to eras stretching from the early medieval period to the late nineteenth century. The most recent of these efforts, which includes a 53-page bibliography, favors the case for the late nineteenth century (Kumar 2003: particularly pp. 202–225).

How can scholars disagree so starkly? This was part of my explanation offered in 'When is a nation?' (p. 100):

A key problem faced by scholars when dating the emergence of nations is that national consciousness is a mass, not an elite phenomenon, and the masses until quite recently isolated in rural pockets and being semi- or totally illiterate, were quite mute with regard to their sense of group identity(ies). Scholars have been necessarily largely dependent upon the written word for their evidence, yet it has been the elites who have chronicled history. Seldom have their generalities about national consciousness been applicable to the masses, and very often the elites' conception of the nation did not even extend to the masses.

In short, evidence of ethnic consciousness among the aristocracy or the literati cannot be accepted as evidence of national consciousness without evidence that it is shared across a broader spectrum of the putative nation.

Smith's response, as noted, is to question the description of the nation as a mass phenomenon. I confess that I do not know how to answer this, because I assumed that all students of nationalism agreed that the nation, when applied to a named people such as the English, German, or French, implied a single group consciousness that transcended in its appeal all lesser divisions within the group. It is in this form that the nation becomes a major force in history, and this is why historians date the age of nationalism to the French Revolution and the Napoleonic Era. A Saxon of the period offered a remarkably perspicacious evaluation and prediction (Palmer and Cotton 1971: 448):

The Revolution has awakened all forces in the French and given to each force its proper sphere of action. ... What infinite power lies sleeping undeveloped and unused within the womb of the nation! Within the breasts of thousands there lives a great genius, but their lowly condition prevents its flowering. ... The Revolution has set in action the national energy of the entire French people, putting the different classes on an equal social and fiscal basis. ... If the other states wish to establish the former balance of power, they must open up and use these same resources. They must take over the Revolution.

In sum, we study nations and nationalism because they have been and continue to be so consequential, and they became and remain so consequential because their appeal has not been restricted to elites but has extended to all major segments of the people bearing the nation's appellation. Smith rhetorically asks: 'must our understanding, indeed our definition, of the concept of the nation be so closely tied to the masses?' (2002: 60). To the degree that 'the masses' suggests a social classification (the hoi polloi, the Third Estate, the common people), the answer is no. The nation, to be a mass phenomenon, must refer to the entire mass, 'the masses' and elites alike.

This brings us to the question of how broadly national consciousness must be shared by the mass before we can describe it judiciously as a nation. Smith describes my position as 'only when the great majority of a designated population has become nationally aware, can we legitimately speak of it as a nation' (2002: 57). Here is what I wrote:

The delay – in some cases stretching into centuries – between the appearance of national consciousness among sectors of the elite and its extension to the masses reminds us of the obvious but all-too-often ignored fact that nation-formation is a process, not an occurrence or event. And this, in turn, further thwarts the attempt to answer the question, 'When is a nation?' Events are easily dated; stages in a process are not. At what point did a sufficient number/percentage of a given people acquire national consciousness so that the group merited the title of nation? There is no formula. We want to know the point in the process at which a sufficient portion of the populace has internalized the national identity in order to cause appeals in its name to become an effective force for mobilizing the masses. While this does not require that 100 per cent of the people have acquired such national consciousness, the point at which a quantitative addition in the number sharing a sense of common nationhood has triggered the qualitative transformation into a nation resists arithmetic definition.

Having thus stressed that 'there is no formula', I did not further address the complexities of this question in my short piece. If I had done so, I would have noted that even the very loose standard of a point sufficient to permit appeals in its name to undergird an effective popular movement may face ambiguities when applied to a given people. Napoleon is customarily credited with being the first major historical figure to have employed such appeals and, as reflected in the foregoing quote from a Saxon contemporary, to have unleashed thereby a new, formidable element into global affairs. And yet we know that some one-third of Napoleon's forces were foreign mercenaries, and that most of the people in rural France did not share a French national consciousness for at least a half-century following Napoleon's death. This is in keeping with my reminder that nation-formation is a process. Did the French people deserve the title of nation during the Napoleonic Era? Or only later in the century? I am very tempted to say 'Who cares?' The preeminent point is that with Napoleon and the *levee en masse* we have our first evidence that national consciousness was no longer restricted to the aristocracy or other elites. Weber's study established that the spreading of this identity was indeed a process still under way between 1870 and 1914. His study also underlined how inappropriate it was for historians to place much credence on a few historical references to a much earlier French nation: very reputable historians had been beguiled into assertions, such as 'the texts make it plain that so far as France and Germany were concerned this national consciousness was highly developed about the year 1100'.[7] An assertion based upon an historical assertion is still just an assertion.

Smith also took sharp exception to a passing reference to dating national consciousness in a democracy (Smith 2002: 57):

Theoretically, Connor's argument is based on the assertion that nations and nationa-lism are mass phenomena and that therefore only when the great majority of a desi-gnated population has become nationally aware, can we legitimately speak of it as a nation. In authoritarian states like Nazi Germany and fascist Japan, we can ascertain their nation-formation after the event, because the population could clearly be mobilized along national lines. But in democracies, mass participation as measured in the elections provides the best indicator of nation-formation, because in a democracy, 'the refusal to permit large sections of the populace to participate in the political process may be viewed as tantamount to declaring that those who are disenfranchised are not members of the nation' (Connor: 99). Thus the English could hardly begin to be described as a nation before the 1867 Reform Act, which gave the vote to some 80 per cent of the adult male population, and certainly not a fully-fledged nation until 1918, when the remaining 20 per cent of men and all women over thirty years of age secured the vote.

He repeats and extends his criticism in his most recent article (Smith 2003: 2).

There is, first, an empirical problem, since one of the key features of the modernist definition is mass participation, that is, the involvement of its members in the social and political life of the nation. Walker Connor has explained this stipulation as requiring a majority of its members to be aware of belonging to the nation, which, in a democracy, would mean that they must participate in politics and therefore be able to vote. So, no nation could be said to exist before the early twentieth century, since in the vast majority of cases women were not enfranchised until after the First World War. But such a radical modernism, besides forcing us to rewrite the very terms of European and American histories, conflates a sense of belonging with political participation and enfranchisement, and militates against Connor's other observation that the nation emerges in stages (even if we cannot so term it until there is mass political participation).

Now this is what I wrote:

In some societies the history of the voting franchise also offers hints of when a nation came into existence. As we are reminded by the history of the rise of national consciousness in, *inter alia*, Japan and Germany, democratic institutions are certainly no prerequisite for nation-formation. However, if a society describes itself as a democracy, then the refusal to permit large sections of the populace to participate in the political process may be viewed as tantamount to declaring that those who are disenfranchised are not members of the nation. If the rights of Englishmen include the right to vote, then what can one say concerning a so-called English nation in which most Englishmen were prohibited from exercising that right? Before 1832, when landlords alone were allowed to vote, it is estimated that only one in sixty adult English males could vote. Following the so-called Reform Bill of that year, one in every thirty male adults would be permitted to do so.

Please note that I do *not* say that in democracies, 'mass participation as measured in elections provides the best indicator of nation-formation'.[8] I am not interested in the level of *participation* but in the restriction to an elite of a fundamental democratic *right* (the franchise which in the case at hand meant a restriction to less than 2 per cent of the would-be-nation prior to 1832).[9] Please note also that I did not mention the matter of woman suffrage. It was not germane to the specific context because the right of women to vote was denied throughout the nineteenth century to all women; had women of the aristocracy and gentry been favored in this regard, it would have been germane. Finally, note that I only suggested that the franchise might 'offer hints of when a nation came into existence,' not that it represents, to quote Smith, 'the best indicator.' Indeed, to be consistent, Smith should embrace this data on the *right* to vote as a conclusive indicator of the absence of an English nation in the early nineteenth century, since it is his definitions of the nation that stress 'common rights and duties'.

Onward and Upward

Nothing in 'When is a nation?' ruled out the possibility of nations existing in pre-modern times. Even the mild closing warning that 'claims that a particular nation existed prior to the late nineteenth century should be treated cautiously' applied only to 'Europe's currently recognized nations'. Perhaps the Iceni who revolted against the Romans under Queen Boudicca in 61 could be shown to deserve being called a nation; but the case must be made on evidence and not on simple assertion. Similarly, the search by Smith and others to find something akin to national sentiments among the elites of earlier ages is to be applauded, if proper regard is paid to how broadly across the named people (French, English, etc.) these sentiments were intended to be shared and were in fact shared. Here I can only suggest that painstaking and imaginative research can go far toward accomplishing this (for more specifics, see Connor 2005). But for most current students of nations and nationalism, such research will require a reordering of primary interest in ascertaining the view of group-self held by elites to that held by the people writ large. Sensitivity to shreds of evidence of the perception(s) that the multitude themselves hold of their group identity(ies) must be developed. Weber's *Peasants into Frenchmen* can aid in this development, as can the works of James Scott with regard to deciphering attitudes on the part of seemingly voiceless peasants (see also Connor 2005). If the nation is a mass phenomenon, then our priority should be to render the mass intelligible.

As for the article 'When is a nation?' that was the focus of both Smith's critique and this response, I believe I would stand by the following:

The chronological fixing of the birth of any nation is usually a matter of great dispute. In some instances, historians have placed the advent of a nation in the Middle Ages, while others have maintained that the same nation's formation came about only in the late nineteenth century. In the case of some putative nations (for example, the Montenegrins), it is problematic whether nationhood has even yet been achieved. The fact that scholars can disagree by hundreds – in some cases several hundreds – of years about the date to be assigned the emergence of a nation or can disagree whether a nation does or does not presently exist underlines the difficulties involved in such calculation. Among the barriers to dating the formation of a nation are:

(1) National consciousness is a mass- rather than an elite-phenomenon, and the masses, until quite recently isolated in rural pockets and being semi- or totally illiterate, were quite mute with regard to their sense of group identity(ies).
(2) The dependence of scholarship upon the written word has necessarily caused undue weight to be given to the opinions and assertions of the literate elite, whose generalizations concerning the existence of national consciousness are often highly suspect; in many cases those declaring the existence of a nation prior to the nineteenth century considered the masses ineligible for membership. The danger posed by over reliance on the written word is underlined by many instances in which individual, contemporary members of the intellectual elite claimed contending national identities for the same people (Macedonian vs. Bulgar, Montenegrin vs. Serb).
(3) There is a lag time of varying, in some instances unending, duration between the espousal of a national consciousness by members of a literate elite and its adoption by the masses.
(4) Nation-formation is a process, not an occurrence, and the point in the process at which a sufficient portion of a people has internalized a national identity so as to make appeals in the name of the nation an effective force for mobilizing the masses does not lend itself to precise calculation.
(5) The process of nation-formation is not sequentially preordained, but capable of terminating at any point and, if not essentially completed, capable of reversal.

(6) The sense of constituting a distinct and ancestrally related people, which is central to the sense of nationhood, often has little relationship to fact, so the ethnographic history of a people is therefore often of little pertinence to the study of nation-formation.

The timelessness of nations

To again risk assuming the persona of Uriah Heep, I do not feel that the issue of 'When is a nation' is of key significance. Although today's nations may in fact be modern phenomena, in a more important sense they defy dating. Stathis Gourgouris, Professor of Comparative Literature and Hellenic Studies at Princeton, has stated this seeming paradox with remarkable brevity and clarity:

My long term research into the nature of national formation and the development of nationalism in both Europe and Greece has taught me two insurmountable historical facts: (1) national symbols are always people's inventions, and (2) people often die for them with the satisfaction of serving eternal truth (Letter to the Editor, *New York Times*, 9 May 1994).

Identity does not draw its sustenance from facts but from perceptions; not from chronological/factual history but from sentient/felt history.

Failure to appreciate that national identity is predicated upon sentient history undergirds a current vogue in the literature on national identity to bifurcate contributors in terms of (1) 'primordialists' and (2) 'social constructivists'/'instrumentalists'/'modernists.' What is missed in all this academic labeling is that, while from the viewpoint of objective history, today's nations are modern creatures, in popular perceptions they are, to borrow a word from Gourgouris, 'eternal', that is to say, 'beyond time', 'timeless'. And it is not facts but perceptions of facts that undergird attitudes and behavior.

Notes

1   Keynote Paper, 'When is a nation?', *Conference on Pre-Modern and Modern National Identity in Russia/the USSR and Eastern Europe*, University of London, School of Slavonic and East European Studies, March 1989.

2   There were, however, troubling references still to the necessity of common citizenship, e.g., on p. 165: 'Central to the concept of the nation is citizenship.' And the multiethnic Swiss were described as 'a solidary nation' (p. 146).

3   In earlier works, I have comparatively investigated the impact of homeland, religion, and economic considerations upon national identity.

4   Smith (2001) actually added a third type of 'nation' (one formed by multiethnic, immigrant societies, such as in 'America, Canada, or Australia') which would be even less influenced by myths of descent.

5   In the eighteenth century, the French statesman, Robert Turgot, complained of such a loose usage, insisting that *nation* continue to denote 'a group of families and peoples who speak the same language' and not 'a state [or] a people living in the same territory and subject to the same authority' (Cited in Margue 1979: 44–5).

6   Smith maintained that his 1991 definition which included, *inter alia*, common rights and duties and a common economy 'sets it clearly apart from any conception of the state. The latter refers exclusively to public institutions, differentiated from, and autonomous of, other social institutions and exercising a monopoly of coercion and extraction within a given territory. The nation, on the other hand, signifies a cultural and political bond, uniting in a single political community all who share a historic culture and homeland.' (Smith 1991: 14–15). Presumably, however, the 'political bond' and the 'single political community' imply a state. In any case, a people divided by a political border would not be considered a nation under Smith's definition.

7   For this and other illustrations of unsubstantiated early claims of nationhood, see Connor (1990: 92). The reference to German nationalism in 1100 is equally unfounded. For evidence that it was a late nineteenth century development (see Hamerow 1969, Hughes 1988, Gagliardo 1969).

8   In some manner unclear to me, Smith ties his interpretation of my passing comments on democracy to what he critically describes as my 'quantitative methodology'. This characterization is made four times (Smith 2002: 59, 62 (twice), and 68). As one who has never squared a chi and who views quantitative analytical studies of comparative nationalism as of little value, I must demur. Smith further pairs this characterization of my work as quantitative with what he sees as an inappropriate overemphasis upon the individual to produce 'methodological individualism' (Smith 2002: 60). Connor 'insists on the primacy of the individual and sees the nation as the sum of its individuals members' (pp. 59–60). I have never insisted or even suggested any such thing. My nation, after all, is 'a mass phenomenon'. It is the 'gesselschaft' – Smith's 'civic nation' – that rests upon individualism (see the above Glossary).

9   The issue of participation may merit a comment. Smith elsewhere attributes my view of nations currently recognized as such as being of recent vintage to three alleged assumptions: 'nations are necessarily mass phenomena; national awareness is tantamount to participation; and, in democracies, participation is measured by voting' (Smith 2002: 69). To the first assumption I plead guilty. The third (which I deny) is treated in part below. The second I do not understand. Certainly I would maintain that before acknowledging the existence of a nation, some evidence for popular national consciousness must be uncovered. But this could be passive resistance by a group to an authority viewed as alien, including the many forms of passive non-compliance brilliantly described by James Scott (See, for example, Scott 1986: 5–35). Or the passive protection extended by a homeland people to a guerrilla movement conducting a war of national liberation or resistance. For a fuller treatment of the varied forms of evidence of the existence/non-existence of a nation, see Connor (2005).

References

Connor, Walker. 1972. 'Nation-building or nation destroying?', *World Politics* 24.
Connor, Walker. 1978. 'A nation is a nation, is an ethnic group, is a …', *Ethnic and Racial Studies* 1: 377–400.
Connor, Walker. 1990. 'When is a nation?', *Ethnic and Racial Studies* 13: 92–103.
Connor, Walker. 1991. 'From tribe to nation?', *History of European Ideas* 13: 5–18.
Connor, Walker. 2005. *Popular Popular Sovereignty*. Cambridge: Cambridge University Press.
Gagliardo, John. 1969. *From Pariah to Patriot: the Changing Image of the German Peasant 1770–1840*. Lexington State of Kentucky, University Press of Kentucky.
Hamerow, Theodore. 1969. *The Social Foundations of German Unification 1858–1876*, Vol.2. Princeton, NJ: Princeton University Press.
Hughes, Michael. 1988. *Nationalism and Society: Germany 1800–1945*. London: Edward Arnold.
Hutchinson, John and Anthony Smith (eds.). 1995. *Nationalism*. Oxford: Oxford University Press.
Kumar, Krishan. 2003. *The Making of English National Identity*. Cambridge: Cambridge University Press.
Margue, Pierre. 1979. *Contre L'Etat-Nation*. Paris: Denöel.
Ostergard, Uffe. 1992. 'Peasants and Danes: the Danish national identity and political culture', *Comparative Studies in Society and History* 34: 3–27.

Palmer, R. R. and Joel Cotton. 1971. *A History of the Modern World*. 4th ed. New York: Alfred Knopf.

Scott, James. 1986. 'Everyday forms of peasant resistance' in *Everyday Forms of Peasant Resistance in South-East Asia*. London: Frank Cass.

Smith, Anthony. 1971. *Theories of Nationalism*. London: Duckworth.

Smith, Anthony. 1986. *The Ethnic Origins of Nations*. Oxford: Blackwell.

Smith, Anthony. 1991. *National Identity*. London: Penguin.

Smith, Anthony. 2001. 'Ethno-symbolism' in Athena Leoussi (ed.), *Encyclopaedia of Nationalism*. New Brunswick: Transaction.

Smith, Anthony. 2002. 'Dating the nation' in Daniele Conversi (ed.), *Ethnonationalism and the Contemporary World: Walker Connor and the Study of Nationalism*. London: Routledge.

Smith, Anthony. 2003. 'The genealogy of nations: an ethnosymbolic approach'. Forthcoming.

Thernstrom, Stephen (ed.). 1980. *Harvard Encyclopedia of American Ethnic Groups*. Cambridge, MA: Harvard University Press.

Weber, Eugen. 1976. *Peasants into Frenchmen: the Modernization of Rural France, 1870–1914*. Stanford, CA: Stanford University Press.

4

Place, kinship and the case for non-ethnic nations

THOMAS HYLLAND ERIKSEN

For many years and through an impressive number of books and journal articles, A. D. Smith has defended his view of the *ethnie* or ethnic community as the sociocultural and historical basis of modern nationalism (Smith 1986, 1991, 1995, 1998). As the readers of this journal are aware, his view is influential but far from uncontroversial. Already Hans Kohn (1955) distinguished between an 'Eastern', ethnocultural and a 'Western', civic form of nationalism, assuming that only the former was based on ethnic identity. Later studies of French and German nationalism (notably Brubaker 1992) have contrasted the consequences of *ius soli* and *ius sanguinis*, indicating roughly that Frenchness can be acquired, whereas descent determines whether or not one is to be considered a German. While Smith's theoretical opponent Ernest Gellner (1983, 1997) agrees with the view that ethnic groups formed the basis of nations – somewhat surprisingly, given his gargantuan emphasis on their constructed nature – the equally influential Benedict Anderson (1983) does not posit such a connection. Several of his main examples, such as Indonesia and the Philippines, were not based on a pre-existing *ethnie*. Current views of possible nations which are immediately relevant to the question of its relationship to ethnicity, include Habermas' notion of *Verfassungspatriotismus* – constitutional patriotism – and Kymlicka's (1995) concept of multicultural citizenship.

The perspective that will be developed here consists in an attempt to overcome the divide between constructivism and primordialism. Just as it can be said that in political philosophy, the liberals have the best arguments while the communitarians have the best social theory, I shall argue that primordialists (or 'perennialists') are right in claiming that community and shared memories are crucial for the formation of national sentiment, while the constructivist emphasis on creativity in conjuring nations into existence is pertinent inasmuch as sentiments of national solidarity can be grown from diverse seedlings, perhaps even sometimes from hybrid germs.

The issue

When A. D. Smith began his research on nationalism, the important academic subculture favouring Marxism and class consciousness seemed to be its most potent alternative; in the early twenty-first century, the challenge comes from a much more general tendency in social theory to emphasise change and movement, the relativity of boundaries, the multiplicity of identities and internal diversity, sacrificing cohesion, stability, homogeneity and structure as key concepts. It is as if the main research tool in much contemporary research on identification consists in a bifocal magnifying glass precluding generalisations and overviews, and favouring minutely detailed accounts of variations and nuances. This has certainly been a dominant tendency in social anthropology, while general social theorists have for years singled out globalisation and differentiation as current academic heartlands. Yet Smith's position on nationalism remains largely unchanged although he has qualified his view on the *ethnie*-nation relation somewhat since *The Ethnic Origin of Nations*; for example, in his recent work he makes it quite clear that he does not question the strength of an 'overarching' American nationalism (Smith 1995: 45), and he accepts that the distinction between civic and ethnic nationalism can be a useful one (e.g. Smith 1998: 212). His theory has nonetheless resisted the temptations from postmodern and postcolonial theories of identification, European integrationism and theories of globalisation and deterritorialisation. Sometimes cast as a primordialist, Smith has always argued that there is continuity between modern nations and a pre-modern past, and that successful national identities presuppose an *ethnie* at their core, that is a historically shaped collective identity incorporating myths of shared origins and cultural sharing. He strongly rejects predictions about the imminent transcendence of nationhood, whether they are based on materialist reasoning (a view represented by Eric Hobsbawm) or on logical arguments about the impossibility of national cohesion in a world which is increasingly recognised as being infinitely diverse (as witnessed in Homi Bhabha's work, see Smith 1998).

Smith's position is not only admirable for its resilience; it is also underpinned by his voluminous and rich writings on nationalism, where he, in addition to presenting empirical cases and developing theory, explicitly discusses alternative accounts of nationalism. His erudition and lucidity make it consistently rewarding to engage with his theorising about nationalism. Clearly, Smith is correct in assuming that national sentiment and solidarity cannot be created *ex nihilo*. As Anderson (1991/1983) pointed out, national identity has more in common with phenomena such as kinship and religion than with secular political ideologies. The question is whether the emotional glue that binds nations together has to be ethnic in character, or whether there are alternative roads to national sentiment. I thus leave questions pertaining to the future of national identity aside, and will also refrain from a discussion of equally important questions concerning multiple identities, transnationalism and ambiguities in national identification, concentrating instead narrowly on the notion of the *ethnie* and its possible emotional and functional equivalents.

What is the *ethnie?*

In his *Ethnic Origins of Nations*, Smith (1986: 22–30, see also Smith 1989) usefully presents an overview of six constituent elements or 'dimensions' of the *ethnie* as he sees it.

1 A collective name. Smith is right in emphasising the importance of ethnonyms for group identity; but of course, many named groups in the past have not qualified as ethnic ones – in many African societies documented in anthropological studies, people identified themselves largely through clan membership – and many African ethnonyms were super-imposed colonial categories, lumping linguistically and culturally related groups together, which were later reified and internalised by the people in question (see e.g. Fardon 1987). In the present world, too, there are naturally many named groups which are not ethnic ones. 'Muslims' is one. 'Bavarians' is another. 'Social anthropologists', I suppose, is a third, although it very rarely (all too rarely?) functions as a corporate entity.
2 A common myth of descent. This is obviously an important criterion of ethnic identity. Smith elaborates the point by saying that there 'are myths of spatial and temporal origins, of migration, of ancestry and filiation, of the golden age, of decline and exile and rebirth'. As Leach (1954) famously showed in his study of Kachin–Shan politics, and many have followed his lead, these myths tend to be ambiguous in that different groups can be constituted in different ways depending on the interpretation of the myth. Since Smith mentions India, it is worthwhile to mention that the recent Hindu nationalist interpretation of the *Ramayana* as an epic focusing on the struggle between good and evil (viz. Hindus and Muslims) is deeply contested among Hindus and other Indians (see e.g. van der Veer 1994).
3 A shared history. Unlike many other authors (e.g. Tonkin et al. 1989), Smith distinguishes between myths and 'shared memories'. He seems to argue that the latter refer to real events, unlike the former; but myths are often believed in, and history – folk or academic – always contains important elements of narrative creativity. As he points out, histories can be divisive just like myths, and it is difficult to see any fundamental difference.
4 A distinctive shared culture. This is a problematic notion. Indeed, as Smith's own examples show, it is a purely empirical question what is considered and accepted as 'shared culture' in the context of group identity. It can be language, it can be religion, or a particular historical experience (such as racism or migration) which is externalised as the cultural emblem of a group, or it could be a unique combination of cultural elements as witnessed in Bangladesh, where the vast majority of inhabitants are unique in that they are Bengali speakers (like Bengali Hindus) *and* Muslims (like Indian Muslims).
5 An association with a specific territory. This is obviously relevant for the kind of group identity in question, but territorial claims are problematic to

deal with in practice owing to migration, mixing and competing claims to the same territory.

6 A sense of solidarity. This is clearly the most important criterion of ethnic identity. Seeing oneself as culturally distinctive, collectively and individually, from other groups, and acting accordingly, is crucial for ethnic identification to endure.

Smith's delineation of the *ethnie*, which he assumes to lie at the foundation of nations, is rather more substantial than common anthropological definitions of ethnicity, which tend to emphasise formal elements, notably the relationship with outsiders, as key factors creating both group boundedness and an awareness of cultural difference (Barth 1969; Eriksen 2002[1993]). Contrasting *vis-à-vis* others is seen, in this intellectual tradition, as the constitutive element of ethnicity. Smith's emphasis on the substantial elements of sharing and internal solidarity represents an important corrective to those who are tempted, following simplistic interpretations of Anderson and Hobsbawm, to see ethnic groups and nations as 'imaginary' (the term 'imagined' is often taken to mean 'imaginary') and traditions as purely 'invented'.[1] The requirement of cultural sharing also not uncontroversially emphasised by Smith, also makes perfect sense. In the pre-modern empires, the imperial state demanded little and gave little in return from its subjects (see Grillo 1998). Cultural pluralism could flourish. The nation-state requires a much greater degree of homogeneity, and its citizens (who are, at least in theory, no longer subjects) demand equality, recognising that a certain degree of cultural similarity, such as command of a shared national language, is necessary for equality to be possible.

Does it have to be an ethnie?

A collective name; a myth of origin; other shared myths/histories; cultural sharing; association with a territory; subjective sense of solidarity: These are Smith's defining criteria of the *ethnie*. He later elaborates ways in which *ethnies* can be turned into nations in the modern world; this will not occupy us here, as I shall, as announced, investigate whether or not other kinds of group can be functional equivalents of ethnic ones in producing national identity. Again, it must be stressed that I am not concerned with the future of the nation-state, its moral legitimacy in the modern world and its alternatives (see Eriksen 1997 for a discussion), but with the question concerning possible foundations for national sentiment and identification.

For the sake of clarity, I shall deal with each of Smith's criteria separately.

First, a collective name or ethnonym. As mentioned above, there are many non-ethnic collective labels which evoke strong sentiments among their members. The question is whether they can serve as the basis for nationhood. The term 'American' seems to be one such, 'Muslim' another in the context of Pakistan, since the main (only?) reason that Pakistanis are not Indians is that they are Muslims. The term 'Pakistan' is itself a modern construction, and it is doubtful if Pakistanis had felt a strong national loyalty without the enmity and competition towards India. In other words, many options will do here.

Second, a myth of origin. In European countries, myths of origin tend to be ethnic, but not invariably so. The French myth of Clovis I, the first Christian king of the Franks, is a spiritual myth more than a genealogical one. Appropriately, it was a French intellectual, Ernest Renan (1982 [1882]), who said that the inhabitants of a nation need shared memories, but they also need to have forgotten the same things. In the same, justly celebrated essay, Renan also pointed out that 'racial considerations have...been for nothing in the constitution of modern nations', adding – much to the exasperation of racial purists – that France, Germany, Italy and Britain were all 'undecipherable medleys' of peoples.

In general, ethnic groups have myths of descent, even if they are often ambiguous and contested. Do nations need myths of descent or of origins? I have earlier argued that nations may thrive on myths of the future (Eriksen 1993), but they also need a shared past. However, this past can be near as well as distant. In Mauritius, a plausible myth of origin is the story of the ethnic riots in the late 1960s, 'the riots to end all riots;[2] in South Africa, the long struggle against racial segregation and apartheid has proven to be a powerful myth of origin for important segments of the otherwise ethnically diverse population. There is no logical reason why the *mythomoteur* often referred to by Smith that is the constitutive myth of the ethnic polity, should necessarily create an *ethnic* group rather than another kind of corporate entity. Again, the postcolonial nations probably give the best examples of alternative, non-biological myths of origin as opposed to biological myths of descent. Another example would be the Muslims of Mauritius (Eriksen 1998). Although they are of North Indian descent, and share their migration history with Mauritian Hindus, the Pan-Arabism of the 1970s led the majority of Mauritian Muslims to redefine their origins in religious terms. In the 1983 Census, most of them claimed that their 'ancestral language' was not Urdu or Bhojpuri, but Arabic. Confronting a Muslim informant with this 'obvious falsehood', I was given the answer that 'we admit that we came from India in a physical sense, but spiritually, our ancestral language is Arabic, and to a Muslim, the spirit is more important than the flesh'. Who is prepared to argue with that? The style of reasoning is reminiscent of General de Gaulle's famous dictum that 'France is not a race, but an idea'.[3]

Third, there is the question of shared memories. Shared collective experiences, codified through narratives which are accessible to the members of the group, are clearly immensely important in the shaping of group identities (and again I agree with Smith at the general level). The refashioning of nations following the upsurge of minority movements, new waves of migration, feminism and postcolonial critiques indicates that the form of content such memories should take is contested, and that they can be re-shaped to fit present concerns (see Hutchinson 1994 for examples). That the memory of certain iconic events in the past needs to be shared by the members of a nation is probably true, but they need not belong to a distant past. In Norway, the memory of German occupation during the Second World War did much to consolidate the sense of national identity, and since it is the only remotely tragic narrative in Norwegian history since the fourteenth century, it plays a significant part in contemporary Norwegian identity.

Then there is the difficult question of shared culture. A degree of sharing is obviously necessary, not least in polyethnic societies, in order to avoid segregation along ethnic lines, which is always a recipe for competition, mutual suspicion and conflict. The question is, how much is enough? How much do the citizens of a given state have to have in common, culturally speaking, in order to form a nation? One thing is for certain, namely that cultural commonalities are not sufficient. The recent histories of culturally rather homogeneous countries like Rwanda, Yugoslavia and Somalia[4] bear witness to this. Moreover, cultural commonalities can be achieved, and are achieved – through education, shared mass media and everyday interaction – by people with discrete origins. National sentiment is rather widespread and strong in a country such as Argentina (Archetti 1999), where it is based on shared migration history, but also on cultural expressions such as the tango, polo and football, as well as cultural practices such as the *asado* (large-scale barbecue). Again, as Calhoun points out in a discussion of the Eritrean–Ethiopian war, it was 'not the antiquity of Eritrean nationalism that mattered in mobilising people against Ethiopian rule,... but the felt reality of Eritreanness' (Calhoun 1997: 35). Eritrean identity is neither historically ancient nor ethno-religious, and during the war, members of the same clan fought on different sides. The importance of trivial everyday experiences – currency, TV news, flags in the street, tipping conventions, conversational styles etc. – has rarely been investigated systematically in studies of nationalism (but see Billig 1995), but contribute substantially to the development of that 'felt reality'. Everyday trivia often goes without saying because it comes without saying, and shared implicit conventions and notions, or taken-for-granteds, create a sense of community which is linked with space rather than time; sharing the same space rather than entertaining notions of shared origins. The moment the children of immigrants begin to speak the vernacular language without a foreign accent, it becomes increasingly difficult for populist politicians to brand them as 'culturally alien'.

Territoral belonging, or at least some association with a territory, is the fifth criterion. With very few exceptions, all the cultural groups known to anthropology have some attachment to a territory or landscape. This is as true of nomads as of farmers, industrial workers and computer programmers. The *form* of belonging naturally varies, and the fixed polity marked by clear, digital, pencil-thin boundaries – citizens inside, foreigners outside – is a modern invention; but place has played a part throughout human cultural history. Mass migration has more often than not been born out of necessity not choice. In the contemporary world, many nonetheless belong not in one place but either in a metaphoric place but in two or more places. Transnational migrants exemplify the latter; Western 'experts' and businessmen the former. Enclaves of Western modernity scattered around the world, incorporating satellite TV, American and French schools, Internet access and cheap air tickets, imply that 'the West' (or even 'the USA') has been deterritorialised to some extent. The main current problem in US foreign policy is that inasmuch as the present regime wishes to pursue the traditional policy of isolationism, defence of American interests and indeed the USA as such seems to imply the necessity of global control, since the USA is everywhere by virtue of its overseas business communities and global economic interests.

More generally, territoriality is seen in many studies of nationalism as a complementary or opposing force to kinship or ethnic identity. Since, according to nationalist ideals, cultural and territorial boundaries ought to coincide, and since they hardly ever do in practice, questions of national identity often concern their mutual relationship: Is one a member of a nation by virtue of a shared ethnic identity/origin, or by virtue of living in the same place (that is, in this context, the same state)? To ethnic nationalists in, say, Norway who argue that immigrants are 'matter out of place' and ought to be sent back, it may be responded that according to their view of nationhood, four and a half million Norwegian live in Norway proper, but some eight to ten million Norwegians – the descendants of emigrants – live abroad, largely in North America. Such a *reductio ad absurdum* of ethnic nationalist claims shows, at the very least, that several forces are at play in shaping national identification, imputed biological origins being only one. This being as it may, territorial identification is definitely an important aspect of national identity; but it can be acquired through migration and settlement, as is evident in the New World, but also among immigrant communities in Europe who claim belonging to particular urban areas. Moreover, territoriality is metaphorical since the nation is an abstract place. In some migrant communities, attachment to the place of origin remains strong even among persons of the second or third generation, who have never been there (see Olwig 1997 for migrants from Nevis). Moreover, the studies presented in a recent book on movement and mixing (Rapport and Dawson 1998a) all in various ways confirm that if movement is endemic to the human condition, so is placeboundness. In the explicitly polemical introductory chapter, the editors first conclude that 'human beings conceive of their lives as moving-in-between', before ending the sentence with the words 'a dialectic between movement and fixity' (Rapport and Dawson 1998b: 33). In the possibly most extreme case study presented in the book, Amit-Talai (1998) describes uprooted expatriates working in the Cayman Islands, unable or unwilling to return home and yet unable to settle in the archipelago permanently, for professional and political reasons. She depicts Cayman society as a transit place, more like an airport than like a town, where expatriates are weakly integrated in the local social systems and voice concerns over their lack of spatial belonging, contrasting their expat lives with 'reality'. If movement is endemic to humanity (and I think it is), then so is spatial identity: It can be dual, metaphorical, big (the USA) or small (a particular neighbourhood in north London), but there is little evidence to suggest that collective and societal identities can thrive without a spatial referent.

The final criterion is the subjective sense of identity. This is presumed to be the outcome of the other factors, and whether or not it exists is an empirical question, but it certainly helps if the five other requirements are satisfied in one way or another. So far, the discussion has indicated that Smith's list of factors defining the *ethnie* is accurate, but also that these elements need not produce *ethnies* but can also produce other kinds of collectivities based on ascription. The concept of the *ethnie* seems too rigid, and too bound up with *la longue durée* and native ideas of bloodlines, to accommodate the entire range of functioning imagined communities. In the words of Brubaker (1998: 301), 'counter-state definitions of the nation may be based on territory, on historical provincial privileges, on distinct political histories prior to incorporation into a larger state and so on'. A certain conceptual flexibility is therefore needed, but it is necessary to resist the temptation to conclude that anything goes. As Smith usefully reminds us there are clear constraints, and to his list of six (or possibly five, if we combine myth and memories) I shall add another two.

Two further dimensions of national identity

One factor which is crucial in shaping community sentiment, rarely considered by sociologists and political scientists writing about ethnicity and nationalism, is that of *interpersonal networks*. The raw material upon which every abstract ideology has to build is everyday experience. The family, the environment of socialisation and the bonds of mutual commitment and trust developed through endless encounters and acts of reciprocity create that sense of 'cultural intimacy' (Herzfeld 1997) which includes insiders at the expense of excluding the outsiders from any group, whether this takes place consciously or unwittingly. The sense of kinship felt by well integrated members of any nation grows out of shared experiences (the cultural commonalities discussed above), but trust is developed through enduring interaction. The extent to which social interaction networks cut across ethnic boundaries determines to no small extent the degree of shared national sentiment in polyethnic societies.

In an evaluation of the 'primordial sentiments' militating against the new postcolonial states, Geertz once wrote: 'One is bound to one's kinsman, one's neighbor, one's fellow believer, *ipso facto*; as the result not merely of personal affection, practical necessity, common interest, or incurred obligation, but at least in great part by virtue of some *unaccountable absolute import* attributed to the very tie itself' (Geertz 1963: 108, my italics). Verging on mysticism, this statement amounts to an intellectual abdication. But clearly, the 'absolute' dimension of the tie referred to by Geertz is nothing but that sense of being in the same boat and living in the same world, with a shared destiny, which results from regular interaction, small exchanges and mutual courtesies, webs of kinship and neighbourly relations. In a word, strong interpersonal ties are far from unaccountable, but derive from the nature of social interaction and local organisation.[5]

The other factor is *contrasting*, which frequently takes the form of negative stereotyping or enemy images of other nations, but which is also omnipresent in everyday arenas such as international sport. Having something in common doubtless helps, but there is also nothing like a common enemy. In the days after 11 September 2001, there were newspaper reports of African-American youths helping old Jewish ladies across the street. Colonial India, to pick another example almost at random, achieved a shared, if precarious (and ultimately doomed) collective identity across a space of huge cultural differences largely because of the shared opposition to the British. Partition, which came on the eve of independence and dampened enthusiasm on every side of the new borders, was not predicated on the Pakistanis having a shared ethnic identity – the Punjabi and the Bengali ethnic groups were actually both divided by partition – but on religion.

National discourses depend crucially on contrasting, which is more widespread than commonly assumed. Take the language of tourism: tourism boards worldwide offer carefully edited, standardised images of the country in question, singling out a few salient elements – Constable country and Buckingham Palace; Grand Canyon and Disneyworld; the *bistro* and the Eiffel Tower; the Kruger Park and Table Mountain – which are intended to 'sell' the country in question, but which also have an important internal function in giving a sense of *relational uniqueness* to the country's own citizens. My village informants in Mauritius would probably not have thought about showing me the coloured earths of Chamarel had they not known that this strange freak of nature was an acknowledged tourist attraction.

Contrasting is also politically important in more immediate ways. Polyethnic and class-divided Britain thus achieved a rare level of national cohesion during the Falklands/Malvinas war in 1982, just as the standardised rituals of international sport regularly enhance national solidarity, however fleetingly. We are not only because we have something in common, but perhaps chiefly because we are not them. Afrikaner group identity in South Africa would obviously have been much weaker if it had not been developed through a hierarchical contrast in relation to other Africans; innumerable other examples could have been invoked to illustrate the same point. Contrasting is not, moreover, merely a political instrument intended to create loyalty and internal homogeneity; it is equally important as a means to achieve recognition in Taylor's (1992, 1998) sense.

Place, kinship and nationhood

Smith's emphasis on shared narratives and territorial belonging as prerequisites for national solidarity is obviously pertinent. Supplemented with an understanding of social networks, trust and reciprocity, it is sufficient as a analytical framework for explaining why communities (which are all in a sense imagined) appear, endure and eventually are transformed or vanish. The question remains whether these communities need to have an ethnic foundation in order to function as nations. To my mind, this would entail stretching the concept of ethnic identity too far. I have therefore argued that there are several ways in which the requirements of nationhood can be met, and that shared ethnic identity is only one, even if it has historically been the most important one.

It is often said that the nation is based on the dual, European heritage of the Enlightenment and Romanticism. The nation can also be said to be connected to more universal dimensions of human existence. Virtually all political identities known to political anthropology are based, in different ways and to varying degrees of course, on place and kinship. The two principles often compete and create divided loyalties (see Gluckman 1982[1956], for a famous presentation of this view), and there are good reasons to assume that patrilineal corporate groups, which fuse political loyalty, inheritance rules and patterns of settlement into one principle, tend to be politically stronger than – all other things being equal – matrilineal or cognatic descent groups, where the principles of place and kinship do not concur. The nation, too, is based on the dual principles of place and kinship, and just as in the traditional African society, they are rarely if ever completely congruent, they compete and lead to divided loyalties.

This much said, it is crucial to keep in mind that both place and kinship are, certainly in the case of huge entities such as nations (with the possible exceptions of countries on the scale of Nauru and Nevis), metaphorical. The sociobiologist Pierre Van Den Berghe, who sees ethnic solidarity as an expression of kin selection,[6] thus nearly gets it right (Van Den Berghe 1981). Kinship and territoriality are very powerful forces indeed in shaping human group identification. What is missing in the sociobiological account is an appreciation of the metaphorical nature of human communities.

The force of nationhood depends on the national ideology's ability to transfer the sentiments and commitments of citizens from their personal experiences to that abstract and imagined community called the nation. When national leaders use kinship terminology ('brothers and sisters', 'fatherland', 'homeland', 'mother tongue' and so on) to designate features of the abstract community which is the nation, they are busy carrying out this work. It could thus be said that the nation expropriates the personal sentiments and experiences of its citizens, transferring them to the much larger and loftier stage of the nation. It is in this sense that a Serb could refer, in the heady 1990s, to the 1389 battle of Kosovo in the first person: 'We [the kin group] lost the battle to the infidels, and we are not going to lose Kosovo again.' It is in the same sense that a crime committed against a member of one's nation is perceived as a crime against one's family members. The rape of a Croatian girl at the hands of Serbian soldiers somewhere in Croatia could justify 'revenge' carried out by any Croat against any Serb, as in a clan feud writ large.

However, the metaphoric kin group of 'Americans' is not based on a folk sociobiological model of origins, yet it can be equally strong. Nations need not have 'navels' (Gellner 1997) even if it helps, and if they do not, they can sometimes create appropriate 'navels' retrospectively.

The nation is, thus, not a kin group but a metaphoric kin group. Similarly, the nation is not a place, but a metaphoric place. As wryly pointed out by Miller and Slater (2000), Trinidad does not stop at the coastline of insular Trinidad, but stretches into England, Canada and the USA, which are the countries with the largest Trinidadian immigrant populations. If anything, Trinidadian migrants feel *more* Trini than the ones who stay put. The everyday abstract image of the nation, taught to children through school atlases and to millions of adults through daily weather forecasts, is another example. Nations (again with a couple of exceptions) as physical entities cannot be observed directly; the citizens have to infer their existence from abstractions such as maps.

None of the above is intended to mean that nations are not real, only that their reality hinges on the efficacy of social constructions relating citizens to one another through fictive kinship, and creating a fatherland through geographical abstractions. In this dual way, the nation can be imagined as a metaphorical kin group residing in a metaphorical place.

The crucial question remains to be answered unequivocally: Under which circumstances do metaphoric kinship and metaphoric place of the national kinds function? This is, I hope to have shown, an entirely empirical question. Kinship, as generations of anthropologists have shown us (beginning, for all practical purposes, with Lévi-Strauss 1949), is not merely about descent and blood lines; it is also about alliances and affinality. In-laws are kin. Women from outside marry into kin groups. Just as it is theoretically possible for anybody to become a 'naturalised' American or Frenchman, rules of exogamy ensure that outsiders are allowed permanent entry into the villages of traditional kin groups. This is not to say that they are entirely open, of course – African peoples have their marriage rules just as Western countries have limits to immigration – but that a shared ethnic identity is not a necessary condition for nationhood.

Exactly who is reckoned as a member of the metaphoric kin group depends on its rules of inclusion and its founding myth. New World societies tend to have founding myths of immigration (as in the case of Argentina), of mixing or *mestizaje* (as in the case of Mexico) or of anti-colonial struggles (as in the case of Jamaica). Old world societies, especially in Europe, tend to have founding myths of shared origins. However, neither the majority of Muslim states nor, of course, African states fit easily into this model. Malays are taught allegiance to their ethnic group *and* to the universal brotherhood of Islam. The polyethnic Malaysian state is thus relegated to an uncomfortably marginal intermediate position. Osama bin Laden's anti-American campaign, moreover, is not a struggle for national liberation (notwithstanding his contempt for the rulers of Saudi Arabia), but a religious struggle. In Africa, there is no doubt that ethnic diversity has emerged as a major source of conflict. However, the bloodiest conflict on the continent in the last couple of decades pitted two groups against each other who were culturally as similar as Croats and Serbs, or for that matter, Eastern Norwegians and Western Norwegians. The Hutus and Tutsis speak the same language and adhere to the same religion. Most Tutsis are sedentary like the Hutus, although their ancestors were pastoralists. Shared culture did not help. Just as in the case of ex-Yugoslavia, culturally similar groups fought bitterly against each other. For a third African example, contemporary South African national identity is deeply based on the struggle against apartheid. In spite of its incomplete integration of all ethnic groups in the country (many problems of identity and loyalty remain to be handled), it cannot be said to be ethnic in any conventional sense of the word. However, it is based on the shared memory of a series of transforming experiences, which thus serve to unite people who are otherwise quite different. The force of a founding myth makes itself felt very strongly indeed.

Place and kinship are nevertheless the prime movers in human collective identification. Living in the same place (physically or metaphorically) entails the acquisition of a wide range of shared skills and notions. During a debate about Norwegian nationhood, I once proposed, as a possible definition, that a Norwegian was someone who lived in Norway and had heard about Henrik Wergeland (a mid-nineteenth century poet known to all Norwegian school-children but to no foreigners). The importance of such shared frames of reference is the reason why no clear-cut distinction between ethnocultural and civic nationalism holds water, as correctly pointed out by Smith (1995: 99). No functioning civic nationalism can be entirely divorced from cultural sharing, but as I have shown, this sharing does not necessarily need to refer to ethnic identity. Regarding kinship, I have emphasised its variable nature and its metaphoric functioning in nationhood, but it is difficult to find an enduring corporate group which does not draw on a notion of relatedness, whether biological or not, in its collective imagery and ideology. The other features listed by Smith – myth, memories, commonalities, subjective feeling of we-hood – follow from place and kinship. Whether or not the resulting collectivities are eventually turned into nations is, of course, another question.

The above argument suggests that the analytical perspective developed by Smith in his writings about nationalism is valid at an abstract level, but that his linking of the traditional *ethnie* and the modern nation is unnecessarily substantial and rules out functional equivalents of *ethnies*. Is this merely a question of terminology? I should think not. It is only when we see that there are empirically functioning alternatives to the ethnic nation that it becomes possible to imagine existing nations as alternative kinds of imagined communities, based not on fictional bloodlines and shared history but on shared futures and multiple pasts; but by the same token, it is only when we heed Smith's words of caution that we understand that the range of options is limited by human experience and, indeed, by human nature.

Notes

Thanks to Aleksandar Boskovic for comments on an earlier version.

1 Surprisingly many of those who have commented on *Imagined Communities* (Anderson 1983) and *The Invention of Tradition* (Hobsbawm and Ranger 1983) have failed to see that Anderson emphasises, on one of the very first pages of the book, that not only nations, but *most communities* are imagined and abstract (which is not to say that they are imaginary), and that Hobsbawm and (especially) Ranger describe invented traditions as a particular subset of traditions, typically created by colonial powers to subjugate and dupe subject populations, incidentally rarely successful in achieving this.

2 As it happened, riots broke out again briefly in 1999.

3 De Gaulle's motivation for saying this, in the mid-1950s, was clearly to tell Algerians that they had no business demanding independence, since they were *de facto* French.

4 Yugoslavia and Rwanda were culturally relatively homogeneous, but they were of course not ethnically homogeneous.

5 An important anthropological account of the relationship between social networks, symbols and community is Cohen's (1985) *The Symbolic Construction of Community*, which concentrates on local and regional, rather than ethnic and national, forms of community.

6 Kin selection is the process, predicted in Hamilton's Rule (Hamilton 1964), whereby close genetic kin support each other because they share most of their genes. If I am infertile, I should thus help to ensure that my siblings and cousins have fertile offspring. The problem with this kind of model, if taken in a literal sense, is that human kinship practices are highly variable and selective.

References

Amit-Talai, Vered. 1998. 'Risky hiatuses and the limits of social imagination: expatriacy in the Cayman Islands' in Nigel Rapport and Andrew Dawson (eds), *Migrants of Identity: Perceptions of Home in a World of Movement*. Oxford: Berg, pp. 39–60.

Archetti, Eduardo. 1999. *Masculinities: Football, Polo and the Tango in Argentina*. Oxford: Berg.

Anderson, Benedict. 1991 [1983]. *Imagined Communities. Reflections on the Origins and Spread of Nationalism*. 2nd edition. London: Verso.

Barth, Fredrik. 1969. 'Introduction' in Fredrik Barth (ed.), *Ethnic Groups and Boundaries. The Social Organization of Culture Difference*. Oslo: Universitetsforlaget, pp. 9–38.

Billig, Michael. 1995. *Banal Nationalism*. London: Sage.

Brubaker, Rogers. 1992. *Citizenship and Nationhood in France and Germany*. Cambridge MA: Harvard University Press.

Brubaker, Rogers. 1998. 'Myths and misconceptions in the study of nationalism' in John A. Hall (ed.), *The State of the Nation. Ernest Gellner and the Theory of Nationalism*. Cambridge: Cambridge University Press, pp. 272–306.

Calhoun, Craig. 1997. *Nationalism*. Buckingham: Open University Press.

Cohen, A. P. 1985. *The Symbolic Construction of Community*. London: Fontana.

Eriksen, Thomas Hylland. 1993. 'A non-ethnic, future-oriented nationalism? Mauritius as an exemplary case', *Ethnos* 58(3–4): 197–221.

Eriksen, Thomas Hylland. 1997. 'The nation as a human being: a metaphor in a mid-life crisis?' in Kirsten Hastrup and Karen Fog Olwig (eds), *Siting Culture*. London: Routledge.

Eriksen, Thomas Hylland. 1998. *Common Denominators: Politics, Ideology and Compromise in Mauritius*. Oxford: Berg.

Eriksen, Thomas Hylland. 2002 [1993]. *Ethnicity and Nationalism: Anthropological Perspectives*, 2nd edition. London: Pluto.

Fardon, Richard. 1987. ' "African ethnogenesis": limits to the comparability of ethnic phenomena' in Ladislav Holy (ed.), *Comparative Anthropology*. Oxford: Blackwell, pp. 168–88.

Geertz, Clifford. 1963. 'The integrative revolution: Primordial sentiments and civil politics in the new states' in Clifford Geertz (ed.), *Old Societies and New States: the Quest for Modernity in Asia and Africa.* New York: Free, pp. 105–119.

Gellner, Ernest. 1983. *Nations and Nationalism.* Oxford: Blackwell.

Gellner, Ernest. 1997. *Nationalism.* London: Weidenfeld & Nicolson.

Gluckman, Max. 1982 [1956]. *Conflict and Custom in Africa.* Oxford: Blackwell.

Grillo, Ralph. 1998. *Pluralism and the Politics of Difference: State, Culture, and Ethnicity in Comparative Perspective.* Oxford: Oxford University Press.

Hamilton, William. 1964. 'The genetical evolution of social behaviour', *Journal of Theoretical Biology*, 7: 1–52.

Herzfeld, Michael. 1997. *Cultural Intimacy: Social Poetics in the Nation-State.* New York: Routledge.

Hobsbawm, Eric and Terence Ranger (eds). 1983. *The Invention of Tradition.* Cambridge: Cambridge University Press.

Hutchinson, John. 1994. *Modern Nationalism.* London: Fontana.

Kohn, Hans. 1955. *Nationalism: Its Meaning and History.* New York: Van Nostrand.

Kymlicka, Will. 1995. *Multicultural Citizenship.* Oxford: Oxford University Press.

Leach, Edmund R. 1954. *Political Systems of Highland Burma.* London: Athlone.

Lévi-Strauss, Claude. 1949. *Les structures élémentaires de la parenté.* Paris: Plon.

Miller, Daniel and Don Slater. 2000. *The Internet: an Ethnographic Approach.* Oxford: Berg.

Olwig, Karen Fog. 1997. 'Cultural sites: sustaining a home in a deterritorialized world' in Kirsten Hastrup and Karen Fog Olwig (eds.), *Siting Culture.* London: Routledge, pp. 17–38.

Rapport, Nigel and Andrew Dawson (eds.). 1998a. *Migrants of Identity: Perceptions of Home in a World of Movement.* Oxford: Berg.

Rapport, Nigel and Andrew Dawson (eds.). 1998b. 'Home and movement: a polemic' in Nigel Rapport and Andrew Dawson (eds.), *Migrants of Identity: Perceptions of Home in a World of Movement*, pp. 19–38. Oxford: Berg.

Renan, Ernest. 1982 [1882]. *Qu'est-ce qu'une nation?* Paris: Pocket.

Smith, A. D. 1986. *The Ethnic Origins of Nations.* Oxford: Blackwell.

Smith, A. D. 1989. 'The origins of nations', *Ethnic and Racial Studies*, 12(3): 341–67.

Smith, A. D. 1991. *National Identity.* Harmondsworth: Penguin.

Smith, A. D. 1995. *Nations and Nationalism in a Global Era.* Cambridge: Polity.

Smith, A. D. 1998. *Nationalism and Modernism.* London: Routledge.

Taylor, Charles. 1992. *Multiculturalism and 'The Politics of Recognition'*, with comments, Amy Gutmann (ed.), Princeton NJ: Princeton University Press.

Taylor, Charles. 1998. 'Nationalism and modernity' in John A. Hall (ed.), *The State of the Nation. Ernest Gellner and the Theory of Nationalism.* Cambridge: Cambridge University Press, pp. 191–218.

Tonkin, Elizabeth Maryon McDonald and Malcolm Chapman (eds.). 1989. *History and Ethnicity.* London: Routledge.

Van Den Berghe, Pierre. 1981. *The Ethnic Phenomenon.* New York: Elsevier.

Veer, Peter van der. 1994. *Religious Nationalism.* Berkeley CA: University of California Press.

5

'Dominant ethnicity' and the 'ethnic-civic' dichotomy in the work of Anthony D. Smith

ERIC KAUFMANN and OLIVER ZIMMER

Arguably the fulcrum of Anthony Smith's research is the ethnie-nation link. One axis of this debate is represented in the early contributions to this special issue, namely, what are ethnies, when did they arise, and what has been their historic relationship to nations. A second – perhaps more contemporary – offshoot of this thinking is the role played by ethnicity within nations in the so-called 'modern' period up to the present time. This is the main problematic with which this chapter will concern itself. Within this framework, two strands of research recommend themselves. These include a) the place of dominant-group ethnicity[1] within contemporary nations; and b) the nature of the 'ethnic versus civic nation' conceptual dichotomy and the dialectic between these two ways of constructing nationalist arguments.

One of the most distinctive vistas which Anthony Smith's work opened up for us as postgraduate students at the LSE in the mid-1990s was the novel way in which he conceptualised ethnicity. Those of us from a sociological tradition, particularly in the English-speaking world, come from an environment in which ethnicity is a difficult phenomenon to study. To begin with, there is the classical-cum-Orientalist and anglo/euro-centric tradition of viewing ethnicity as residing exclusively in the exotic 'Other'.[2] This has then been overlaid by a strongly normative, New Left discourse which sought to reverse the patronising and negative tendencies of Orientalism. Though the new radicalism claimed to be making a sharp break with the anglo-centric tradition, it actually represents a continuation of many of the earlier exoticist themes. Thus, for example, the idea of exotic cultures as repositories of mystery and meaning (in opposition to a dessicated Western rationality) remains in both romantic and radical versions. One subtext is that authenticity and *ethnicity* – a relatively new term in the English language – resides in those strange foreign peoples who have retained something that we Western moderns have lost.[3]

A second, related theme is that ethnicity is possessed by those who are politically or geographically marginal. Hence the link between ethnicity and an egalitarian politics. Here it must be stressed that many early Orientalist writers and travellers were far from the intolerant crusaders or rationalistic imperialists of caricature. Many were among the more cosmopolitan and tolerant of their time – though they are judged differently today. Take the American example. The so-called 'Parliament of Religions' held in Chicago as part of the Columbian exposition of 1893 featured representatives of many world religions and sects, largely from colonial lands in Africa, Asia and the Middle East. Though derided as a classic example of the colonial mindset, many of the supporters of this venture were representatives of the city's liberal cultural vanguard, members of freethinking *cénacles* like the Free Religious Association. They were among the few in their society who supported a more relativistic attitude toward other faiths (Arieli 1991).

Later, the Liberal-Progressive 'Settlement' movement and the bohemian 'Village Renaissance' in New York urged Americans to study the ways of the derided European immigrant groups and become more appreciative of the cultural 'gifts' these groups had to offer as opposed to the 'over-organised' nature of Anglo-Saxon Protestant modernity. Following this strand through the Chicago school of Robert Park in the 1920s through to Donald Young's pioneering *American Minority Peoples* (1932) and finally to the federal Ethnic Heritage Studies program of 1972, we can see definite linkages between the romantic exoticism of the nineteenth century and the multiculturalist radicalism of today.

The Austrian-Jewish social psychologist Gustav Ichheiser famously remarked that if the Jews obtained a state of their own, they would behave in much the same way as other ethnic groups. Here Ichheiser was mischievously firing a shot across the bow of the cosmopolitan mainstream within diaspora Jewry which viewed the Jews as uniquely placed – by virtue of their alienation from a state – to provide universal intellectual and moral leadership. He is also noteworthy for the way in which he remarked that many popular beliefs, though often heavily skewed by prejudice, are predicated upon a kernel of truth (Ichheiser 1949).

Here there is a parallel with Anthony Smith's work. Like his co-religionist Ichheiser, Smith's work runs against the normative grain of his contemporaries. It does so in two important ways. First, in eschewing the tendency of modernist scholars like Hobsbawm, Gellner or Anderson to sever nations from their ethnic pasts, Smith, like Ichheiser, is implicitly suggesting that the counterintuitive explanation, while cognitively impressive, is not necessarily correct. The popular belief that nations have continuity with pre-modern roots thus has an Ichheiserian core of truth which turns out to be quite substantial. Second, and more germane to this discussion, Smith successfully disembeds ethnicity from the ideologically-charged, anglo-centric discourse of ethnic relations and places it in historical context. Ethnic groups are no longer defined by their exoticism or marginality, but rather by characteristics (i.e. popular name, myth of shared ancestry, concept of homeland, ethno-history) which are attributable to oppressors and oppressed alike. This notion greatly influenced

Yael Tamir, whose *Liberal Nationalism* reflects many of the theoretical advances made by Smith (Tamir 1993).

This latter departure *is* a useful example of counterintuitive reasoning in that it questions taken-for-granted ideas about the 'ethnic' as Other.[4] Yet, unlike the arguments of constructivists, this readily rings true with our investigation of the empirical world. 'Yes', we might say, the idea of an English ethnie in Britain or French ethnie in France makes sense and can be usefully compared with, for example, the Japanese in Japan, Persians in Iran or Javanese of Indonesia. In recasting the ethnie-nation distinction on the basis of pre-modern v. modern rather than periphery v. metropole, Smith allows us to usefully compare ethnies and nations and the myriad connections between them.

This approach is also clearly superior to the efforts of political theorists like Will Kymlicka, who view the ethnie-nation distinction as hinging purely on the issue of territoriality (Kymlicka 1997: 59). Thus an American Jew who steps off a plane in Tel-Aviv leaves her ethnicity at the airport, to be recollected for the return journey. Kymlicka also informs us that ethnic groups really are cosmopolitan entities uninterested in 'ethnic descent' while nations are content with an official high culture and are otherwise infinitely elastic in their accommodation of difference. By relying on this conceptual sleight-of-hand, Kymlicka connects the dots of his theory, but detaches it from the reality. Meanwhile, the ethnic realities which Kymlicka does acknowledge are exclusively minoritarian (Kaufmann 2000).

Smith's reconceptualisation of ethnicity, by contrast, de-centres it from its Anglo-European moral centre, thereby opening up space for 'us' as well as the 'others' to possess ethnic identity. In rescuing this term for generalised use, he renders his theory useful as a template for case study or comparative research. This is precisely the kind of meso-level theorising which some suggest as a critical way forward in bridging the solitudes of social theory and empirical research (Mouzelis 1995). To be sure, Schermerhorn spoke of dominant majorities and dominant minorities as early as the late sixties (Schermerhorn 1970). Yet this important work only really concerned itself with the political charge of ethnic relations. Lost in the discussion of the 'dominant' aspect of dominant ethnicity was any discussion of the *ethnic* part of the equation. To do so would entail a consideration of the interiority of dominant ethnicity, of the ontological connections between ethnicity and nations and the nature of charter ethnic group myths and symbols.

The first attempt to probe the cultural-ontological dimension of dominant ethnicity appeared with Smith's *Theories of Nationalism* (1971). Here he speaks of 'revivalist' nationalism as the alter-ego of 'reformist' nationalism. Smith argued that the Janus-faced character of nationalism could either lead the nation outward toward 'reformist' modernisation in the pursuit of scientific credence, or inward, toward its ethnic particularity, in search of spiritual legitimacy (Smith 1971: 246–54). This theme resurfaced in *The Ethnic Revival* (1981) with the idea that ethnic revival – whether within or outside the nation – provided meaning and continuity in a post-religious age. Notice that the question of political hegemony is largely tangential to this debate, hence its originality. Smith's investigation into the 'revivalist' nature of dominant-group ethnicity influenced the work of John Hutchinson, who postulates that ethnic groups seek revival in response to what their intellectuals perceive as a weakening of the group's cultural self-awareness (Hutchinson 1987).

The landmark *Ethnic Origins of Nations* (1986) presents us with the first exposition of Smith's axial thesis regarding the ethnie-nation link. We see, for the first time, explicit mention of the term 'core ethnie' and a consideration of how such ethnies become nations. Core ethnies are mentioned as dominant in both cultural and political terms (Smith 1986: 138). Later, Smith refined his ideas to emphasise that nations are built around 'ethnic cores' or 'dominant ethnies' which furnish it with legitimating myths, symbols and conceptions of territory. In Smith's words: 'Though most latter-day nations are, in fact, polyethnic, many have been formed in the first place around a *dominant ethnie*, which attracted other ethnies or ethnic fragments into the state to which it gave a name and cultural charter...the presumed boundaries of the nation are largely determined by the myths and memories of the *dominant ethnie*, which include the foundation charter, the myth of the golden age and the associated territorial claims, or ethnic title-deeds' (Smith 1991b: 39, emphasis added).

Smith's work is often cited as representative of a perennialist or primordialist theoretical pole. Smith resists such characterisations, instead preferring the label 'ethno-symbolist'. Unfortunately, too much of this exercise is concerned with the timing of nations' emergence onto the historical stage, though the question of social motivation is, to our minds, more important. This issue is addressed more subtly in Smith's work. Numerous fragments from his *oeuvre* suggest that the motivation behind ethnicity is not biological or neuro-psychological, as in the work of Van den Berghe, but rather emerges from a blend of cultural-historical path dependency, lived existence and psychological alienation. Thus we are motivated to become ethnic by traditions embodied in our cultural-historical institutions (including the family) and by our 'diurnal round of work and leisure' in our particular *habitus*. These push factors are necessary but not sufficient, however, since, as Smith makes clear, the ethno-historicist quest is powerfully motivated by a nostalgic and romantic longing to escape the alienation of a profane and disenchanted modernity and to find continuity, *pace* Debray, in the tales of ancestors which reach back into the past and forward into the future[5] (Smith 1986: 175–176).

This captures an element of dominant ethnicity which escapes standard political accounts. Namely the idea that political or economic domination may satisfy pecuniary motives but provides no answer to the quest for meaning and continuity in the face of modern disenchantment. If the latter matters, as Smith suggests, then ethnic revivals are apt to occur among both dominant and subaltern groups, even in the absence of political imperatives. The multiple ethnic revivals that have taken place among the majority in locations as disparate as Korea or Ireland bear witness to this (Kendall 1998). In short, the tacit assumption that identity politics, recognition and authenticity are minority sports needs urgent revision. Indeed, we may surmise that ethnic revivals can readily take place – often repeatedly – within the dominant group in a nation-state.

Often, manifestations of dominant group ethnicity are labelled 'ethno-nationalism'. The two concepts overlap a great deal, but they are not identical. Dominant ethnicity can occur in a pre-modern or imperial context, with few links to the idea of the nation. (i.e. Mohajirs in Mughal Empire, Germans in the medieval Baltic, the British in Kenya). The political dominance of Afrikaners in South Africa or economic dominance of Anglo-Protestants in Quebec provide more recent examples. More importantly, today's norms of Western cultural liberalism (Soysal's 'universal personhood') are increasingly forcing dominant ethnic groups to define 'their' nations in inclusive ways that draw an ever firmer line between a once hidden dominant ethnie and its national covering (Soysal 1994). This makes it extremely important to finger dominant ethnicity as an independent political player.

In approaching contemporary dominant ethnicity, we encounter relatively uncharted territory, a vast field of inquiry which has been bypassed by the legions of scholars armed with conventional citizenship studies, nationalism and ethnic politics paradigms. Despite his more nuanced approach, this is also where some of the limits to Anthony Smith's work appear. Smith certainly recognises the current interplay between dominant ethnies and the nation. He notes the challenges posed by the globalisation of capital, the rise of minority secessionist movements and heightened international migration (Smith 2004). However, whereas Smith's work on the emergence of the modern nation from its dominant ethnic chrysalis is well-delineated, his work on contemporary dominant ethnicity remains more theoretical and exploratory.

Smith's approach to the role of nations betrays a curiously ambiguous stance with respect to dominant ethnicity – an equivocation which is less evident elsewhere in his writing. Though firm in his defence of the nation and its resilience in our global era, Smith nowhere states that dominant ethnies have a similar tenacity. At times, when discussing anti-immigration politics, there is the suggestion that dominant ethnicity resists centripetal forces. When considering the challenge of minority ethnic revival, multiculturalism and secession, however, Smith seems to veer toward a different position. Now, national identity becomes far more flexible, able to be 'recombined' in such a way as to supersede dominant ethnic symbols and boundaries (Smith 2004). To a degree, this ambiguity is reflected in the way Smith speaks of civic nations, with ideological (as opposed to genealogical) myths of descent as equally capable of capturing the affections of the mass of the population. His reading of 'immigrant nations' as lacking a dominant ethnie, but possessing an ideological founding myth which coalesces successive waves of immigrants into a nation, is part of this train of thought (Smith 1984; 1991b: 40).

For instance, Smith avers that 'immigrant nations' like the Americans or Australians differ from the nations of the Old World in their self-conceptions.

But a glance at the history of either nation in the twentieth century shows that the nation was defined in an ethnic 'British' or 'WASP' manner which was more effectively executed than in many 'old world' nations. Britain or France, for example, never implemented a racial and ethnic quota system like the American 'National Origins' scheme of 1924–65 nor were they gripped by the kind of dominant ethnic fraternalism represented by the American Protective Association or (second) Ku Klux Klan in the USA or Orange Order in Canada.[6] The phenomenon of 'white flight' in the USA is also far more developed than in Europe, where racial mixture and co-residence is more common (Frey 1996). Furthermore can one seriously doubt the electricity of, for example, Mexican *Mestizo* or Guyanese Creole dominant ethnicity in the present day?

Smith suggests that dominant ethnies furnish the nation with its myths, symbols and public culture, and that this constrains the degree to which new immigrant groups can alter the national culture. But on the critical question of ethnic boundaries, Smith remains ambiguous – he speaks of the new migration as modifying both 'immigrant' and 'older' nations and introducing elements of pluralism into the national fabric. He adds that both ethnic and civic models of the nation (based on a 'civil' religion and public culture) are viable forms. Once again, the limits of civic national pluralism are not clearly specified. For if civic traditions are elastic and adaptable, then it is not immediately clear why the post-colonial 'nations by design' cannot succeed as well since these present civil religions and public cultures to their diverse ethnic citizenry (Smith 1995b: 107–111).

Smith partly evades the issue of the future of dominant ethnicity because his primary concern is to consider the viability of nations in relation to other forms of cultural-political organisation like supranationalism and globalisation. There are periodic ethno-nationalist backlashes in civic nations, writes Smith, but these are presented as complementary rather than antagonistic to the main thrust of his argument: that nations are resurgent. By betting on both the ethnic and civic horses, Smith buys himself out of the conundrum of why there seems to have been a shift from ethnic to civic modes in post-industrial Western nationalism.

Such equivocation is less noticeable in Smith's excellent riposte to the avatars of globalisation, first expressed in 1990, in which he contends that globalisation makes 'possible a denser, more intense interaction between members of communities who share common cultural characteristics …'. He adds that a memory-less, eclectic global culture, wrapped in the universal packaging of a standardised global economy and techno-scientific discourse, has little chance of achieving popular resonance (Smith 1990a: 171–191). Smith's writings on globalisation and cosmopolitanism provide a much-needed corrective to the lofty pronouncements of globalists like Malcolm Waters, Anthony Giddens and Kenichi Ohmae. In this regard, it serves a very useful function. However, Smith could engage more deeply with the subtler globalisation or social psychology literature which speaks of the nation as one of the layers of governance (and of identity) between the local and global (Held 1995; Hirst and Thompson 1996). The critical question is therefore not whether the nation will survive, but whether it can retain its place as the *primary* seat of political power and cultural identity.

More also needs to be conceded to those who claim that there has been a decided change in the ideological context in which nationalism operates. Traditional religiosity (except at the elite level), neo-classicism, romanticism, social Darwinism, fascism and even state socialism make better bedfellows with nationalism than neo-liberal cosmopolitanism and expressive individualism. The latter are not entirely new, but have emerged as the ideological victors of the post-Enlightenment epoch, reaching far wider strata than ever before. The rise of scientific history, the eclipse of nationalistic historiography and the concomitant pressure to redefine the nation inclusively were forces which had their origins in the late eighteenth and early nineteenth centuries (i.e., Catholic Emancipation in Britain) but crested in the post-1960 period.

Likewise, large-scale changes in popular attitudes toward race and religion (not to mention drink, sex and other mores) have been repeatedly documented in social attitude surveys between 1945 and the present. These beliefs have trended in a liberal direction on cultural questions for decades, even as economic questions elicit responses that vary back and forth over time (Inglehart 1990; Mayer 1992). The individualism that spawned higher rates of divorce, psychotherapy and out-of-wedlock marriage has led to a decline in 'social capital', the connectedness embodied in associations like churches, patriotic societies and ethnic fraternities. This has eroded long-standing electoral cleavages and reduced political participation, causing political realignments. Should we be surprised that this trend also leads to more inter-ethnic, inter-religious and inter-racial marriage? The result appears to be a growth of a symbolic 'pick and mix' approach to individuals' ethnic and religious heritage. This seems to point, over time, to a post-ethnic attenuation of these historic identities (Putnam 2000; Gans 1994; Alba 1990).

The possibility that trans-national 'lifestyle' enclaves and subcultures, with their cultural boundaries, cues, superficial narratives and residential segregation, can usurp ethnic-national identity is very real and needs to be considered (Bellah 1996 [1985]; Chaney 1996). With the increasing diversity of Western cities, their liberal-egalitarian ethos and the upward mobility of ethnic minorities, we can expect to see an increasing disjuncture between lifestyle enclaves and ethnicity. Naturally, those members of the dominant ethnie who do not make it into the university-educated 'New Class' will reject the multicultural order and support the ethno-nationalist right. But the forces of liberal-egalitarianism have greater access to social and political capital and maintain politico-cultural hegemony in a much more secure manner than their predecessors of the inter-war period.

The social differentiation of today vastly supersedes the functional specialisation noted by Spencer, Durkheim and Parsons. The antinomian, 'modernist' cultural ethos of the latter twentieth century focuses on novelty,

difference, change and immediacy (Bell 1976). Thus, in addition to occupa-
tional specialisation, we now have a fragmentation of meaning, generated by
individuation, which splinters public culture and taste into more specialised
segments. This produces lifestyle frames like 'hippie', 'bobo' or 'yuppie' which
often have primary meaning for modern individuals. The 'ethnic' segment of
the dominant ethnie is increasingly marginal in the West: concentrated among
its lower-educated and peripheral members. This hard core represents an
important minority, but, at least in the West, it has lost the hegemony it once
possessed and the Far Right does not seriously threaten the existing order.[7] At
the mainstream level, even minority nationalists (i.e. Scots, Catalans,
Quebecois) feel compelled to define their projects as 'civic'.

This major shift of the past 30–40 years – from ethnic to civic, from
dominant ethnic to multicultural, from *gemeinschaft* to individualism – needs
to be recognised and incorporated into a more wide-ranging contemporary
theory of dominant ethnicity and nationalism. This should take account of the
new egalitarian individualism, of instances of ethnic and national decline, of
assimilation as well as differentiation. Though many corrections must be made
to Smith's notion of perpetually-reviving nationalism, the case is far from lost.
A careful specification of the limits of current liberal-egalitarian trends in
particular contexts can provide the needed corrective to the utopian rhetoric of
hyper-globalists like Waters or universal-individualists like Fukuyama.

The foregoing discussion has highlighted the importance of questions of
'civic versus ethnic' types of nations/nationalism more generally in Anthony
Smith's writings. Given the centrality of this topic in recent research (see
Brubaker 1992; Soysal 1994; Fahrmeir 1997; Schnapper 1998; Gosewinkel
2001; Zimmer 2003b), it is worth examining Smith's own contribution to this
scholarly debate in somewhat greater detail. Yet before doing so it might be
useful to locate its place in relation to the central concern of Smith's work,
namely the possible connections and continuities between pre-modern
ethnic communities and modern nations. The first point that needs to be
noted in this regard is that, like the discussion concerning dominant ethnicity,
the debate over civic and ethnic forms of nationhood is almost exclusively
focused on the modern period. A glance at Smith's definition of 'nation' makes
this obvious in that many of the elements he attributes to the modern nation – a
mass, public culture, a common economy and common legal rights and duties
for all members (Smith 1991a: 14) – form the institutional core of the civic
nation-state. The latter is commonly underpinned by a civic ideology that
stresses the need to create, foster, and constantly improve the national
community, its institutions and public culture. This is not to say that ethnic
understandings of the nation become irrelevant under modern conditions,
but they will almost certainly be counter-balanced by the rhetoric of
civic nationalism.

In more specific terms, the conceptual differentiation between civic and
ethnic forms of nationhood has played a part within two separate (if closely
related) areas of Smith's work. The first relates to his concern with nationalist

movements and with the formation of nations and nation-states, while the second pertains to his interest in the ideology of nationalism and in the construction of nationalist arguments. Smith has approached the former theme from a more sociological and typological perspective, while in his treatment of the latter he has often adopted a more explicitly historical and inductive method. Although the two themes are closely linked in his *oeuvre*, making this distinction will allow us to identify changes in his work that affected his writing on civic-versus-ethnic dichotomy.

The first of these changes was mainly of a methodological nature. Whereas in many of his earlier works Smith tended to concentrate on the formation of nations and the role of nationalist movements in an attempt to create typologies suited to the comparative study of nationalism (see Smith 1973, 1983, 1986), his more recent publications reveal a more marked concern with the ideology of nationalism in its various historical manifestations (Smith 1991a, 1995a, 2000). This shift was closely related to his adoption, from the mid-1990s, of a more dynamic understanding of the key concepts of nation, nationalism, and national identity. Quite obviously, this partial re-orientation grew out of his emphatically critical engagement with Eric Hobsbawm's concept of 'invented traditions' and Benedict Anderson's view of nations as 'imagined communities' (Smith 1991a; Hobsbawm 1983; Anderson 1991). While rejecting their radical constructivism, Smith nonetheless began to look more systematically at the relationship between nationalist actors and their ideologies on the one hand, and national identity on the other.[8] This led to a clearer differentiation between two themes that had not been separated in his earlier work: the formation of nations, national movements and nation-states in the long historical durée, which Smith now often discusses under the label of 'perennialism'; and the construction and reconstruction of nationalist arguments along 'voluntarist' and 'organic' lines.

The more typological approach is clearly visible in Smith's pioneering *Theories of Nationalism* (Smith 1971 and 1983). In chapter 8 on typologies, Smith posits the need to identify the diversity within the unity of nationalism. Yet it is characteristic of this early work, which is still under the influence of what in a later study he would call 'classical modernism' (Smith 1998), that Smith is primarily concerned with nationalist movements, and only secondarily with their ideology. Unlike Ernest Gellner's, Smith's scepticism of theories of nationalism that concentrate on ideology (an approach applied most radically by Elie Kedourie in his seminal book *Nationalism*) is not rooted in an adherence to any kind of materialism (Gellner 1983; Kedourie 1993). Rather, Smith's early critique of the history-of-ideas approach flows from his emphasis on the political nature of nationalism. After all, in the early 1970s Smith was convinced that a sociology of nationalist movements and their leaders along Weberian lines offered the most promising way forward. For example, in chapter 8 of *Theories of Nationalism* he challenges a number of prominent idealist accounts (by such scholars as Hugh Trevor-Roper, Carlton

Hayes, and Hans Kohn). Smith is particularly sceptical of some of the causal correlations proposed in these works between nationalist ideology and the social position of nationalist intellectuals, such as Hans Kohn's view that the differences between 'Western' and 'Eastern' nationalism reflect a contrast between a rational French and English bourgeois middle class and the bookish yet socially marginal sons of German clergymen and civil servants (see also Smith 1991b: 80–82). But Smith's main point is that these historical taxonomies need to be replaced by sociological ones that concentrate on movement rather than ideology. This leads him to separate pre-independence from post-independence nationalist movements, both of which, he argues, can be underpinned by an ethnic or a territorial type of nationalism (1983: 199–210).

Perhaps it was in his illuminating yet little known essay on 'Neo-classicist and Romantic Elements in the Emergence of Nationalist Conceptions' (Smith 1976: 74–87) that Smith for the first time examined different patterns of nationalist ideology in a manner directly relevant to the civic-versus-ethnic dichotomy. In this essay, which effectively represents a theoretically informed piece of intellectual history, Smith explores the origins and early development of European nationalism in the period from 1770 to 1815. He argues that a transformation took place, during the 1770s and 1780s, from the neo-classical veneration of antique themes and role models to a more Romantic concern with ethnic origins. These two visions roughly correspond with the civic and ethnic patterns of communal identity in that the first emphasises political voluntarism while the second stresses organic growth. As the reader soon realises, however, the main point of this chapter is to question that the transition from the neo-classical to the ethno-historicist was as clear-cut as some historians of ideas had previously suggested. The neo-classical and Romantic viewpoints, Smith insists, were often fused in the thought of early nationalist thinkers and, in spite of important disagreements, neo-classicists and early Romantics shared a number of common features. To begin with, they were both opposed to the status quo and to 'all authority that is external and imposed' (Smith 1976: 86). In more strictly ideological terms, they represent varieties of eighteenth-century historicism in that both located the source of a community's energy and unity in its origin. Lastly, each of them attributes a central place to education as a means to accomplish communal regeneration. And it is here, in the sphere of education, that the fusion of the voluntarist and organic elements becomes most apparent in the writings of some of the foremost critics of the French Enlightenment. Hence for Rousseau, education appeared as a means to rediscover, cultivate and strengthen that which was 'authentic' and 'natural' in a community (Smith 1976: 83–85).[9]

In *The Ethnic Origins of Nations* (1986), his most seminal book, Smith combines the sociological analysis of nation formation with an examination of nationalist ideology. Here he also engages, much more explicitly than in his previous works, with the differentiation between different types of nationalism first advanced in the classic accounts of Friedrich Meinecke and Hans Kohn. Building on their scholarly precedents, Smith distinguishes between 'territorial and ethnic principles and components', which he sees as the products of two distinct patterns of nation formation. Where the state developed earlier and more vigorously, as was the case in the Western core states of England and France, groups in control of the state (whether a pre-modern aristocracy or a modern bourgeois class) fostered and promoted a national self-image that was predominantly civic or territorial. Here the emphasis was on boundaries, legal institutions, rights and duties, citizenship and common culture. Where the road to state-formation was more protracted and contentious, as was the case in the East, national self-definitions took on a more ethnic form. This often meant that the intelligentsia of a marginal community ruled by a dominant ethnic group in an imperial context drew on ethnic symbols and myths to legitimate its claim to autonomy or, where the nationalist movement was more advanced, to an independent state. Here the stress is on 'genealogy, populism, customs and dialects, and nativism'. Ethnic nationalists seek to revive, politicise and extend these elements, while they are less concerned with the kind of institutions and rights that are so prominent a concern for those adhering to the civic vision of the nation (1986: 136–137).

Yet Smith nonetheless objects to the widespread tendency of confusing ideal types with actual historical phenomena. In the real world, he insists, the elements associated with the civic nation – territoriality, political and legal institutions, citizenship rights, a common civic culture and ideology – are not universal but embedded in particular historical communities. The concept of a national territory makes this obvious. While territories possess a formal and universalist dimension, manifest in concepts such as 'boundary' or 'frontier', they are also highly particularistic. This more particularistic dimension finds expression in terms such as 'historic land' or 'homeland'. Another key element of the civic nation – a shared public culture – reveals the same duality. Although modern civic cultures are to some extent created and promoted from the centre, they also historically evolved or, at any rate, must be seen as consonant with existing historical myths, symbols and memories if they are to resonate within a wider population. The same applies to political and legal institutions. If they are to evoke the necessary emotional attachments and loyalties from a given population, they must be seen as historically evolved rather than merely invented or constructed. 'Nations', Smith tells us, 'always require ethnic "elements"' because they would be 'inconceivable without some common myths and memories of a territorial home' (1991: 40). Conceptually, the nation has come to 'blend two sets of dimensions, the one civic and territorial, the other ethnic and genealogical, in varying proportions in particular cases' (1991: 15). He drives home the same point when he states that nationalism, rather than a secular ideology, is merely the 'secular, modern equivalent of the pre-modern, sacred myth of ethnic election' (1991: 68–70).

But what precisely, we may ask, caused these changes in the public definition of national identity? What determined the particular blending of civic and ethnic elements in a particular case? How precisely do nationalists define the nation in the face of social and political change? We believe it was Smith's realisation that his existing concepts would make it difficult to examine these questions adequately that prompted him, in some of his most recent works, to replace terms such as 'civic', 'territorial' and 'ethnic' with 'organic' and 'voluntarist' (Smith 2000 and 2001). This indicates more than a terminological shift. The former terms are rooted in his typological method and reflect his ambition to construct a conceptual framework that could be used for broad diachronic and synchronic comparisons at the macro level of society. The latter terms, by contrast, are indicative of Smith's search for concepts that can adequately capture the process-like and fluctuating nature of nationalism and national identity. In a recently published introduction to nationalism, Smith examined the complex blending of voluntarist and organic elements in the works of such thinkers as Renan, Burke, Lord Acton, Max Weber, with each fostering a vision of nationhood that tends to lean more towards either of the two ends on the voluntarist-organic continuum (2001: 13–15).

Smith undoubtedly deserves a great deal of credit above all for having emphasised the janus-faced nature of nationalist ideology and for moving the debate surrounding civic and ethnic nationalism away from the strong normative connotations typical of the classical as well as some recent accounts on the subject (see Viroli 1995; Ignatieff 1993).[10] Nor can there be any doubt that his approach and analyses on this subject are superior to those accounts that associate civic and ethnic nationhood with particular 'traditions' or 'mentalities' or tend to classify entire 'nations' as either 'civic' or 'ethnic' (culminating in highly simplistic assumptions about 'the-Germans'-and-their-obsession-with-blood-and-the-soil versus 'the-French'-and-'the English'-and-their-appreciation-of-rationality-and-civic-liberty). Yet if our concern relates to the discontinuously occurring public redefinitions of national identity rather than to long-term developments, intellectual debates, or citizenship legislation, then the limitations of his approach are revealed. These have become particularly obvious to historians and social scientists studying national movements and political ideologues rather than focusing on a handful of selected thinkers and intellectuals or taking a broadly comparative approach.

One might be able to overcome these problems if 'voluntarist' and 'organic' are conceived not in terms of conceptions, principles or ideas, but in terms of mechanisms or metaphors that actors use as they construct nationalist arguments by drawing on particular resources. The resources that nationalists commonly draw upon in different contexts to address particular problems – political institutions and values, cultural traditions and codes, communal history, even geography – can be processed in either voluntarist or organic ways: as the product of human action or, alternatively, as forces that determine the collective 'character' of a nation. Some adherents of organic nationalism, for example, rejected the voluntarist connotations commonly attached to the modern nation-state. Instead, they saw the state in naturalistic terms, as an expression of the evolutionary development of the national community, not as a set of deliberately created institutions. The same is true of 'nature' and 'geography'. They too need not be conceived in organic (i.e. deterministic) terms, although this has admittedly often been the case where nationalists made references to the natural environment. Even so, for some eighteenth-century neo-classicists the natural environment was cherished because it could serve as a projection of human ingenuity and an expression of national character. But perhaps the most instructive example is language. While in the French republican tradition language is conceived in voluntarist terms – as something that can be taught, learned, and acquired, for a right-wing nationalist like Albert Sorel language was organic and deterministic.[11]

Conclusion

This chapter suggests that Anthony Smith has made important contributions to the literatures on both dominant ethnicity and the 'ethnic-versus-civic' nationalism debate. In terms of the former, he has successfully redefined the American term 'ethnicity' (as well as 'nation') in a more consistent manner than his exoticist and radical predecessors. In so doing, he has opened up space for an exploration of the phenomenon of dominant ethnicity within modern nations. A limitation of Smith's work, however, is his incomplete specification of the role of dominant ethnicity (as opposed to nations) within post-industrial Western societies. In terms of the 'ethnic-civic' discourse, Smith's work has again successfully abstracted a key concept away from its overly normative and idealist matrix and employed it as a useful sociological typology. Nonetheless, this approach could be improved by a stronger focus on 'voluntarist' and 'organic' processes as mechanisms rather than ideas – a transition which could improve their utility in empirical situations which are marked by discontinuities in symbolic strategies and social action.

Notes

1 For more discussion, see Kaufmann 2001.
2 There is some purchase in considering this tendency in the light of Roman characterisations of outsiders as 'natio', or in disparate foreign words like Welsh, Vlach and Viet (Smith 2004).
3 Ogburn's theory of cultural lag provides an explicit theorisation of this reasoning.
4 The new White Studies literature only partly redresses this issue since it remains firmly wedded to the idea of an Anglo or European bogeyman which serves as a moral centre for further discussion (Ceaser 1998).

5   Smith's notion of a 'diurnal round of work and leisure' has parallels with Bourdieu's notion of habitus or Habermas' use of the term 'lifeworld'.
6   The Orange Order's largest jurisdiction in the first half of the twentieth century was Canada, where membership levels, in per capita terms, equalled those of Northern Ireland and far exceeded anything seen in Scotland or England (Kaufmann 2002).
7   The 35 per cent of the popular vote attained by Georg Haider in Austria and the strong showing of the FN in the first round of presidential elections in France represent the high-water mark for the European far-right. In all locations, the combined effort of the media, established political parties and economic interests as well as the popular mood have limited the progress of politicised dominant ethnicity.
8   He discusses this relationship most explicitly in his article, 'Gastronomy or geology? The role of nationalism in the reconstruction of nations' (Smith 1995).
9   Smith has provided a more systematic account of the role of historicism in ch. 6 of his book, *The Ethnic Revival.* See Smith 1981.
10   For an incisive critique of the normative point of view, see Yack 1996.
11   For a fuller outline of these ideas and examples, see Zimmer 2003a.

References

Alba, Richard D. 1990. *Ethnic Identity: the Transformation of White America.* New Haven, CT: Yale University Press.
Anderson, Benedict. 1991. *Imagined Communities. Reflections on the Origin and Spread of Nationalism.* London: Verso.
Arieli, Yehoshua. 1991. 'Individualism and national identity', in Richard O. Curry and Lawrence B. Goodheart (eds.), *American Chameleon: Individualism in Trans-National Context.* Kent, OH: Kent State University Press, 151–87.
Bell, Daniel. 1976. *The Cultural Contradictions of Capitalism.* New York: Harper Collins.
Bellah, Robert N. 1996 [1985]. *Habits of the Heart,* 2nd ed, London: University of California Press.
Brubaker, Rogers. 1992. *Citizenship and Nationhood in France and Germany.* Cambridge, MA: Harvard University Press.
Ceaser, James. 1998. 'Multiculturalism and American liberal democracy' in Arthur M. Melzer, Jerry W. Weinberger and M.Richard Zinman (eds.), *Multiculturalism and American Democracy.* Lawrence, KS: University Press of Kansas, 139–155.
Chaney, David. 1996. *Lifestyles.* London: Routledge.
Fahrmeir, Andreas. 1997. 'Nineteenth-century German citizenship: a reconsideration', *Historical Journal* 40: 721–52.
Frey, William H. 1996. 'Immigration, domestic migration, and demographic Balkanization in America: new evidence for the 1990s', *Population and Development Review* 22(4).
Gans, Herbert J. 1994. 'Symbolic ethnicity and symbolic religiosity: towards a comparison of ethnic and religious acculturation', *Ethnic & Racial Studies* 17(4): 577–92.
Gellner, Ernest. 1983. *Nations and Nationalism.* Oxford: Blackwell.
Gosewinkel, Dieter. 2001. *Einbürgern und Ausschliessen. Die Nationalisierung der Staatsangehörigkeit vom Deutschen Bund bis zur Bundesrepublik Deutschland.* Göttingen: Vandenhoeck & Ruprecht.
Held, David. 1995. *Democracy and the Global Order: from the Modern State to Cosmopolitan Governance.* Cambridge: Polity.
Hirst, Paul and Grahame Thompson. 1996. *Globalization in Question: the International Economy and the Possibilities of Governance.* Cambridge: Polity.
Hobsbawm, Eric. 1983. 'Introduction: inventing traditions', in E. Hobsbawm and T. Ranger (eds.), *The Invention of Tradition.* Cambridge: Cambridge University Press.
Hutchinson, John. 1987. *The Dynamics of Cultural Nationalism: the Gaelic Revival and the Creation of the Irish Nation-State.* London: Allen & Unwin.
Ichheiser, G. 1949. 'Misunderstandings in human relations: a study in false social perception', *American Journal of Sociology* LV, special monograph, 1–70.

Ignatieff, Michael. 1993. *Blood and Belonging: Journeys into the New Nationalism*. London: Vintage.

Inglehart, Ronald. 1990. *Culture Shift in Advanced Industrial Society*. Princeton, NJ: Princeton University Press.

Kaufmann, Eric. 2000. 'Liberal ethnicity: beyond liberal nationalism and minority rights', *Ethnic and Racial Studies* 23(6): 1086–1119.

Kaufmann, Eric. 2001. 'Dominant ethnie' in Athena S. Leoussi (ed.), *Encyclopedia of Nationalism*. London: Transaction, 51–3.

Kaufmann, Eric. 2002. 'The decline of sectarianism in the West? A comparison of the Orange Order in Canada, Ulster and Scotland', in N. Singh and T. Vanhanen (eds), *Ethnic Violence and Human Rights*. Delhi: KIRS.

Kedourie, Elie. 1993. *Nationalism*, 4th edn. Oxford: Blackwell.

Kendall, Laurel. 1998. 'Who speaks for Korean shamans when shamans speak of the nation?', in Dru Gladney (ed.), *Making Majorities*. Stanford, CA: Stanford University Press.

Kymlicka, Will. 1997. 'The sources of nationalism: commentary on Taylor', in Robert McKim and Jeff McMahan (eds.), *The Morality of Nationalism*. Oxford: Oxford University Press, 56–65.

Mayer, William G. 1992. *The Changing American Mind: How and Why American Public Opinion Changed between 1960 and 1988*. Ann Arbor, MI: University of Michigan Press.

Mouzelis, Nicos P. 1995. *Sociological Theory: What Went Wrong*. London: Routledge.

Putnam, Robert D. 2000. *Bowling Alone: the Collapse and Revival of American Community*. New York: Simon & Schuster.

Schermerhorn, Richard A. 1970. *Comparative Ethnic Relations: a Framework for Theory and Research*. New York: Random House.

Schnapper, Dominique. 1998. *Community of Citizens: on the Modern Idea of Nationality*. London: Transactions.

Smith, Anthony D. 1971. *Theories of Nationalism*. London: Duckworth.

Smith, Anthony D. 1976. *Nationalist Movements*. London: Duckworth.

Smith, Anthony D. 1981. *The Ethnic Revival*. Cambridge: Cambridge University Press.

Smith, Anthony D. 1983. *Theories of Nationalism*, 2nd ed. London: Duckworth.

Smith, Anthony D. 1984. 'National identity and myths of ethnic descent', *Research in Social Movements, Conflict and Change* 7, 95–130.

Smith, Anthony D. 1986. *The Ethnic Origins of Nations*. Oxford: Blackwell.

Smith, Anthony D. 1990a. 'Towards a global culture?', *Theory, Culture & Society* 7, 171–91.

Smith, Anthony D. 1990b. 'The supersession of nationalism?', *International Journal of Comparative Sociology* XXXI(1–2): 1–25.

Smith, Anthony D. 1991a. 'The nation: invented, imagined, reconstructed?', *Millenium, Journal of International Studies* 20(3): 353–68.

Smith, Anthony D. 1991b. *National Identity*. London: Penguin.

Smith, Anthony D. 1995a. 'Gastronomy or geology? The role of nationalism in the reconstruction of nations', *Nations and Nationalism* 1(March): 3–14.

Smith, Anthony D. 1995b. *Nations and Nationalism in a Global Era*. Cambridge: Polity.

Smith, Anthony D. 2000. *The Nation in History: Historiographical Debates about Ethnicity and Nationalism*. Hanover, NH: University Press of New England.

Smith, Anthony D. 2001. *Nationalism: Theory, Ideology, History*. Cambridge: Polity.

Smith, Anthony D. 2004. 'Ethnic cores and dominant ethnies', in Eric Kaufmann (ed.), *Rethinking Ethnicity: Majority Groups and Dominant Minorities*. London: Routledge.

Soysal, Yasemin. 1994. *Limits of Citizenship: Migrants and Postnational Membership in Europe*. Chicago, IL: University of Chicago Press.

Tamir, Yael. 1993. *Liberal Nationalism*. Princeton, NJ: Princeton University Press.

Viroli, Maurizio. 1995. *For Love of Country: an Essay on Patriotism and Nationalism*. Oxford: Oxford University Press.

Yack, Bernard. 1996. 'The myth of the civic nation', *Critical Review* 10(2): 193–212.

Young, Donald Ramsey. 1932. *American Minority Peoples. A Study in Racial and Cultural Conflicts in the United States*. New York: Random House.

Zimmer, Oliver. 2003a. 'Boundary mechanisms and symbolic resources: towards a process-oriented approach to national identity', *Nations and Nationalism* 9(2): 1–23.

Zimmer, Oliver. 2003b. *A Contested Nation: History, Memory and Nationalism 1761–1891*. Cambridge: Cambridge University Press.

6

Ethnicity and supra-ethnicity in corpus planning: the hidden status agenda in corpus planning

JOSHUA A. FISHMAN

Introduction

The sociology of language is indebted to Heinz Kloss (1904–1987)[1] for the seminal distinction between corpus planning (planned efforts to change the lexicon, grammar, phonology, orthography and/or writing system of a given language) and status planning (planned efforts to change the societal functions – governmental, educational, mass media, legal, religious) (Kloss 1952 and 1967) within the all-inclusive effort denoted as language planning. Language planning *per se* has been defined as 'the authoritative societal assignment of scarce resources to language'. However, although this distinction is now half a century old it still remains unevenly elaborated. Status planning has received the lion's share of attention since it is of greater popular interest, as well as of interest to social scientists (primarily political scientists and sociologists) who outnumber linguists by far. It is the purpose of the present paper to add to the societally relevant discussion of *corpus planning* (for my own previous two efforts along these lines see Fishman 1983 and 1987). At this time I propose to raise several questions as to the relationship between status and corpus planning as well as to indicate several alternative directions and ideological paths that the latter may take.

Relationships: primum mobile, direction and reversal

Kloss' original discussion indicates that he thought of corpus planning and status planning as two necessarily co-present aspects of any total language planning effort. Like the two sides of a coin they are obviously both necessary and co-present and any effort to influence one of the two cannot be engaged in without having necessary implications and repercussions for the other. Helpful as this observation may be (see Figure 1), it still leaves a number of crucial issues unanswered, and fosters the unfortunate impression that the two, corpus planning and status planning, are clearly separate entities. 'Which side is up' is,

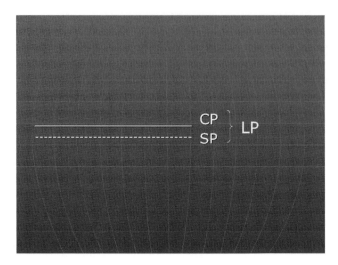

Figure 1. Corpus planning (CP) and status planning (SP) constitute two sides of the same language planning (LP) coin.

of course, a purely perspectival issue: when one is examining corpus planning, it is 'up'; and when one is examining status planning, it is 'up'. However, considering the language planning process *per se*, does this mean that 'which is first' (which is the 'motor' or where does the process start) is also irrelevant (that one or the other can come first without reason or consequences)? Does one *have to* change when the other changes, or are the two sometimes out of sync? Also, any questions as to substantive directionality or kinds of change remain unanswered, which is a pity since not all changes are necessarily equivalent, whether in underlying goal, rationale or consequence.

One post-Klossian assumption is that (successful) status planning is the real stimulus to subsequent corpus planning. Without appropriate status gains for language X, the corpus planning engaged in by its educated and aspiring speakers, writers and/or linguists is all for naught and no more than an empty game that intellectuals sometimes play. This view is supported by the experience of many corpus planning specialists who have created or rediscovered unused and even unknown corpuses for mathematics (or for chemistry, or physics, or astronomy etc.), only to have them languish on language academy shelves because of the lack of corresponding status change which authoritatively assigns to language X a societal function for which that corpus is necessary, or, at least, advantageous, within a specific speech community or network. Figure 2 is a schematic representation of how status planning pushes corpus planning, so that the latter can catch up to and adjust itself to the former. I myself have formerly been a supporter of this particular directional point-of-view.

Of course, the diametrically opposite directional assumption also obtains, namely, that corpus planning pre-dates status planning. In my 1997 study of positive ethnolinguistic consciousness, I discovered, to my own great surprise,

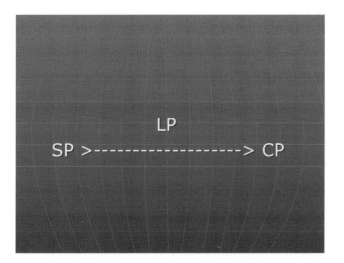

Figure 2. Status planning is the motor (the dynamo) of the language planning process.

that the dates of most corpus citations that I had accumulated, language by language, were often (and appreciably) older than their corresponding status citations (Fishman 1997 [Appendix]). The underlying dynamic in the latter scenario, one which has reoccurred in every part of the world, may be that of prohibited status planning. Because of that prohibition the seemingly more innocuous corpus planning is the only activity which is permitted by the repressive authorities governing the functions of language X. The First International Congress for the Catalan Language (1910) may be taken as a case in point (Marti' y Castell 1993). Literally thousands of laymen attended a conference lasting several days that was devoted to such apparently esoteric topics as Catalan phonology, morphology, syntax and orthography which only a handful of those in attendance could actually follow. Obviously, the conference conveyed a covert message pertaining to the status of Catalan that attracted most of those in attendance: the message that Catalan, which was prohibited in such functions by the Madrid regime, could aspire to and discharge all of the functions of modern urban life, including those of the highest power-related functions in econotechnical and governmental pursuits. Such a predating of corpus planning is found for Hindi, Quechua, Afrikaans and many other late-modernizing and governmentally 'once-frowned-upon' varieties.

A more complex model

The above-mentioned models are, at most, unidirectional. A more complex model can be fashioned by combining both of the uni-directional ones referred to immediately above. Such a model posits that regardless of where our account of language planning begins, one stage feeds into the next in an ongoing feedback

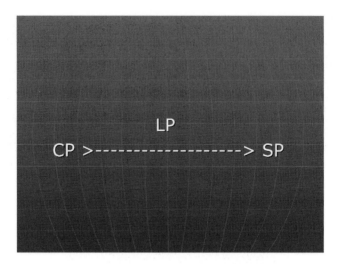

Figure 3. Corpus planning anticipates, facilitates and/or stimulates status planning.

sequence. Status planning successes prompt further corresponding corpus planning and corpus planning achievements facilitate or lay the groundwork for subsequent status planning. The first spiraling graphic implies that increasingly higher (power-related) stages are involved, whereas the circular graphic (Figure 4b) does not take a position on this particular issue and stresses mutual feedback. The second spiraling model (Figure 4c) implies both ups and downs of different degrees and as well as lengths of time. Ataturkian CP in Turkey, e.g., lasted relatively briefly, was soon overturned and then only partially reinstated, while during all of this time Turkish SP was constantly being advanced, regardless of the fate of Ataturkian orthography and nomenclature (Landau 1993). Further study is needed to determine whether linear and circular developmental paths have different consequences for language planning either as a whole or in part.

The substantive content and directionality of corpus planning

Thus far we have dealt only with the issues of 'what comes first and what are the consequences thereof', whether under the conditions of linearity, circularity or cycularity. However, it is time to recognize that CP itself is not all of one piece structurally, i.e., in substantive or ideological terms. A review of various documented CP dimensions will reveal that although they may be quite similar technically (i.e., insofar as involving linguistics and language planning as scientific pursuits), they differ radically along four different bipolar ideological dimensions through which their technical efforts must be filtered. These dimensions will now be introduced one at a time and then related to each other.

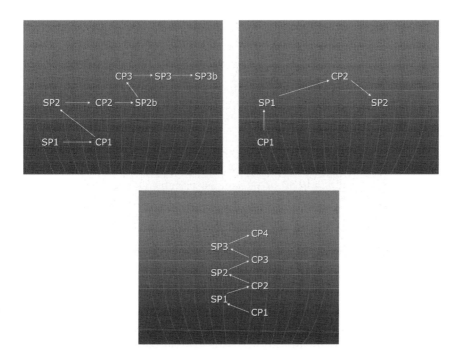

Figure 4. Various circular or spiraling models.

Purity vs. Vernacularism

One very frequently encountered claim among language planning (language correction, language management) agencies and their supporters is that they pursue 'language purity goals' in conjunction with their efforts. With respect to lexicon, orthography and grammar they purportedly seek to follow a substantive language planning model which rejects influences from outside languages. The fact that such a pursuit is regarded as a will-of-the-wisp by modern linguistics is neither here nor there for the other, more powerful, authorities that are in control of guiding the very substantive ideological agenda not only of corpus planning but of sociocultural planning and identity planning more generally. As the above mentioned Catalan case suggested, the rank and file members of sociocultural aggregates are not really interested in corpus planning for its own sake. To the extent that they have any interest in corpus planning at all it is subject to status planning direction and veto. The 'Purity' concern rejects influences, old or new, that are associated with impinging ethnocultural entities or influences via language spread, conquest, travel, trade or other kinds of interpersonal and intergroup interaction. Perhaps the best-known proponent of purism today is France, whose phobia against 'anglicisms' (such as parking, lunch, fast-food, hotdog, fax, camping, etc., not to mention the recent flap over 'e-mail') remains at an officially high alert level. Other relatively recent examples of 'Purism' have been exemplified by Norwegian Nynorsk and by Icelandic (vis-à-vis Danish), as well as by Turkish (only the 'uncontaminated' language of Anatolian peasant women was considered pure enough to serve as a model for modern Turkish). Historical examples may be found in the anti-'inkhorn' (anti-learned and essentially anti-French influences) campaign on behalf of 17th century British English; the related pro-'Amerikan' campaign in mid-nineteenth century American English; the anti-Yiddishism and anti-Europeanism campaigns that guided the revernacularization of Hebrew; the anti-foreignisms campaign that has recently marked turn-of-the-millennium Russian; the anti-Americanism campaigns in many parts of the world either in former years (e.g., Pilipino (Sibayan and Gonzalez 1996) or in Sudanese Arabic (Wagi'alla 1996) in the sixties) or today. Note that the object of opposition need not necessarily be either a cognate or a former colonial language and, indeed, can shift in focus from time1 to time2, to time3.

The opposite tendency, vernacularism, is represented by Robert Hall's famous dictum ('leave your language alone!'), captured in the titles of his 1951 and 1961 books. This is a view well known to and generally popular among American academic linguists who have long believed neither in the necessity for nor in the efficacy of language planning. On 'the man in the street' level, the vernacularism view is one that was eagerly championed by Vuk Karadzic, the earliest proponent of 'write the way you talk' in connection with modern Serbian language planning, by the major governmental advocates of Filipino (not Philipino), and of the very earliest stages of language planning in conjunction with various pidgins, Creoles, and lingua francas the world over. Sociolinguistics prides itself on studying oral varieties (e.g., Afro-American Vernacular English [AAVE]) and, indeed, must do so if it is to validly differentiate between the varieties within a speech community's repertoire and their respective functions (Lanehart 1999). However, when the hitherto untutored and unregulated vernacular subsequently increasingly becomes the object of language planning and of literacy training (as it has again and again throughout the centuries of European modernization), the 'write as you speak' stage may effectively be considered as on its way out. *Language planning is primarily related to the language of literacy* and even schools that start off using strictly vernacular varieties of the language, transition out of it gradually, in upper grades (Fishman and Salmon 1972), when cultivated writing and the more formal speech become the usual goals as is amply demonstrated by the experience at school with AAVE, Bilbaoan Basque, Valencian Catalan, Low German and other dialectal varieties today. *The Purity-Vernacular dimension is a bipolar alternative that all corpus planning must come to terms with. Folk-linguistics* (Preston 1999, Fishman 1997) *and its associated puristic ideology (sometimes, as in India, related to ritual purity and caste purity as well) play inevitable roles in setting up boundaries to the diffusion of unfettered influences that may derive from power inequalities between language groups.* In addition, 'purity' has much wider and very multifaceted societal precedents and concomitants in art and literature ('pastoralism'), intergroup relations

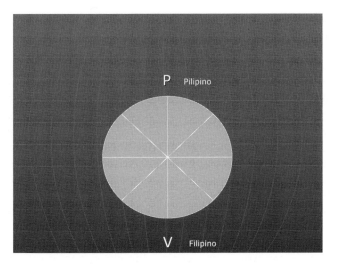

Figure 5. The purism vs. vernacularism dimension.

(apartheid), politics (immigration policy), and wherever xenophobia is rife and racism is in vogue. All things considered it is a boundary setting stance, whether between peoples or their languages, and one that is inevitably reinforced by literacy and by language planning as a whole.

Uniqueness vs. Internationalization

Uniqueness is a corpus planning direction that is similar to but yet different from Purism. Uniqueness goes beyond Purism in that it emphasizes specificity, i.e., not only distance from foreign models but even distance from any cognate indigenous terms or constructions that may resemble those declared undesirable. However, that being said, the oppositionality of uniqueness is primarily inward searching, whereas that of purity is outward oriented. Within its own corpus, uniqueness attempts to foster terms and usages that are (relatively) unknown, archaic, provincial, dialectal or, at least, as yet unknown to the written language. The extreme example of this approach is that attributed to Johannes Aavik (1880–1973) who even utilized randomly constructed syllables in the modernization of Estonian during the early twenties of the previous century (Aavik 1971). The syllables preserved Estonian vowel-harmony and traditional CVC/VCV word formation but were otherwise purely meaningless to begin with. Although this approach may be in fundamental agreement with linguistic theories of the original associations between sounds and the meanings given to them around the world (as opposed to the popular 'ding-dong' and 'heave-ho' onomatopoetic pseudo-theories), it effectively cuts off all post-planning formulations from the prior history of the language and its cultural oral traditions, recorded literature, public and family records, etc. In learning new terminology, learners literally 'haven't a clue', even if they are accomplished native speakers. Thus, uniqueness exacts a high price from the very intergenerational continuity which it seeks to foster, complicating both intragroup and intergroup communication.

The other extreme along this dimension is that of maximizing interlingual similarity with one or another of the major languages of the Western world, either by directly adopting their models or by doing so indirectly via models drawing initially upon a major local purveyor of internationalisms (e.g., the Hispanosphere, the Sinosphere, the Sanskritosphere, the Bahasasphere, etc.) instead of immediately drawing primarily upon the Graeco-Latin model that the West itself employs. Calling such language planning innovations 'internationalisms' removes or counteracts the onus of courting and employing foreignisms. In the case of Ataturk it was even compatible with purism. His 'Great Sun Theory' considered all European languages to be derived from Turkish and, as a result, borrowing from French, for example, merely entailed the re-acceptance or re-admission of a long lost or strayed Turkish word.

The realm of modern econotechnical life is the one most impacted by internationalisms, whether we look at Hausa, Wolof, Quechua or Vietnamese. In this realm, for sure, it is necessary for specialists and all westernized folks more generally to interact easily and frequently with the modern world. The facilitation and maximalization of such interaction is the underlying and often unspoken goal of internationalism-prone corpus planning (particularly as it pertains to the natural and applied sciences). It is no accident, therefore, that the languages that epitomize modern power and econotechnical superiority are favorite models of language planning throughout the world under the less threatening disguise of internationalisms. As a result, Americanisms have come to be most frequently emulated (the English 'e-mail' becomes 'emeel' in Frisian, 'e.mail' in Basque and 'emel' in parts of the hispanophone world, even though

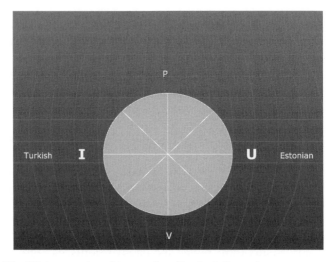

Figure 6. The U(niqueness) vs. I(nternationalization) dimension.

loan-translations of 'electronic mail' are also widely considered '[hyper-] correct'). French, therefore, faces the double challenge of rejecting Anglicisms for reasons of purity and accepting 'the inevitable' under the guise of internationalisms, so as not to fall even further behind its omnipotent 'Anglo-Saxon' competitors. The globalization of culture and of products has remade the world into a smaller linguistic pie and the adoption of internationalisms is often seen as a less objectionable and, perhaps, a less self-destructive step in that direction. Furthermore, the simultaneous pursuit of 'uniqueness-oriented' and of 'internationalism-oriented' language planning has become well established, each orientation being supreme in its own functionally specific direction.

The Classicization vs. Sprachbund dimension

A good bit of the world is still blessed(?) with a classic tongue through which it can have a locally validated association with its own antiquity and with the domains of higher literacy and even sanctity. Such languages are not easily set aside, if for no other reason than that the entire world, including the much emulated Western world, has come to honor and respect them, at least in theory, above and beyond their more strictly local and regional claims to fame. But such languages are also not easily vernacularized (actually: revernaculari-zed) either, precisely because of their sanctity and removal from the work-a-day world. Nevertheless, culturally associated vernaculars can draw upon their own classicals (whether or not they are now cognate with them) for language planning purposes. This gives rise to the phenomenon of classicals being utilized to advance local modernization goals vis-à-vis an associated local vernacular. Thus, modern Israeli Hebrew draws upon Biblical/Talmudic/Rabbinic Hebrew, vernacular Middle Arabics all draw upon Koranic Arabic, 'Chinese' (Potinghua) upon Classical Mandarin, Hindi upon Sanskrit, Tamil upon Classical Tamil, demotic Greek upon Katharevusa, etc., even much more so than do the modern Slavic languages upon their respective Old Church Slavonics or the modern Romance languages upon Latin. Clearly, such an approach to modernization amounts to having one's cake and eating it too, since the modern (i.e., the modern too) can be clothed in classical garb and the classical can live again for modern econotechnology. Apparently, this is neither impossible nor even terribly difficult to accomplish, since classical tongues frequently have a wealth of linguistic resources and their utilization for modernization yields a perspective on modernization that perspectivally integrates it with prior intracultural experience. Modernity is not, therefore, a deleterious 'foreign import', but, rather, a further indication of the eternal superiority of the classical ('particularly for important purposes').

Just as classicals reverberate with a uniquely exalted and mythically embellished antiquity, so the approach of Sprachbund reverberates with a shared regional past that may be roughly equally unique, mythical and exalted. It points to shared glories (the distant pan-Slavic, pan-Germanic or pan-Turkic pasts, the prehistoric and possibly imagined Malphilindo (a purported Malay-

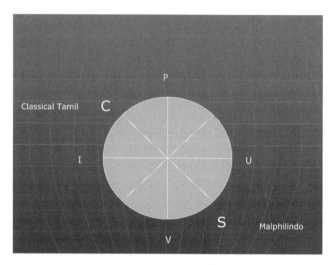

Figure 7. The classicization vs. sprachbund dimension.

Philippine-Indonesian Empire of a dimly remembered past)) as vibrant sources of inspiration that can still be ingeniously recovered, operationalized and benefited from in the difficult pursuit of modern problem solving. Sprachbund borrowings have the advantage of being obtained from distant relatives ('all in the family') and, therefore, of not being as inbred as classicals are, but also of not being as indebted to the totally strange and foreign as internationalisms can often be. Thus, sprachbund corpus enrichment was advocated, drawing upon Arabic and the other Semitic tongues, for the modernization of Hebrew, only after all of the internal resources of at least two millennia of Hebrew had been exhausted but before the offerings of the modern West were resorted to. The phonological and morphological similarities shared by all languages within one sprachbund, based upon their endless years of common origin, interaction and problem-sharing, give them good prospects of having acceptable word-formations with a 'feel good' advantage. Of course, they require a non-threatening image as well, and this, regretfully is often the problem when the borrowing language is much weaker than its essentially more famous and very similar big-brother. Sprachbund may be a useful and broadening 'sometimes thing', but as a major source of constantly ongoing corpus planning it runs into the realization that too much of a neighboring influence (e.g., the ultimately unwelcome influence of Danish as a lingua franca upon all of its neighboring Scandinavian 'cousins') can sometimes be very worrisome indeed. The man who came to dinner is ultimately expected to go home.

Ausbau vs. Einbau as directions of corpus planning

Many avid practitioners of corpus planning are mortified by nothing more than the charge that the language which is so dear to them is 'merely a dialect' of their more powerful, more widely known but structurally quite similar and often threatening Big Brother. Any such charge (or even suspicion) of less than desired local autonomy is often experienced as a major problem by smaller and less well known varieties vis-à-vis their stronger and more prestigious big brothers. The 'dialect' charge, as popularly and non-technically employed, is viewed as an invidious charge of lack of well-educated internal-norm-setting authorities. Where one levels the charge of 'dialect', this is meant to imply a dependent rather than a free-standing language designation. A 'dialect' is a variant (particularly an informal and unschooled vernacular variant at that) of another variety which is accorded the status of a 'real language'. Since this is experienced as a put-down, it is natural that it be resisted and corpus planning is one of the prime arenas where such resistance transpires and via which advances in 'autonomy' can be noted and promoted.

Ausbau (the building away of a weaker variety from a stronger but very similar, fully recognized and therefore bone-fide 'language', in order to provide ample evidence that the 'dialect' charge against the former in comparison to the latter is unfounded, pointing as it does to myriad palpable differences between the two), is a preoccupation of Urdu vs. Hindi, of Bosnian vs. Croatian and of Croatian vs. Serbian, of Byelorussian vs. Russian, of Frisian vs. Nederlands (Dutch), of Yiddish vs. German, of Gallego vs. Portuguese, etc.

Since the two varieties, the weaker and the stronger, are so very similar to one another, this building away process is not an easy goal to attain. One possible approach is to adopt or retain a totally different writing system (Yiddish vs. German, Croatian vs. Serbian, Urdu vs. Hindi) so that the difference between the two varieties is at least visually unambiguous, while drawing upon the independent religious traditions and literary elites that writing systems ultimately link back to. Another approach to procuring 'autonomy motivated distancing' proceeds by developing a standard based on as different (or as distant) a dialect base as possible vis-à-vis the standard of the stronger variety. Both of these approaches pertain primarily to the languages in print (rather than to the languages in popular and private speech), but in all settings language planning itself pertains first and foremost to the printed, i.e., the more bookish and, therefore, formal variety, with the formal spoken variety following somewhat behind in terms of attention from language planners. The more informal the varieties of the two languages, e.g. the market place varieties of Hindi and Urdu or of Serbian and Croatian, the less the Ausbau between them that can be attained or even attempted. Planning and spontaneity do not go together.

The contrasting tendency in corpus planning is the one that emphasizes bringing two varieties together, so that they will fuse. Such polices were followed by Norway, which required both Nynorsk and Landsmal to fuse into Samnorsk, even after each had already established its own standard and was regulated by its own authorities (not without years of prior political effort and sociocultural antagonism). Similar policies of fostering 'dependency based approximation' have been followed in Spain (vis-à-vis Asturian), in Russia (vis-à-vis Byelorussian) and in Catalunya (vis-à-vis Valencian). Languages are more than born and not unlike the angels on Jacob's ladder they move up and down endlessly.

Since Ausbau and Einbau involve diametrically opposed political and philosophical positions it should come as no surprise that they sometimes (often?) follow one another in tandem, with one approach being replaced by the other as differently oriented authorities come into and go out of favor and power. This can be seen in the case of Yiddish in Eastern Europe (Kerler 1999), which went through in-tandem stages of de-Germanization and re-Germaniza-tion during the nineteenth century, followed again by de-Germanization thereafter, as well as in the cases of 'Soviet languages' like Moldavian, that first went through Ausbau from Romanian, as Soviet control was instituted after World War II, and then Einbau to Romanian, after Soviet domination ended subsequent to the crumbling of communism. In Yugoslavia, the differences between formal Croatian and Serbian were first governmentally decreased ('minimized, in favor of Serbian') by the Tito regime, but then, after Yugoslavia broke apart, each variety is now being engineered in more individualistic directions (as has also been the case with the closely related newly established language 'Bosnian'). Indeed, wherever closely related regional varieties ('dialects') become polarized in different political directions, the probability of Ausbau tendencies in corpus planning is radically increased, as is the reversal of such tendencies when political fortunes become drastically changed. Americans, who tend to be dismissive and sarcastic about Ausbau and Einbau, would do well to remember that, after the Revolution, Noah Webster advocated the official establishment on these shores of what he variously called the 'American Language' or 'Federal English', with an academy of its own, because the USA now deserved to have 'a language that was as independent of England

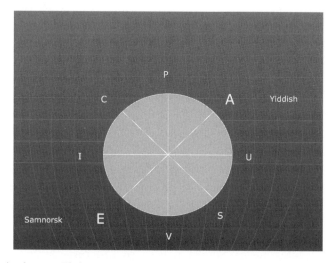

Figure 8. Ausbau vs. Einbau as corpus planning dimensions.

as were its political institutions'. This recommendation has been repeated in the nineteenth and even in the twentieth centuries and has even been recognized by a number of state constitutions, e.g., Illinois, 1930 (see Fishman 1997 for the full text of its constitutional amendment), and still remains unchanged, to the effect that 'The official language of the State of Illinois shall be known as the "American" language and not as the "English" language'.

The eight mini-directions and the two maxi-directions of
LP 'ideological orientation'

Most, if not all, of the eight mini-directions derived from the polar extremes of the four dimensions that we have been discussing can be pursued simultaneously.[2] This is so because corpus planning and status planning authorities may not be in agreement with each other (particularly over time) or even consistent among themselves over time. But, in addition, there is often an inherently built-in conflict within the entire corpus planning enterprise. Corpus planning that seeks to attain both 'ethnic authenticity' (often the initial ideological home of corpus planning) and 'maximization of desired interaction with (and acceptance by) the West' (often a subsequent but equally urgent co-priority) is likely to be pulled in two directions. Sometimes this is even done by the very same governmental authorities, not to mention being done by rival and mutually opposed authorities. The nature of this built in tension between sentiments of ethnic 'purity' and 'authenticity', on the one hand, and the aspirations for international interaction and acceptance, on the other hand, may result in compromises that favor different directional emphases in

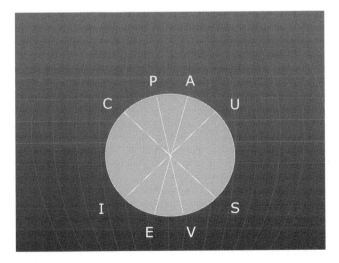

Figure 9. The distancing and the interaction sub-clusters.

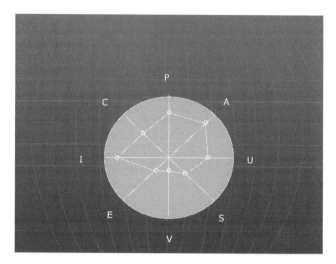

Figure 10. A profile of the self-evaluated activities and emphases of a recognized corpus planning agency today.

language planning taken as a whole, each oriented to the different and often incommensurable imperatives of ethnocultural and econotechnical life.

There are also other factors that lead to 'mixed tracks' in corpus planning. One of these is the intrusion of outside influences and events (conquest, political and/or economic influences, language spread, tourism, study abroad, in-migration, population transfers and exchanges, ethnic revivals, religious revivals [fundamentalism vs. modernization], etc.). All of these factors possess the potential to bring about a redirection and re-balancing of previous emphases in corpus planning. As societies change their ethnocultural and political directions, their corpus planning is redirected so as to more adequately express the then-current hopes and goals of new authorities that come to be recognized by their respective speech-and-writing communities. Ethnonational concerns wax and wane, within any given society, within the region with which it is most intimately linked and throughout the world as a whole. As Clyne (1997) has already noted, much of language planning actually consists of *re*-planning or *de*-planning the planning of the past. Now we can see that such efforts are not only further divisible but also relatable to a higher order factor of opposite but apparently linked ethnicizing and de-ethnicizing needs and efforts.[3] Each of these higher order factors also provides opportunities for changes of 'track' while remaining true to the underlying goal of the broader factor *per se*.

As Figure 10 reveals, the agency portrayed therein substantially pursues both Internationalism and Uniqueness (which some might consider incommensurable but which are obviously both prized by this agency) and also shows a predilection for Classicization, Ausbau and Purification. Thus, it scores itself (i.e., a participant observer scores it) to be high on four out of four distancing/

authenticity polar extremes and only on one out of four interaction/ modernization polar extremes. Such ratings may be perspectival and self-serving, as may be all ratings of self or of others, but they do enable one to compare raters as to their views (and changes in their views) of the directionality of corpus planning in particular language planning contexts. Both the inter-rater consensus (reliability, agreement) and the validity of such ratings still remains to be examined, but now we may have a tool with which to begin to do so. The benefits to be potentially derived from this approach are those of demonstrating that corpus planning definitely has a status planning agenda, rationale and implications, no matter how inconsistent or changeable that agenda may be.

Conclusions

The contrasting and complementary efforts of modern societies to withdraw from foreign ethnocultural impositions and yet be effective participants in the world of modern power and econo-technical interactions, efforts well-documented by Anthony Smith and other specialized students of ethnicity and nationalism, have their counterparts on the language planning scene as well. This has long been recognized in connection with status planning. It has been the goal of this paper to illustrate how corpus planning too participates in this constant approach-avoidance relationship and to do so by showing that all corpus planning has a status planning dimension, hidden though that may frequently be.

Notes

1   Although Kloss has recently been unmasked as an early and committed Nazi (Hutton 1999) who had long disclaimed and hidden any such involvement from me and from other post-WWII colleagues in North America, I nevertheless believe that he made several worthwhile and non-discriminatory contributions to the sociology of knowledge. The corpus/status distinction on which I base this paper (expanding the original notion to subsume various kinds of corpus/status interaction) may well be one of these.

2   All dimension in four-dimensional space can be orthogonal to each other. Dimensions that appear graphically next to each other (on our necessarily two-dimensional graphs) must not be considered to be any more similar to one another than dimensions that are drawn so as to appear further apart.

3   Although both Ausbau and Einbau may be considered as reflecting ethnic self-differentiation, the former is entirely authenticity motivated whereas the latter at least requires a re-negotiation or re-conceptualization of that concept (viz. the current 'return of Byelorussian' to Russian proper) in conjunction with the possible reunification of two polities.

References

Aavik, Johannes. 1971. *Uheksa aastakummet: puhendusteos Johannes Aavikule*. Tallin: Valgas.
Clyne, Michael (ed.). 1997. *The Undoing and Redoing of Corpus Planning*. Berlin: Mouton.

Fishman, Joshua and Erica Lueders-Salmon. 1972. 'What has the sociology of language to say to the language teacher?: On teaching the standard variety to speakers of dialectal or sociolectal varieties, in Courtney B. Cazden et al. (eds.), *Functions of Language in the Classroom*. New York: Teachers College Press, 67–83.

Fishman, Joshua. 1983. 'Modeling rationales in corpus planning: modernity and tradition in images of the "good corpus"', in Juan Cobarrubias and Joshua A. Fishman (eds.), *Progress in Language Planning*. The Hague: Mouton, 107–118.

Fishman, Joshua. 1987. 'Reflections on the current state of language planning' in Lorne Lafarge (ed.), *Proceedings of the international colloquium on language planning*. Quebec City: Laval University Press, 406–28.

Fishman, Joshua. 1997. *In Praise of the Beloved Language: a Comparative View of Positive Ethnolinguistic Consciousness*. Berlin: Mouton.

Hall, Robert A. 1951. *Leave Your Language Alone!* Ithaca, NY: Linguistica.

Hall, Robert A. 1961. *Linguistics and Your Language: Leave Your Language Alone*. Garden City: Anchor.

Hutton, Christopher. 1999. *Linguistics and the Third Reich*. New York: Routledge.

Kloss, Heinz. 1952. *Die Entwicklung neuer germanischer Kultursprachen von 1800 bis 1950*. Munich: Pohl.

Kloss, Heinz. 1967. 'Abstand languages and Ausbau languages', *Anthropological Linguistics* 9: 29–41.

Kerler, Dov-ber. 1999. *The Origins of Modern Literary Yiddish*. Oxford: Clarendon Press.

Landau, Jacob. 1993. 'The first Turkish language congress', in Joshua A. Fishman (ed.), *The Earliest Stage of Language Planning*. Berlin: Mouton, 271–92.

Lanehart, Sonja L. 1999. 'Afro-American Vernacular English', in Joshua A. Fishman (ed.), *Handbook of Language and Ethnic Identity*. New York: Oxford University Press, 211–25.

Marti' y Castell, Joan. 1993. 'The first international Catalan language congress, Barcelona, 13–18 October, 1906' in Joshua A. Fishman (ed.), *The Earliest Stage of Language Planning*. Berlin: Mouton, 47–68.

Preston, Dennis R. (ed.). 1999. *Handbook of Perceptual Dialectology*. Philadelphia, PA: Benjamins.

Sibayan, Bonufacio P. and Andrew Gonzalez. 1996. 'Postimperial English in the Philippines', in Joshua A. Fishman et al. (eds.), *Post-Imperial English*. Berlin: Mouton, 139–62.

Wagi'alla, Anwar. 1996. 'English in Sudan' in Joshua A. Fishman et al. (eds.), *Post-Imperial English*. Berlin: Mouton, 339–56.

7

From ethnic group toward the modern nation: the Czech case

MIROSLAV HROCH

The Czech national movement is generally regarded as a 'success story'. The ethnically defined Czech national identity received, during several decades of national agitation, general acceptance from the masses of the Czech-speaking population. This happened under the conditions of the oppressive Metternich regime and against German cultural and social superiority. In my earlier comparative research, it was demonstrated that this success can be explained neither by the Herderian influence (as the traditionalist, above all German, historians supposed), nor by the force of the idea of 'nationalism' as a free-floating actor. At least, the oft-quoted author of the concept of nation as the product of nationalism, Ernest Gellner, proved that successful 'nationalism' had its deep historical roots in the social and cultural process labelled by him erroneously 'industrialization'. According to my earlier research, the transition from the Phase B of national agitation to the Phase C of mass movement was possible only under several conditions, which were independent of the wishes of its actors, the 'nationalists': firstly, strengthening social communication and mobility; secondly, a coincidence of national demands and social (political, cultural) interests, i.e. under conditions of a nationally relevant conflict of interests; thirdly, the pre-existing linguistic and cultural community, sometimes accompanied by a memory of old 'national' statehood.

This contribution does not intend to repeat earlier published results and recall generally known data on the transition of the national movement from Phase B to Phase C, i.e. to the mass movement. It aims to go one step back and try to interpret the transition from the learned Phase A dominated by nationally 'neutral' scholars to the nationally engaged, agitating Phase B. This chapter offers an attempt to explain motives: why some intellectuals decided to construct a new national identity and to propagate it among the members of their ethnic group. Expressed in the terms used by Anthony Smith, we try to explain the decision to transform the ethnic community into a modern nation. For good or ill, the actors of this procedure understood themselves as protagonists and 'awakeners' of the real existing nation and they regarded the non-existence of statehood in most cases (except the Balkans) as unimportant or as not decisive.

This turn to national agitation occurred in the Czech case (and above all in Bohemia) in the period between 1790 and 1815, contemporaneous with similar developments in Hungary, Norway and Greece, and much earlier than most other European national movements.

Our analysis chooses as its point of departure a hypothesis proceeding from social psychology that the need for a new identity has to be understood as a result of the crisis or loss of old identities, as an answer to the dissolution of old values and social ties, under conditions of uncertainty caused by social and political changes and transformations. This hypothesis will be verified through the analysis of empirical data from Czech history.

Our procedure follows three steps, answering three questions:

1. 'the constants': what were the basic factors of stability under the conditions of the old regime?
2. What changes and reforms destabilized or eroded old factors of stability?
3. 'the answers': How did members of the Czech ethnic community react to these changes?

During the second half of the eighteenth century, the way of life of the inhabitants, their beliefs, habits and identities were formed and maintained by several constant relations and institutions. These invariables or 'constants' had survived without significant change since the seventeenth century, in some cases even since the Middle Ages.

The medieval Kingdom of Bohemia gradually lost its independence under the rule of the Habsburgs, but it did not disappear: its name, its borders, its capital Prague survived, and also some institutions, like the Landtag, Court of Justice and even the constitution from 1627. Most aristocratic families were not Czech by origin (they usurped the confiscated lands of Protestants, who were expelled after their defeat in 1620), but their later members accepted an identity with the 'Lands of the Crown of Bohemia'. A new feeling of identity emerged among many members of the nobility in opposition to the centralist policy of Vienna and they tried to retain old privileges: the 'Landespatriotismus'. As a part of this process, the memory of old statehood of the Crown was retained. Nevertheless, for the most part, the majority of this nobility regarded the Austrian dynastic identity as the dominant one and many aristocrats supported Habsburg centralism.

Since Protestantism in Bohemia had been defeated, the Catholic Church had controlled all the religious, spiritual and cultural life in the country. Its organization corresponded to the old political structure: Bohemia remained an autonomous ecclesiastical unit with the archbishop in Prague as its head. Similarly, Moravia was an archbishopric with its capital in Olomouc. The Catholic hierarchy kept elements of the 'land'-identity and some among its members (and above all among the lower clergy) developed a Bohemian baroque patriotism, as a positive attitude to the land, and even regarded the Czech language as a symbol of Bohemian or Moravian individuality. The cult of St.Vaclav (Wenzel) I as 'Protector' of the Crown of Bohemia and of other 'national' saints represented an important element of this patriotism. Naturally, the Church asserted until the middle of the eighteenth century, beside its monopolistic control of education and all spiritual life, a privileged position in the economy and politics.

The most expressive social constant was signified by the rigid system of serfdom in the countryside and guilds in towns. Aristocratic domains, still strongly influenced by their feudal origins, created the basic unit of administration, taxation, and jurisdiction. All individuals were firmly included into the more or less effective system of Church and state administration. This meant that inhabitants of non-noble origin were subordinated to the state, to the Church and to their lordships. They had no right to self-administration and at the same time, they were the only tax-payers. Nevertheless, the inequality of human beings, predestined by birth, was still generally accepted by all strata of the non-privileged population as a self-evident feature of their life.

What about the ethnic constants? Since the Middle Ages, both Bohemia and Moravia were inhabited by a majority Czech-speaking and a minority German-speaking population. The written Czech language developed during the fourteenth century and remained, until the seventeenth century, the official language of administration. The new constitution of 1627 gave the German language an equal position with Czech, but in reality German became the dominant language in administration, the economy and cultural life. The Czech-speaking population was aware of its language, at least, since it remained the language of the Church. We have proof for some degree of ethnic identity, which – with very few exceptions – did not include xenophobia or spontaneous patriotic enthusiasm. The social structure, the 'Stand', was still decisive. An example of this was the fact that the Czech- and German-speaking peasants participated side by side in the great peasant war in northeast Bohemia and there is no evidence of any relevant conflict between insurgents from these two *ethnies*.

In general, one could gain the impression that this society was stabilized and based on currently accepted inequality, religious legitimacy and everyday oppression. Nevertheless, this was only on the surface. Within society, immanent tensions and signs of crisis increased. To prevent conflicts, to ameliorate the situation and to avoid a crisis, the enlightened absolutist rulers initiated efforts to modernize society through reforms. These famous reforms, introduced by the late Maria Theresa and above all by Joseph II, brought significant changes which brought old constants into question.
Their impact can be summarized in five points:

1. The hitherto monopolistic and uncontrolled power of the Catholic Church was limited not only by the introduction of religious tolerance and by diminishing its intellectual control, but also by the reduction of Church property by the state.
2. The state decreased the power of landlords, above all through the abolition of serfdom and through increasing state control in local and state administration.

3. The progress of jurisprudence and the reform of legislation, based on principles of equal value of all citizens, was the first step to abolish – at least in the theory – the inequality of classes.
4. The new concept of education and the school system tried to spread elementary education to all and to open higher schools to all inhabitants.
5. The state administration increasingly supported the spread of enlightened principles and scientific research, diminished the rights of censorship and contributed to the creation of a new secular public.

All these reforms, even though not generally welcomed, influenced sooner or later everyday experience, but their immediate importance was larger: they demonstrated not only to the educated classes, but also to the people that the conditions and circumstances of their life were not unchangeable and that they could be ameliorated.

Naturally, an opposition emerged against these reforms, led above all by a part of the nobility and by the Church hierarchy. This opposition – irrespective of its reactionary character – included a mobilizing impact: it demonstrated a phenomenon which seemed until this time unthinkable, i.e. public opposition against the will and the orders of the ruler and of the state authority. The image of the inviolability of the ruler's will was impaired. All this played a role as a factor which started to disturb old constants and old identities.

Beside this general impact, each of the five groups of reforms included changes which influenced – usually without having intended to – the preconditions for the strengthening of a new national identity.

The religious tolerance brought an end to more than one hundred years of persecution and ostracism of the Reformation tradition in Czech cultural life: non-Catholic books written in Czech and published before the triumph of the Counter-reformation had until this time been forbidden and destroyed and their authors had to be forgotten as 'heretics'. Only now was it possible to offer a full picture of the history of Czech-written literature since the fifteenth century. The religious tolerance allowed now even reprints of some important works written by Czech non-Catholics. In this context, some new historical sources could be published and this contributed to a better knowledge of the country's past, understood sometimes as 'national history'.

The abolition of serfdom was regarded by traditional historiography as the starting point of the migration from the Czech-speaking countryside to the German towns. Recent research has revised this opinion in two respects: firstly, the immigration from the countryside had already started before the abolition of serfdom; secondly, the towns in the core territory of Bohemia were ethnically not as strongly Germanized as in Moravia. Nevertheless, more important from the point of view of identity crisis was the difference in the experience of personal freedom between the Czech-speaking and the German-speaking peasant. The German peasant entered a society whose official language was similar to his local dialect. The Czech peasant entered a society whose official language he was unable to understand. The difference in possibility of social advancement – and also in the search for a new identity – became apparent.

The reform of jurisdiction was discussed but not finished until after 1800. For this reason, it had a limited impact on the masses of people. Nevertheless, the educated public, partially Czech by origin, was well informed and accepted the principle of equality of human beings. The abolition of serfdom itself was regarded as a great demonstration of the principles of equality, which opened the possibility of new social relations (and identities).

The new school system was also an expression of this trend towards equality. From the point of view of the change of identities, its impact was ambivalent. In theory, all higher schools and the university in Prague were open to everyone regardless of social origin. On the other hand, the replacement of Latin by German as the language of instruction created a new inequality. German native speakers and also sons from bilingually educated families were in a more advantageous position in comparison with those who were born in Czech-speaking families.

The elementary schools received – unlike all higher schools – the 'local language' as the language of instruction. This was an important point of departure not only for the improvement of alphabetization, but also for the awareness of ethnic identity. Somehow, it could also be regarded as an important sign for the prestige of the Czech language.

While the elementary schools remained under ecclesiastical control, the majority of higher schools became secularized: the proportion of secularized themes increased and new scientific knowledge was allowed to enter education. Themes from history and geography achieved an unintended importance for the awareness of the specificity of one's own region, country, and nation.

The secularization of education together with the liberalization of intellectual and scientific life influenced the profile of the new emerging social strata – the secular 'intellectuals' (or better 'intelligentsia') who lived off contracted work or through free professions and who became partly independent of the state and religious control, even though the degree of independence of various professions differed from a totally loyal clerk in state service to a relatively independent attorney or surgeon. Naturally, this new category of educated people, without the disadvantage inherited in their birth, sometimes had difficulties in the search for a position which would correspond to their qualifications. It is not surprising that some of them defined a new understanding of social and material interests and were strongly interested in the search for identity.

That is to say, most of these new intellectuals did not belong to any established estate or self-conscious traditional professional group. Even those who were originally educated as priests or friars did not regard their affiliation to the Church as a decisive identity. Some of them identified with their aristocratic sponsors (and with the Bohemian nobility), with a limited chance to be accepted as members of this noble class. Some of them identified with the modernizing centralist state, in so far as they found jobs in state services. It was difficult for them to accept other traditional identities and so the search for a new identity seemed 'inevitable' for them.

The internal and institutional reforms of social and cultural life were only one part of the changes that shook the traditional social relations and identities of the old regime in the Habsburg monarchy. The other category of shocks were external in origin, did not depend on the state policy, and came from outside.

The most famous and influential among them originated from the French Revolution and were strengthened by the interventionist wars against it. In these wars, the Habsburg armies played the central role and could not be omitted in the system of communication in their Empire. Given the conditions of Central Europe, it was impossible to introduce a total blockade of information on the French Revolution, as was realized, with some success, in Russia and in Spain.

Since revolutionary terms like 'liberty' and 'equality' could not be ignored because they were an integral part of daily news, the governmental ideologists tried to adopt them and use them as positive values – naturally, not to announce the fall of the old regime, but on the contrary, as natural features of this regime. 'True' liberty and equality is realized not in the 'falsified' sense in France, but in the Habsburg lands. Later, the revolutionary term, 'la patrie', was adopted as 'Vaterland'. On the other hand, the term 'la nation' did not become an object of dynastic revaluation – maybe because it was not regarded as a danger to the stability of the old regime.

Even though the wars against revolutionary France affected the lands of the Crown of Bohemia only marginally, the German and Czech reading public was regularly informed about the battles and military campaigns and the 'French danger' was present, at least indirectly. The psychological and educational impact of these reports was immense: never before had the population received such detailed information about the war. Reports presented the war not only as the ruler's war, but also as 'our war', a war against a common enemy and this enemy was often defined ethnically: 'the French'. War reports were in some sense an instrument of identification, but they also offered a schooling in imagination: you never knew the consequences of military operations, of battles won or lost – the only thing you could do, was to imagine the different alternatives.

Beside this, the reading public – and indirectly also the people – received through war reports an immense amount of geographical information about foreign countries, peoples, towns, rivers etc. Some of these names the Czech and the German reading public had never heard of and, above all, this was a practical training in imagination: imagining the existence of 'the other', people could imagine their own group, their own country.

Later on, especially during the Napoleonic wars, another factor of identification was offered by military billeting and transits. For the first time, Czech peasants and urban inhabitants met others who spoke a language different from the usual Czech or German: French, and also the Slavic languages, like Russian. We know from contemporary comments that the

Czech people oscillated between sympathy with soldiers who spoke a similar language, and aversion against the parasitic demands of foreign (and not only foreign) armies.

It is significant that all other innovations happening in the neighbourhood were overshadowed by the Revolution and wars. The process of dissolution of the Old Empire received only a marginal place in newspapers and contemporary comments. We can interpret this marginalization of the Reich as a partial success of the efforts of the Viennese government to strengthen the Austrian identity of both Czech and German speakers in contrast to the identity based on the Old Empire. The events in the 'Reich' were interpreted as events which happened abroad, in foreign countries.

In the end, we have to mention some events which did not change the life and institutions in the Empire, but mobilized the attention of the broad masses insofar as they also influenced the search for identities. Three great political festivities at the beginning of the 1790s played this role. Chronologically the first was the public transfer of the Bohemian Crown Jewels to Prague from Vienna, where they had been kept since the time of Maria Theresa. The transportation of the Crown Jewels of the Kingdom of Bohemia was accompanied by festive processions and meetings, where the feeling of Landespatriotismus were demonstrated, sometimes explicitly as a reaction to Viennese centralism.

The reason for transportation was the second festivity: the coronation of Leopold II as king of Bohemia in 1791 and one year later – after his unexpected death – another coronation, that of his son Franz. Both coronations were opportunities for great ceremony not only for the nobility but also for the people. Thousands of peasants and artisans were invited to come from the provinces to Prague for this occasion.

While these three festivities corresponded to the traditional patterns of the old regime, the attempt to awaken Bohemian patriotism in 1808 intended to mobilize all strata of society, aiming to strengthen the people's will to resist an eventual French invasion of Bohemia. As part of these patriotic activities, the old medieval Kingdom was celebrated and even the Czech Hussites were presented as an example of bravery and of the love for fatherland. After the defeat in 1809 patriotic agitation was stopped. Nevertheless, this short period offered to the small group of Czech patriots an opportunity to strengthen the arguments for, and to improve instruments and forms of, national agitation.

At least one negative experience with governmental 'innovations' has to be mentioned: the catastrophic failure and bankruptcy of state finances in 1811, which struck almost all inhabitants of the Monarchy. The loss of savings through the decision of the state did not provoke any larger social unrest, but it affected the search for identities, because it urgently reminded all state subjects that they lived in the same country and shared the same fate.

In the last part of this contribution, we ask, how did people respond to the challenge of all these historical events? How did all these changes and innovations influence the identity crisis and the search for new identities?

We have to resist a simplifying temptation to draw a teleological line from the identity crisis provoked by enlightened reforms to the creation of the modern Czech national identity. During the critical period, we distinguish several activities based on different and mutually overlapping identities. The aristocratic Landespatriotismus survived as an activating medium of scientific research on history of the kingdom, its old literature and the Czech language itself. Analogically, baroque patriotism, with strong religious affiliations, also survived the period of enlightened absolutism, stressing the traditions of the autonomous kingdom. Although both variants of old patriotism were based on anti-modernist feelings, they were partially compatible with the new identity which emerged with enlightened regional patriotism. This enlightened patriotism regarded the patriotic individual (usually an intellectual) as responsible for the wealth and prosperity of the region and its population: he had to improve the situation through school education, scientific research, and cultural activities.

During the last decade of the eighteenth century, this regional patriotism, originally intellectual, exclusive and in most cases German-*writing*, diverged into several streams. One of them kept the concept of a purely economic improvement of the country, disregarding linguistic aspects. Another integrated into the learned activities of Landespatriotismus. The third regarded its main responsibility as improving the cultural standard and education of the most neglected part of the population – the Czech-speaking part. This patriotism started to support Czech publishing not only on economic matters but also on the past of Bohemia, on its heroes, on the present situation and also descriptions of foreign countries as 'other'. A specific component of these edu-cational efforts offered to the Czech public were translations (and increasingly also original works) of fiction, mostly 'popular' reading and in some places (above all in Prague) Czech-speaking theatre, with both translated pieces, and pieces from the history of Bohemia. This was the environment in which some intellectuals wrote enthusiastic 'defences' of the Czech language.

The enlightened patriotic activities were in most cases written in German, as it was the usual language of communication in the Habsburg monarchy at the end of the eighteenth century. The minority of Czech-*writing* enlightened patriots demonstrated that they accepted – beside a regional and professional identity – some kind of ethnic identity. Nevertheless, the use of Czech language was also compatible with baroque patriotism and eventually also with aristocratic Landespatriotismus. In spite of this overlapping of identities, they evidently differed in their social background. The Czech-*writing* patriotism of that time could hardly count on material or moral support from the ruling elites. The Czech-*writing* engagement could, in other words, bring no profits to the patriots. Some degree of selfless enthusiasm was a necessary precondition of this branch of patriotism and the activists could at best earn their reward in the immaterial field of prestige.

However, this patriotic attitude expressed the heritage of the basic moral principles of enlightened patriotism: self-denying and active love for the fatherland without regard to any material profit. Prestige was then regarded as some kind of moral, spiritual substitute for profit. Symptomatically formulated on the threshold of the nineteenth century by Bernard Bolzano, Professor in Moral Philosophy at the University in Prague, was a concept of regional patriotism, where the enlightenment and religious traditions were combined: patriotism was an expression of Christian charity imposed upon the people by God. In his understanding, all kinds of patriotic activities were fully in accord with religious moral principles.

Beside this combination of the enlightened and baroque patriotic traditions, another combination emerged at the very same time, Austrian state-patriotism, proposed in the above mentioned crisis year of 1808. The love for the fatherland was presented as an integral part of the love for the Emperor, who was presented as 'father' of his subjects. The official propaganda offered a twofold identity: the broader one with the Emperor and his Empire, the narrower one with the concrete historical Land. The new identity, offered by official Austrian state-patriotism, was accepted as a central one by a very small stratum of the state bureaucracy in Bohemia and partly among aristocrats. Nevertheless it was immanently or explicitly accepted also by the broader masses of population but not as their central identity.

For those patriotic intellectuals who tried to define their 'national' or regional identity in a new way, one central question had to be answered: how to define and describe the fatherland, 'patria', as an object of care and love? Where is the homeland of one's fellow-countrymen? Three answers can be distinguished at the threshold of the nineteenth century, corresponding to different types of old patriotism and to their modified versions.

The surviving concept of regional patriotism was related to a region, defined by political (or historical) borders, without regard to its internal structure and also without regard to the ethnic borders. Ethnic identities of the inhabitants were respected as a specific feature of the region. This old concept implied some overlapping with Landespatriotismus and with baroque patriotism and its linguistic or ethnic 'neutrality' meant that German was its basic language of communication and that its impact was limited and acceptable above all for German-speaking enlightened elites, while the Czech-speaking population remained almost untouched.

Those intellectuals, ethnic Czechs by origin, who felt responsible to their ethnic countrymen, defined the 'patria' in a different way. The most important among them, Josef Jungmann, defined the fatherland (for the first time in 1806) as a territory, where people speak the same language, 'my' language. In this context, they used as synonym of fatherland the term 'narod' – nation. This term was not a neologism invented by them, but an old term used in the Czech language since the sixteenth century and understood at least since the seventeenth century as a community characterized by common history, living place and also by common language.

The third concept of fatherland was formulated at the same time by Professor Bolzano as a vision of one nation comprising all the inhabitants of Bohemia, who would be able to use or understand both Czech and German, i.e.

a bilingual society. This vision seems to be very up-to-date, even fashionable today; nevertheless, the future proved, very soon, that it was only a utopian vision. Even if Bolzano was in his time more popular (above all among students) and influential than Jungmann, it was not his, but Jungmann's vision, which was accepted by young educated men in their search for a new group identity.

If we ask why this linguistic concept of national identity became the most attractive one, we have to take into account that these newly educated intellectuals and students proceeded from the lower middle classes; they were sons of artisans, small shopkeepers and peasants. Most of them kept in contact with their families and the localities where they were born, and were well aware about their way of life and about the impact of enlightened reforms.

The Czech-speaking artisan or peasant was, thanks to these reforms, personally free and regarded as an equal human being, he was often wealthy enough to acquire some degree of self-consciousness and for this reason he realized a humiliating fact, which was not relevant for his parents or grand parents: that he was excluded from the new emerging society of 'equals' because the language he spoke was rejected by this society as inferior. As long as the horizon of Czech-speakers was limited by the feudal estate, this inferior status of his language played no important role: the only linguistic difference he experienced as 'naturally' inferior to him was that in relation to the German-speaking landlord and his servants. As soon as he or his son overstepped the bounds of the local estate, he experienced his Czech ethnicity as a handicap or even as a source of humiliation. 'We are foreigners in our own land', commented one educated peasant as early as the 1780s.

It is evident that among those who experienced this inequality were young sons who started on the difficult process of achieving higher education. Even though they were personally able to learn German sooner or later, the only language of education, they were not able to achieve better social positions and jobs. This feeling of injustice provoked in some of them a need for total assimilation, but another reaction became increasingly frequent: the decision to struggle for linguistic equality in Bohemia, i.e., to accept and support the ethnic concept of national identity and of the nation, proposed by Jungmann.

The traditional historians regard this programme as Herderian and 'romanticist' – and for the same reason, some social scientists denounce it. Naturally, Herder played an important role as inspiration and as a source of arguments and similarly, German Romanticism was welcomed by Jungmann as validation of his concept, which was, however, formulated and written earlier than the famous 'Reden' of Fichte and the pamphlets of Ludwig Jahn.

There is no doubt that there were also emotional motifs behind the decision to accept an ethnic national identity. The 'irrational' love for language was derived from the more understandable love for his countrymen, for those inhabitants of the country he felt identity with. In this respect, Jungmann's proposals represent rather the heritage of enlightened patriotism than the influence of 'romanticism'.

Very soon, this ethno-national identity started to diverge into a moderate and a consistent stream. The moderate patriots regarded the Czech language as a loved symbol of community, they enjoyed using and developing it, but they regarded the demands for its equality with German as utopian and even as unnecessary. To adore the Czech language and to be proud of Czech national history did not negate their pessimisim concerning the chance of the Czech language becoming a modern written language. For this reason, German had to maintain its domination in Bohemia.

The consistent stream aimed to achieve a real and not just formal equality between both languages. Sooner or later, the Czech language had to be able to express all modern feelings and thoughts and to describe complicated connections. For this reason, it had to be accepted as a language of instruction in schools and as a language of communication in public life. Even if this vision seemed to be a utopian one in the eyes of contemporaries, these claims cannot be interpreted as a mere project of romanticism. Neither can they be explained as a tool in the struggle for political power, as was the case a century later.

The interpretation has to take into account that the enlightened concept of equal human beings was later accompanied by the proto-liberal concept of equal opportunities for every man. These principles, however, could not be fulfilled – at least according to the opinion of these patriots – under conditions of differential prestige and unequal possibilities of different languages. So far, the decision to embrace the linguistic national identity had not been very far from the emerging ideas of civil society and equality of its members. Additionally, the struggle for equality of languages (and their speakers) has something to do with the need for prestige and acknowledgement felt by the Czech-speaking intellectuals.

For a better understanding of this attitude, let us exemplify it by comparing the arguments used in favor of the Czech language by enlightened patriots in their 'Defences' from the 1780s and 1790s, with the arguments used by Jungmann in favour of the Czech language in 1806. In the eighteenth century Defences the Czech language was celebrated above all for its beauty, rich vocabulary and its age (as a language spoken by medieval Czech kings, etc.). Its practical use was recommended to the elites of that time: the landlord needs it for better understanding of his (Czech) servants or serfs, the officer can better understand his soldiers, the surgeon his patients. The general position of these Defences was a call addressed from below to the higher classes of Bohemian society.

Jungmann also praised historical and aesthetic values of the Czech language, but his most important argument was that it was above all the Czech people who needed the improvement of their language. It was not important to him which language was used by the nobility; what was important was that the Czech speaker, if he did not know German, had no chance for any social advancement.

The search for new identities proceeded in Bohemia at the time around 1800 in different ways and offered different identities. Naturally, it was always a matter of individual decision, which alternative was preferred, or how the hierarchy of old and new identities was constructed. To avoid the criticism of being under the influence of the concepts of 'teleolology' and 'ethnicism', let us put the concluding question, concerning the chances of different alternatives to be realized as the generally accepted modern national identity.

The non-ethnic regional patriotism kept its position as an identity accepted by German-speaking and bilingual intellectuals for several decades. Nevertheless, since it did not aim at any mass-mobilization, it was unable to compete with other identities, but could survive as a marginal identity in connection with another one. The same could be said about regional identity as a component of a national one, even though the regionalists tried to mobilize the population. So, for example, the Moravian regionalists opposed, until the second half of the nineteenth century, full integration into the Czech nation with the result that the national identity of the Moravian population existed alongside the regional identity not as an alternative but as an additional identity.

The alternative of the 'Bohemian' bilingual nation had a real chance of success only if accepted not only by Czech but also German speakers. Czechs, so far as they achieved higher education, fulfilled the claim for bilinguality, but only a few Germans by origin did the same by learning the Czech language so as to become consciously bilingual 'Bohemians'. Nevertheless, with the emerging national movement in German states, an increasing number of German intellectuals in Bohemia decided to accept the linguistic concept of German identity and regarded themselves as members of the German nation. This decision was for the first time demonstrated in 1848 in the dispute about participation in elections for the parliament in Frankfurt. Once this decision was taken, a bilingual nation in Bohemia ceased to be an alternative.

The old surviving Landespatriotismus also rejected Frankfurt and German identity, but it was socially exclusive and its aristocratic representatives only in very few exceptional cases supported the efforts to improve the Czech language as an integral part of their identity with the land. The decisive part of the nobility did not renege on their German language – not as a symbol of their national identity but as a symbol of their social superiority.

Consequently, the linguistic definition of a new national identity in Bohemia was the victorious alternative, because it was the only real way which could integrate an intellectual patriotism with the Czech- (but also with the German-) speaking population. This does not mean that this population inevitably followed the 'national' call. Only if several conditions were fulfilled, could the real possibility of Phase B turn to the reality of Phase C. This is, nevertheless, already another problem.

Bibliographical note

English historians writing on the Czech national movement were mostly interested in the period of political conflicts, but there are very few contributions to its initial phase. The best analysis is that of Hugh LeCaine Agnew, *Origins of the Czech National Renascence*, University of Pittsburg Press (1993) (with a rich bibliography). Among earlier authors, relevant is Robert Joseph Kerner,

Bohemia in the Eighteenth Century. A Study in Political, Economic, and Social History with Special Reference to the Reign of Leopold II., 1790–1792, New York: Macmillan, 1932. More specialized is Janet Wolf Berls, *The elementary school reforms of Maria Theresia and Joseph II in Bohemia*, PhD. diss. Columbia University (1975); Paul P. Bernard, *Jesuits and Jacobins: Enlightement and enlightened despotism in Austria*, Urbana, Chicago 2nd London, University of Illinois Press, 1971; Joseph F. Zacek, 'The French revolution, Napoleon and the Czechs' in *Proceedings of the Consortium on Revolutionary Europe 1750–1850, Tallahassee,* Florida: Florida State University Press, 1980, pp. 254–63. The same author gave a general view of this period in 'Nationalism in Czechoslovakia', in Peter F. Sugar and Ivo John Lederer, *Nationalism in Eastern Europe*, 3rd ed. (1994), pp. 166ff. For the linguistic aspect, see George Thomas, *Linguistic Purism*, London: New York (1991).

8

Myth against myth: the nation as ethnic overlay

JOHN HUTCHINSON

Introduction

A central theme of Anthony Smith's encyclopaedic scholarship is the relationship between premodern ethnic communities (ethnie) and modern nations.[1] In his classic text *The Ethnic Origins of Nations* (1986) and subsequent writings he attacks the dominant modernist orthodoxy that perceives nations as essentially novel political entities, created by the ideology of nationalism. Although most nations have many modern components, they are built on premodern ethnies, and, indeed, there is a strong causal relationship between ethnies and nations.

Smith, like John Armstrong (the other great scholar of nation-formation in *la longue durée*), also explores the layered nature of the ethnic past, and how nationalists are directed and constrained by myths and memories in the process of constructing the nation (see Smith 1995). How is this emphasis on the persistence of ethnic identities compatible with the innovative, even revolutionary, character of nationalism and the rise of the territorially extensive, socially mobile, and mass political units that we call nations? How are nationalists able to overcome ingrained tradition? This is what I will address in this chapter, elaborating on Smith's recognition of the cultural role of romanticism.

I will argue that national revivalists, shaped by neo-classical as well as romantic cultural movements, developed a dynamic view of the role of ethnic communities in history that has appealed to new educated groups. These realised that in order for their ethnic communities to survive in a world of ceaseless change they had to be modernised (turned into nations). I will explore first the ideas of this national revivalism and then two important strategies of social transformation. The first is 'inner': the attempt at a transformation of the accepted concept of the past so that it took on new activist meaning. The second is 'external': the creation of a cult of sacrifice for the nation by a revolutionary elite whose moral authority would then enable them to override existing myth structures and systems of authority. As I shall argue, both have resulted in an overlaying rather than an obliteration of ethnic traditions. In many contexts there remains a tension between national and older ethnic traditions.

Romanticism and national revivalism

Central to romanticism was the conception of a living not mechanical universe, in which all natural entities were animated by a force that individualised them and endowed them with a drive for realisation. For Herder one of these organic entities was the nation, a primordial and unique cultural and territorial community through which individuals developed their full potential as moral and rational beings. Herder portrayed humanity as essentially diverse, and world progress as a result of the mutual interactions of nations, each of which had its own unique contribution to make. This polycentric *Weltanschauung* which rejected Christian exclusivism and the rationalist universalism of the enlightenment had revolutionary consequences. It presented a new dynamic and democratic view of humanity, made history a weapon of social innovation, intensified and extended identification with territorial homelands, vernacularised cultures, demoticised politics and inspired counter culture movements of educated youth dedicated to moral and social transformation.

Polycentric interactionism

A primary motivation of romantic intellectuals was the regeneration of European cultures. From the late eighteenth century, European intellectuals, convinced that their civilisation was deracinated, sought new sources of inspiration outside an ossified Christianity and the mechanistic philosophies of the enlightenment. Philhellenes found this source in Greek antiquity, but others looked to the 'founding' civilisations of Egypt, Persia, and the Arabs. One outcome was momentous: the 'discovery' in the 1780s by British Orientalist scholars in Calcutta, led by Sir William Jones and Henry Colebrooke, of a Hindu Aryan Sanskrit civilisation in North India developing from the second millennium BC, which they proclaimed as the 'original' civilisation of humanity (Schwab 1984: 51). Jones' conjecture that Sanskrit was the mother language of Europe, was given 'scientific' status in Franz Bopp's Indo-European language classification in 1816.

A vision of a human family tree based on ethno-cultural principles inspired an internationale of thinkers and scholars to rediscover and record the most distant origins of peoples of the world and their interrelationships, as a way of making sense of the present, thereby stimulating the rise of archaeology, philology, folklore and comparative religion. This had several consequences.

Firstly, it subverted the existing status orders within Europe and between Europe and the rest of the world. Within Europe prestige had been based on the relationships of rulers and peoples to Biblical figures or Graeco-Roman antiquity. Jones's discovery was interpreted by the Schlegel brothers as declaring the Asian origins of the European peoples (the

Greeks, Romans, Celts, Germans, and Slavs) who had migrated from the East in successive waves (Poliakov 1974: 198). German romantics claimed direct descent from 'pagan' Aryans and cultural leadership of contemporary Europe against the imperial pretensions of Napoleonic France, which legitimised itself as the new Roman imperium. These ideas had a deep impact outside Europe on the intellectuals of overseas European empires in Egypt, India and elsewhere who would claim their rights to freedom and dignity as heirs of civilisations that had predated modern Europe.

Secondly, this quest resulted in the transfer of modern academic resources from European advanced centres to the rest of the world, providing intellectuals in the latter with the means to 'reconstruct' their own histories and cultures. Germany became the heartland of romantic nationalism and its thinkers and universities inspirations for the intellectuals of the stateless peoples of Europe, from Finland to Slovak territories, and beyond. Outside Europe British Orientalist scholars in Bengal saw it as their duty, because of their perception of Britain's debt to ancient India, to inform Indians about their forgotten golden age. In 1816 Hindu College was established to educate the Calcutta elite, promoting a regeneration of the Indian heritage together with the study of a secular Western curriculum (Kopf 1969: ch. 5).

Thirdly, a sense of ethnic or cultural affiliation led romantic intellectuals to play an important part in the cultural struggles of 'reviving' nationalities. A sense of their Greek heritage inspired co-operation among European intellectuals and public opinion in support of the Greek struggle for independence against the Ottoman Empire, depicted as the struggle of European liberty against Oriental despotism.

Finally, by presenting world civilisation as the product of national cultures, each of which played a special role, it justified a mutual borrowing of cultures. Nationalists might claim that, although currently backward, their nation had once been a teacher of the nations, so that borrowing from the advanced nations was no more than reclaiming their patrimony. This undermined an ethnocentric resistance to change and enormously expanded the repertoire of options available to modernising elites. At the same time revivalists rejected an uncritical adoption of external models: such borrowing had to work to enhance distinctive nations, not to efface them within a single conception of development. Against what they saw as the uncritical adoption by Russian westernisers of French liberal revolutionary principles, conservative Slavophiles extolled the model of early nineteenth century England where the landed gentry sponsored moderate reform. Such a perspective encouraged nationalist groups within independent non-European states such as Japan, the Ottoman Empire, and China to look world wide for models by which to reconstruct their societies and stave off the European imperial challenges.

History

In this vision, power was transformed from God (or his representatives) to originating peoples and their mythos. History replaced religion as the guide to collective identity and destiny. Historical scholars, Palacky for Czechs, Hrushevsky for Ukrainians, Iorga for Rumanians, became fathers of the nation. Romantic nationalists undermined existing ethnic traditions by recreating the past as one of continuous creativity. This was achieved by placing the origins of the group back in time, discovering multiple pasts with alternative repertoires and role models, and, above all, by identifying a golden age that authenticated innovation.

In search of collective authenticity romantics focused on the earliest emergence of peoples when their original character was most clearly displayed. The poet Henrik Wergeland in 1834 declared in a famous speech 'In Praise of the Ancestors' that the Old Norse sagas, translated in the late eighteenth century, were 'the Norwegian patent of nobility among the nations', portraying a Viking warrior people, a great state, heroic kings and explorers, an extensive code of law, an expressive pagan religion, and impressive poetry, epic and lyrical (Sørensen 1994: 26–29). The recording of older pagan origins before the arrival of Christianity (or other religions) and present dynasties, validated the rise of a heroic conception of the community of which the later coming of a world religion was just another expression.

The core of the nation, however, was revealed in its golden age when the creative genius of the nation flowered. This was a period of high cultural achievement, harmonising all dimensions of human experience (religious, scientific, artistic, military and economic), when the nation was in active contact with other great centres, and making a permanent contribution to human civilisation. Although Arab nationalists might present the coming of Mohammed as inaugurating a golden age, they viewed Islam as the creator of the Arab nation, as the content of its culture and the object of its collective pride (Gershoni 1997: 8–9), one that defeated Western crusaders and became a centre of achievement in mathematics, medicine, philosophy and the sciences.

Historical memory could stimulate revival through invidious comparisons with the decadent present. A Greek national consciousness developed amongst diaspora Greeks of the early nineteenth century, aware of the humiliating contrasts European Philhellenic visitors made between the Hellenic progenitors of Western civilisation and the backward peasant subjects of the Ottoman Empire (Campbell and Sherrard 1968: 29–30). Above all, the golden age inspired a rising generation to throw off the 'paralysis' of tradition, recreate the nation as a politically autonomous and self-reliant society, and make it a model to the world.

History then evoked a call to action. By rooting themselves in an ancient and self-renewing collectivity that had survived countless disasters, a new educated middle class found confidence they could overcome a world of revolutionary uncertainty. They acquired stature in the modern world through membership of a nation whose heroic age had contributed to the civilisation of humanity. They found their own special mission as a generation who by heroic sacrifice would restore the links in the chain to this great past, thus renewing the destiny of their nation.

Homelands

Although ethnic groups typically view themselves as linked 'ancestrally' to the land, romanticism intensified, extended, diffused and embedded a sense of belonging to a homeland, larger in scale than before, and it proclaimed the defence and the regaining of the national territory as a sacred duty.

For romantic nationalists nations were outgrowths of nature, and thus explained by the characteristics of the land they work. Equally the land national communities named and worked was an expression of the nation and its history. In pantheist fashion they viewed the homeland as a repository of a unique moral vision and primordial energies, since each nation's homelands had distinctive characteristics that gave the community its individuality.

As part of the discovery of their collective self, nationalists thus must undertake cultural voyages to record the distinctive qualities of their habitat and its cultures. This *extended* spatially the sense of homeland, filled out a sense of the life and activities of the communities who worked the land, and historically *deepened* the sense of attachment by exploring the layers of the past that 'scaped' the land. Nineteenth century Danish archaeological discoveries of the lur and golden horn (musical instruments), the sunwagon, and the 'barrow' burial mounds became important symbols of a primordial folk culture (Sørenson 1996).

One result was the unexpected 'discovery' of remote areas of natural beauty, or of great cultural significance, that because of their 'wildness' and 'hidden' quality became mysterious reservoirs of the national spirit. Inspired by this sense of rebirth, travelling nationalist artists, musicians and poets saw it as their duty to *diffuse* and represent this moral vision. Irish poets like Mangan and Yeats using folk images personified Ireland as a beautiful young woman, Cathleen Ni Houlihan, to whom devotion was due.

Such regions became ramparts of the nation to which groups, especially alienated urban educated middle classes, could turn to escape assimilation into foreign values and experience moral regeneration, thereby *embedding* themselves in the land. The defence of these regions from foreign cultural or political threat galvanised powerful nationalist movements. During the late nineteenth century tens of thousands of young members of the Finnish middle classes visited Karelia to tap its poetry; and after Finnish independence the Finnish nation-state fought two wars with the USSR in order to claim this sacred region for the nation (Wilson 1976: 47, 141–143).

The cult of the land bound a new mobile middle class of the cities to a larger territorial unit, by rooting them in a defence of a highly individualised homeland. New imperatives bound this group, the territorial unification of all members of the nation, freeing the land from foreign rule, and ridding the land of aliens who by their presence adulterated its cultural purity.

Vernacular culture

Romantics pioneered a general vernacularisation of high culture, creating a unified field of exchange by which new educated elites sought to integrate a society that was differentiating through the division of labour.

This vernacular revolution went much deeper than language, which was one of several means to a larger goal: the resurrection of the *Volksgeist* that expressed the unique creative genius of the nation in all its plenitude. Because of national decay, this *Volksgeist* was submerged and lost to sophisticated society, but the remnants could be found in the untamed imaginative life of rural folk living close to nature. In shaping these fragments into a unified whole, romantics might turn to many sources – fairy tales, songs, melodies, and proverbs. But James Macpherson's 'discovery' of the Ossianic Lays (1762) triggered a competitive craze throughout Europe to rediscover early epic literature, whose myths and legends were portrayed as the earliest and purest expression of the anonymous genius of the people.

If historians provided a map of the national identity, it was the artist who had a special mission to restore the ancient unity of being lost to the modern world by the division of labour, returning individuals to their national archetype, and thereby recreating a unified way of life. Kollar for Slovaks, Mickiewicz for Poles, Yeats for the Irish, Bialik for Jews, Wagner for Germans, had iconic status within their national movements. As creative artists they could not simply reproduce the past: they had to find new cultural genres and institutions appropriate to their changing society, one that was increasingly literate but also increasingly diverse.

An influential genre was the drama – inspired by Shakespeare who was likened to Homer and Ossian in his artlessness, protean energy, sense of mystery, and social range (Bate 1997: ch 6). Yeats argued that a theatre, by bringing individuals into a collectivity and immersing them in the national legends, could perform for a literate age the equivalent of the ancient epics, whose communal recitations had bound older oral societies (Hutchinson 1987: 134). Wagner, like Yeats, hoped that from legends of the *Nibelungenlied* he could create a single collective national personality. In Finland the *Kalevala* epic, after its 'discovery' in Karelia in 1832, became the lodestar around which a unified but also diversified national identity was constructed. During the campaigns against cultural and political Russification in the late nineteenth and early twentieth century, the poet, Leino, the painters Gallen-Kallella and Halonen, and the composer, Sibelius, turned to the *Kalevala* and the Karelian landscape to create a distinctively national high culture (Wilson 1976: 58–60).

In this way this vernacular project sought to unite and guide a society undergoing rapid differentiation under the impact of technological change. All activities would express a national vision based on popular traditions. Societies were formed to promote native dress, national sporting associations, gymnastic, arts and crafts societies. The physical was to be developed in sporting association with the spiritual, as a preparation for the service of the nation, paving the way for cohorts of a virile and revolutionary shock force.

A political community of sacrifice

Romantic nationalists revolutionalised politics by transferring authority from state to a national community animated from below, encouraging an upsurge of populist energies. They gave rise to grass roots organisations in localities outside existing power structures that could influence existing power holders in nation states or act as centres of disaffection from which to mount a revolutionary attempt on the state.

The nation was not viewed in rational terms as the sum of unmediated individuals, but as an organic unity differentiated by regional, gender, religion and occupation identities. National revivalists rejected the centralising bureaucratic state as a threat to the life forces of the community. Equally, the forces of tradition had to be overthrown in each social sector which must be animated by the national will. Social decay came from within from a loss of national identity that resulted in anomie and social conflict as the nation dissolved into its constituent interest groups. A healthy national identity, the Irish revivalist, Thomas Davis, maintained was not something that crystallised in the rational exercise of political power (through voting or participating in political institutions). Heroes rather than mere citizens were the key to national survival and progress. Only the formation of a heroic leadership in each national sector would ensure the formation of a solidaristic community protected against the anomie and class conflict of modern life (Hutchinson 1987: 104–105).

Theirs was a grass roots strategy of educational permeation. Revivalists spoke of a return to the people and valorised those whom they regarded as the custodians of the nation's continuity, usually the peasantry. In practice, their politics was pragmatic and directed at the educated from whatever social group. They found sympathisers in groups of religious and social reformers, particularly lower clergy seeking a revitalising of their religion by directing it to the welfare of the people. Their core constituency was among young middle class men who became the political cadres of nationalist organisations. As the names of these organisations suggest (Young Italy, Young Poland, Young Ireland, Young Egypt) nationalism was an ideology of the educated young. Alienated from their traditional values by their secular education and imbued with new expectations of social and political mobility, they sought to reconnect with their society by leading it from backwardness. Yet, only too often, they found themselves blocked by established holders of power and status. Nationalism offered them an alternative moral vision of integration achieved by a novel form of training, conveyed by the term *bildung*, a drawing out of the essence of the individual through an immersion in the life energies of the nation, as captured in its history, arts, customs and whole way of life.

Revivalism created a new symbolism and set of ceremonies and an overlapping range of cultural and social agencies (literary societies, musical choirs, sporting associations) as part of this holistic construction to train body and mind into a life of sacrifice for the nation (Mosse 1976; 1989: chs. 1, 2). Such movements evinced a fervent religious character exalting the spiritual glories, physical beauties, heroic qualities of the native history, language, literature, and customs and the infernal corruptions of other cultures. Oaths of sacrifice to a Kali (as 'national' Goddess) in India; impassioned public testaments to the born again effects of adopting the Gaelic language in Ireland; commemorations of heroic battles and of the fallen soldier; and pilgrimages of the young German members of the early twentieth century *Wandervogel* to battle fields, religious shrines, and the birth place of famous artists of historic significance – these public displays of commitment to certain behaviour and rejection of others bound diverse individuals to a distinctive moral community and to the institutions necessary to maintain it.

This, however, was very much a minority enthusiasm of intellectuals dependent on an educated stratum. How can we explain the capacity of such movements to become hegemonic?

Firstly, this elite-based national-identity construction took a wider though limited social hold through a process of *moral innovation*, that presented populations with new maps of identity and political prescriptions at times of social polarisation when established traditions were shaken by modernisation. Smith's dual legitimation thesis (Smith 1971: ch. 10) offers a stimulating discussion of the cognitive and institutional reactions to the challenges of modernisation.

Secondly, revivalist nationalism created a counter community knit by a cult of heroic sacrifice for the nation. Periodically, throughout the modern period political systems have been faced with extraordinary crisis, at which these counter communities became the launch pads of revolutionary action, generating myths that legitimised the hegemony of new governing elites and nation-state structures. But these national myths were but an overlay on existing myth structures that continued to exert a hold.

Moral innovation

What allowed national revivalism to challenge traditions, ethnic and otherwise, were the continuous and unpredictable external and internal challenges and shocks to the existing social order unleashed by secular modernisation. Although traditional autocratic regimes regarded with horror the liberal democratic ideas of the French revolution, they realised the mobilising capacities (especially military) of the national model. As European states expanded world wide, even the great non-Western Russian, Ottoman and Chinese empires felt compelled to introduce limited reforms (expanding education, emancipating serfs, and opening access to public offices and so forth) to ensure the survival of their regimes. As they reformed, conflicts erupted between traditionalists and modernisers. The traditionalists initially sought to block out 'the West' and the ideas of progress that threatened to destroy indigenous values. Many modernisers in nineteenth century Russia, China, and India adopted a radical anti-traditionalism, arguing that the only salvation of their society was to copy the models of the advanced West, if needs be abandoning the great traditions of Orthodoxy or Confucianism or Hinduism that doomed their peoples to backwardness and poverty. But such projects could result in intense social conflict as well as a creating a sense of demoralisation *vis-à-vis* the external enemy.

Romantic revivalism offered a third way, by preaching a modernisation from within. We find national revivalists regularly establishing formal institutions at times of conflict. They found an early constituency in religious reform movements that sought to abandon dogmas, laicise teachings, develop vernacular languages, and advance 'scientific' agriculture in order to make (religious) tradition a living force among the people. Both nationalists and reformists sought a solution to the internal conflict by evoking a national golden age and studying the experience of other countries.

For this reason I have described such nationalists as moral innovators, providing new directions at times of social crisis (Hutchinson 1987; 1999). The golden age of such nationalists was a time when the nation was a dynamic high culture, harmonising all dimensions of human experience (religious, scientific, artistic, military), in active contact with the other great centres, and making a permanent contribution to human civilisation. This evolutionary historical vision claimed to present an innovative solution that would reconcile the interests of traditionalists and modernisers, thereby redirecting energies away from destructive conflict into a co-operative reconstruction of the national community. The golden age was used to transform the accepted meanings of tradition and modernity so that they were one and the same, and thereby persuade their adherents to ally in the national project.

To traditionalists, national revivalists argued that it was a misunderstanding to conceive of tradition as a passive repetition of custom. Traditionalists must recognise that tradition had continually to be renewed, sometimes by adapting the ideas of others, and its authentic expression was to be found in the golden age when the national community was a dynamic modernising civilisation confidently exchanging ideas and technologies with other cultures. For example, Swami Vivekananda's neo-Vedantic movement, formed in the 1880s, sought to undermine the authority of Hindu tradition by evoking as the authentic India, an Aryan civilisation that had allegedly instructed two of the great world centres of learning (Greece and Persia) and that denied there were inherent barriers between the sexes, castes or between religious and secular learning.

He rejected the religious taboos on contacts with foreigners and the caste hierarchies as later inventions of the Brahmin priesthood, which were deviations from this dynamic democratic civilisation (Heimsath 1964: ch. 7).

To modernisers who uncritically admired foreign models, revivalists argued that the greatest embodiment of a successful modernity was to be found in the golden age of their nation, which had instructed the then backward 'West'. Whatever the West now had was borrowed from their nation, and hence they should look to their own traditions for inspiration. Liang Qichao, one of the leaders of the Chinese reform movement, thus claimed that China was a primary world civilisation when the West was still barbarous, hence the West was once no better than the Chinese were now, and whatever of value in the West had been taken from China. At other times he would argue that it was foolish to imitate blindly Western values, for its progress had arisen out of its own unique patterns of growth and decay. Indeed, the West was now in decay, for it had overdeveloped the material in relation to the spiritual and was now faced with internal dissolution. History had reserved a special mission for the Chinese who had retained their ancient religious and aesthetic traditions and were well placed to lead the world as they had in the past to a new golden age in which the moral and the material would be integrated (Levenson 1959: 93–94).

In search of solutions, Chinese revivalists looked outward to world historical studies of polities ancient and modern that had disappeared from history, and they analysed in their journals contemporary anticolonialist Boer and Indian movements, the struggles of the Young Turks to modernise the Ottoman Empire, and the successes of the Meiji Reformers in Japan, especially after Japan's defeat of the Tsarist Empire in 1905. The reformers disagreed in their analyses, some stressing the importance of a strong state, others the creation of a powerful ethnic consciousness, but by 1911 educated opinion had come to believe that the answer to the Chinese crisis was the transformation of a foreign-led (Manchu) dynastic Empire into a national state, led by a patriotic elite. Increasingly they saw China as leader of an Asian civilisation against the West (Karl 2002: chs. 2, 4–6). These were the undercurrents that preceded Sun Yatsen's revolution of 1912.

Although usually small in scale, they establish a counter culture movement, based on a network of independent institutions, international linkages, the possession of higher education and the use of new forms of communication (newspapers, academies, and cultural societies). That this gave them a reach into the literate strata of the population. In colonial societies like India, C. A. Bayly (1996) has argued, the nationalist intelligentsia of lawyers, officials, and journalists had a power out of proportion to their numbers with respect to the British state and traditionalist leaders because they uniquely combined a mastery of the languages and techniques of modernity (often as officials within state administration) and of the traditional discourses and networks of their indigenous societies.

National sacrifice and mythic overlaying

However, the revivalist strategy of inner reform had limitations. Revivalism might find allies in reforming state elites who saw nation-creation as the road to social modernisation. But in seeking to permeate powerful social institutions, they were often in danger of being co-opted by them: by religious and gentry interests who sought to retain their patriarchal hold over the people and by states that might use them to obtain support for reform without empowering their peoples. By themselves they lacked the resources to gain majority support, especially against the state, able to diffuse its values through the education system, bureaucratic career structures, and police power.

How then did revivalism succeed in making national identities hegemonic in contexts where it faced resistance from dominant institutions? The answer lies in constructing a community of sacrifice with its separate mythos, capable of overriding established mythologies. Although revivalism for the most part promoted a peaceful permeation of the community, it created through its overlapping institutions (language associations, theatres, sporting associations) a counterculture of young activists, imbued with a religious sense of mission to the nation, and contemptuous of their degraded society. A switch to sacrificial struggle remained a strategic option to which nationalists could turn when the 'nation' seemed threatened by internal crisis and/or when the state was faced with a systemic crisis such as war or social revolution.

The French revolution and the subsequent military resistance to French domination in the German territories and elsewhere institutionalised in nineteenth century Europe the romantic mystique of the national hero, willing to sacrifice himself for the nation. The unpredictable upheavals of the modern period of warfare, social revolution, and economic dislocation periodically generated millenarian expectations of a general overthrow of established structures. In the 1820s, 1830s and 1848 Europe was hit by waves of national as well as social revolts. Although these mostly failed, a revolutionary tradition of 'martyrs' was established in countries such as Ireland, Poland and Italy, who embodied the willingness of each generation to sacrifice themselves for the nation. The apocalyptic world wars of the twentieth century resulted in a wave of nationalist revolutions in Central and Eastern Europe following collapse of the Romanov, Habsburg and Ottoman Empires in 1918–19, and in Asia and Africa after 1945 following the defeat of the Imperial European powers.

Because of their sense of historical destiny, national revivalists were hardened to adversity and they viewed a large scale crisis as a sign of a prospective rebirth of the nation. At such times as alternatives to a failing system, they had a directive effect in a situation of increasing fluidity and confusion in several ways. They threw up leaders, sometimes endowed with a charismatic cultural authority, outside established structures untainted by the past and they energised demoralised populations by offering positive alternative social pathways. When this resulted in a revolutionary rising or a war of independence, this collective experience became the basis of new set of national legends that could legitimise the formation of a national social and political order.

We can observe this process in modern Ireland where through revolt and a war of independence a nationalist elite established a national mythology overriding existing ethnic traditions by a process of *mythic overlaying*. By overlaying I refer to the creation of fresh myths by the new nationalists embodied in extraordinary contemporary collective sacrifice against a traditional 'enemy' that can be presented as a renovation of a national continuum when the old myths have failed. In so doing, the new elites were able to legitimise themselves to the collectivity. But the old mythic structures were not obliterated, but, to use Anthony Smith's geological metaphor (Smith 1995), pushed into a substratum, available to resume their hold on collective loyalties, should the new conceptions prove wanting.

The Easter Rising of 1916 was the fourth of a series of significant nationalist revolts (in 1798, 1848, and 1867) against British authority in Ireland, and exemplifies a pattern. The revolts of 1798, 1848 and 1916 ended a period of revivalism whose early ambitions had been a peaceful nationalisation of the competing communities in Ireland but which had switched to insurrection in an atmosphere of social and political instability. Wolfe Tone's failed 1798 rebellion erupted when Britain was at war with revolutionary France and hoped for French support; Thomas Davis's 1848 rebellion occurred during the desperation of the Irish famine, which appeared to threaten the destruction not only of nationalist hopes but of the Irish nation. Although these failed, the Fenian Brotherhood (who rebelled in 1867) building on their memories created a mystique of martyrdom and permanently institutionalised an underground revolutionary tradition.

The late nineteenth century Irish revivalists had rejected physical force in advocating an Irish language and literary renaissance. Their goal was to replace dominant otherworldly Catholic conceptions of Ireland as a martyred nation that they claimed had weakened Irish resistance to the encroachment of secular British industrial values. Inspired by Celtic high cultural achievements in the early medieval ages, they sought to recreate Ireland as a rural but dynamic Gaelic-speaking democratic community that would take its part in modern Europe. After initial successes in mobilising a new Catholic educated middle class, the revival ran out of steam by 1914, outflanked by a neo-traditionalist Catholic resurgence in the countryside and by the continued 'Anglicisation' of Irish society. At this point, a small group of Irish revivalists, led by Patrick Pearse and Thomas MacDonagh joined with the revolutionary movement, and developed a cult of the legendary Irish warrior hero Cuchulain, but the majority of revivalists supported a constitutional nationalist campaign for a Home Rule parliament that they hoped would support revivalist programmes. However, the outbreak of World War One led to the British government shelving Home Rule and incorporating Ireland into the war effort, initially with popular support.

Despair at this co-option of Irish political and religious elites into the war effort (and hopes of German support) led to the Easter Rebellion in 1916. Patrick Pearse, one of its leaders, created the canonical legend of the 'Rising' as a self-conscious act of religious sacrifice to redeem Irish sins, drawing parallels to Christ's crucifixion and Cuchulain's triumphant death facing his enemies. The execution of the rebel leaders by the British confirmed the myth and inspired the subsequent successful war of liberation against Britain that radicalised the population. The Easter Rebellion and the subsequent guerrilla war created the potent founding myth of the new nation-state in 1922 and of the new governing class, two thirds of which entered politics through the revivalist organisations. By creating new cultural icons (great writers such as Yeats, a heroic war generation, and the Irish language) the revival had forged a new secular definition of Irish identity.

Here we find a clear example of the successful nationalist construction of myth based on collective sacrifice that overrode older ethno-religious legitimations and justified the revival of the Irish language and the Irish-speaking west. Nonetheless, the national myth was an overlay not a replacement. For the myth had itself fused national and religious symbolism (as in the choice of Easter), and the nationalists dramatised the British atrocities in the course of a brutal guerrilla war as a continuation of the historic 'martyrdom' of a helpless Catholic nation. The secular linguistic nationalism of the new state proved to be elite-based and thin, as Ireland after independence found itself still confronted with economic and cultural competition from a powerful British neighbour. To reinforce its national character, the new state rooted itself in historic ethnocentric religious and rural sentiments. The Catholic Church was given official status, and the Irish state developed until recently a distinctive puritanical social policy, effectively prohibiting divorce, contraception, and abortion (Hutchinson 1987: ch. 9).

Conclusion

Anthony Smith's work has pointed to the important *cultural* dimension of nationalism that it is too often neglected by scholars when focusing on the dramatic political and socio-economic changes of the past two centuries. But the precise strategies employed by nationalists to transform the moral language that legitimises novel forms of collective action remain under researched, as are the means by which the foundation myths of nation-states are married to existing ethnic traditions. The above analysis supports his criticisms of those who view the nation as an invention or as a (statist) construction. It is better to speak of revivalists as moral and cultural *innovators* who seek to engineer change by a 'regeneration' rather than an eradication of collective traditions (ethnic and otherwise). Even when they are able to seize the state and to implement their programmes, the process of nation-formation is complex, leading one to speak of an *overlaying* of tradition rather than an invention. We might suggest that where ethnic traditions are absent, the problem of nationalists is still more difficult: they have greater room for manoeuvre but without the raw materials on which to build, they are dependent on long drawn out processes of intergroup conflict in order to achieve a sense of collective identity.

Note

1 He defines an ethnic community (or ethnie) as 'a named unit of population, with common ancestry myths and shared historical memories, elements of shared culture, a link with a historic territory, and some measure of solidarity, at least among the elites'. A nation has, in addition, 'a mass public culture, a common economy and common legal rights and duties for all members' (Smith 2001: 19).

References

Bate, J. 1997. *The Genius of Shakespeare*. London: Picador.
Bayly, C. A. 1996. *Empire and Information: Intelligence Gathering and Social Communication in India 1780–1870*. Cambridge: Cambridge University Press.
Campbell, J. and Sherrard, P. 1968. *Modern Greece*. New York: Praeger.
Gershoni, I. 1997. 'Rethinking the formation of Arab nationalism in the Middle East, 1920–45' in J. Jankowski and I. Gershoni (eds.), *Rethinking Nationalism in the Arab Middle East*. New York: Colimbia Unversity Press.
Heimsath, C. 1964. *Indian Nationalism and Hindu Social Reform*. Princeton, NJ: Princeton University Press.
Hutchinson, J. 1987. *The Dynamics of Cultural Nationalism*. London: Allen & Unwin.
Hutchinson, J. 1999. 'Re-interpreting cultural nationalism', *Australian Journal of Politics and History* 45(3): 392–407.
Karl, R. E. 2002. *Staging the World: Chinese Nationalism at the Turn of the Twentieth Century*. London: Duke University Press.
Kopf, D. 1969. *British Orientalism and the Bengali Cultural Renaissance*. Berkeley, CA: University of California Press.
Levenson, J. 1959. *Liang Ch'i -ch'ao and the Mind of Modern China*. Berkeley, CA: University of California Press.
Mosse, G. 1976. 'Mass politics and the political liturgy of nationalism' in E. Kamenka (ed.), *Nationalism: the Nature and Evolution of an Idea*. London: Edward Arnold.
Mosse, G. 1989. *Fallen Soldiers: Reshaping the Memory of the World War*. Oxford: Oxford University Press.
Poliakov, L. 1974. *The Aryan Myth*. New York: Basic.
Schwab, R. 1984. *The Oriental Renaissance: Europe's rediscovery of India and the East 1680–1880*. New York: Columbia University Press.
Smith, A. D. 1971. *Theories of Nationalism*. London: Duckworth.
Smith, A. D. 1986. *The Ethnic Origins of Nations*. Oxford: Blackwell.
Smith, A. D. 1995. 'Gastronomy or geology? The role of nationalism in the reconstruction of nations', *Nations and Nationalism* 1(1): 3–23.
Smith, A. D. 2001. 'Nations in history' in M. Guibernau and J. Hutchinson (eds.), *Understanding Nationalism*. Oxford: Polity, 9–32.
Sørensen, Ø. 1994. 'The development of a Norwegian national identity during the nineteeenth century' in Ø. Sørensen (ed.), *Nordic Paths to National Identity in the Nineteenth Century*. Oslo: Research Council of Norway, 17–36.

Sorenson, M. L. 1996. 'The fall of a nation, the birth of a subject; the national use of archaeology in nineteenth century Denmark' in M. Diaz-Andreu and T. Champion (eds.), *Nationalism and Archaeology in Europe*. London: UCL Press.

Wilson, W. A. 1976. *Folklore and Nationalism in Modern Finland*. Bloomington, IN: Indiana University Press.

9

Anthony D. Smith on nations and national identity: a critical assessment

MONTSERRAT GUIBERNAU

Introduction

It is a great pleasure to contribute to this volume devoted to the work of Anthony D. Smith. In this paper I engage with his path-breaking contribution to the study of nations and nationalism. In so doing, I wish to highlight the importance of his theory and examine what I consider some of its most significant limitations.

The paper is divided into two parts. The first provides a critique of his concepts of nation and national identity. It begins by offering a brief introduction to ethnosymbolism and, after a critical discussion of Smith's classical definition of the nation, it highlights the relevance of his latest changes to this concept. The paper then moves on to consider his definition of national identity. It argues that by including 'citizenship' as one of its defining features, Smith associates national identity with membership of the state ignoring that, although all nations have a national identity, not all of them have a state of their own.

In the second part, I offer an alternative definition of national identity, which draws on some aspects of Smith's work on the relevance of history, territory and culture. I also examine the political dimension of national identity, absent from Smith's theory.

Part One
Ethnosymbolism

The ethnosymbolist theory developed by Smith has offered fresh and illuminating insights into pre-modern forms of collective cultural identity such as those embodied in *ethnies*. Its contribution is located between stark modernist theories defending the recent, invented and constructed nature of nations and nationalism (Gellner 1983; Hobsbawm and Ranger 1983; Anderson 1983), and perennialist theories emphasizing the permanence of nations (van den Berghe 1978; Geertz 1973; Armstrong 1982).

The study of *ethnies*, 'named human populations with shared ancestry myths, histories and cultures, having an association with a specific territory, and a sense of solidarity' (Smith 1986: 32), is fundamental to the ethnosymbolist theory formulated by Smith. Its relevance stems from the *ethnie's* status as the precursor of nations. Smith explores the origins of nations and national identity and finds them in ethnic identity as a pre-modern form of collective cultural identity. In his view, 'Collective cultural identity refers not to a uniformity of elements over generations but to a sense of continuity on the part of successive generations of a given cultural unit of population, to shared memories of earlier events and periods in the history of that unit and to notions entertained by each generation about the collective destiny of that unit and its culture' (Smith 1991: 25). Smith adds: 'there is a felt filiation, as well as a cultural affinity, with a remote past in which a community was formed, a community that despite all the changes it has undergone, is still in some sense recognized as the "same" community' (Smith 1991: 33).

Smith's work on the relevance of the ethnic origins of nations becomes central to his understanding of 'why and where particular nations are formed, and why nationalisms, though formally alike, possess such distinctive features and contents' (Smith 1998: 191). His research on the role of myths, memories, values, traditions and symbols, as powerful differentiators and reminders of the unique culture and fate of the ethnic community, is fundamental to his analysis of national identity.

Ethnosymbolism focuses on the cultural aspects of nations and nationalism. The political aspects are left practically untouched. But, is it possible to offer a full account of nations and nationalism while ignoring their tremendous political leverage in modern societies? Can culture be dissociated from politics when examining national identity? Is it possible to ignore the role of the state in the construction of national identity? What are the political consequences of being recognized as, or claiming to be, a 'nation' in the modern world? In this paper I argue that a fully-fledged theory of nationalism ought to examine the political as well as the cultural aspects of nations and national identity.

My objective here is not to undermine the ethnosymbolist's contribution. Instead, I wish to argue that the ethnosymbolist approach, due to its narrow focus on the cultural aspects of nations and nationalism and the scant attention it pays to the study of the nation-state, remains insufficient to offer an integral view of nations and nationalism in the twenty-first century. It is my concern that a systematic and thorough political analysis has to complement the richness and insights provided by the ethnosymbolist approach.

Having said this, it is crucial to be aware that while emphasizing its cultural nature, ethnosymbolism is not 'apolitical'; on the contrary its findings contain powerful political implications. The myths, symbols, traditions, heroes and holy places studied by ethnosymbolism are key components of any nationalist doctrine and, by studying them and bringing them to the fore, I argue that ethnosymbolism provides powerful arguments to those who seek to reinforce the political legitimacy of their nations and the power of the states claiming to represent them. For instance, the findings of ethnosymbolism, in an intended or unintended manner, are likely to turn into formidable cultural assets to be employed as legitimizing elements for a nation demanding self-determination. Proving that the community has pre-modern roots and that its culture shows a certain degree of continuity is a key objective for the creators of the nationalist doctrine.

The Nation

In my view, the most fundamental flaw in Smith's theory, which contains significant repercussions for his approach to national identity, stems from his conflation of nation and state. Although he claims to distinguish between the two, I set out to prove that he fails to do so.

In his book *National Identity* (1991), Smith formulates his classical definition of the nation as 'a named human population sharing an historic territory, common myths and historical memories, a mass, public culture, a common economy and common legal rights and duties for all members' (Smith 1991: 14). In contrast, in his article 'When is a Nation?' (2002) Smith emphasizes the 'ideal-type' nature of his definition of the nation and, in an almost unprecedented move, he introduces very substantial changes to it. He defines the nation as 'a named community possessing an historic territory, shared myths and memories, a common public culture and common laws and customs' (Smith 2002: 15).

Three major changes can be identified when comparing the two definitions. In the most recent one: (1) the 'mass' character of public culture has been eliminated; (2) reference to a 'common economy' has also been removed; and (3) 'common legal rights and duties for all members' have been replaced by 'common laws and customs'.

Why has Smith changed his classical definition of the nation?

(1) I understand that the elimination of references to the 'mass' character of public culture is somehow connected with Smith's ongoing debate with Walker Connor, who, in his seminal essay 'When is a nation?', stressed that nationalism is a mass – not an elite – phenomenon, an assertion raising fundamental questions about when the emergence of a nation should be located in time.

If Smith were to continue arguing that a nation requires a 'mass' public culture as he has done for over ten years, then, how could he maintain that 'it was possible to find examples of social formations in pre-modern periods, even in antiquity, that for some decades or even centuries approximated to an inclusive definition of the concept of the "nation"'? (Smith 1998: 190). This statement would be simply untenable because Smith is not merely arguing that there is an ethnic origin of nations to be found in pre-modern times, rather he affirms that some 'nations' did exist prior to the modern period. Furthermore, how should 'mass' be defined? As including the 'whole' people? The 'majority' of the population? And if so, what type of 'majority'? Simply a large section of the population? Over 51 per cent?

Smith is aware of the potency of Connor's argument since 'pre-modern' nations never enjoyed a 'mass, public culture'. In 'When is a Nation?' Connor argues: 'A key problem faced by scholars when dating the emergence of nations is that national consciousness is a mass, not an elite phenomenon, and the masses, until quite recently isolated in rural pockets and being semi or totally illiterate, were quite mute with regard to their sense of identity(ies) ... and very often the elites' conception of the nation did not even extend to the masses' (Connor 1994a: 159). A similar point is made by Ernest Gellner who emphasizes the distance between the high culture of elites and the low culture of the masses: 'In the characteristic agro-literate polity, the ruling class forms a small minority of the population, rigidly separate from the great majority of direct agricultural producers, or peasants... Below the horizontally stratified minority at the top, there is another world, that of the laterally separated petty communities of the lay members of the society... Even if the population of a given area starts from the same linguistic base line – which very often is not the case – a kind of culture drift soon engenders dialectal and other differences' (Gellner 1983: 10).

Smith's elimination of references to the 'mass' character of public culture allows him to claim that a nation exists even if its particular culture is not shared by the mass of the population. A 'public culture' is fundamentally different in scope from a 'mass' culture and much easier to attain.

(2) References to a 'common economy' have also vanished from Smith's most recent definition of the nation. The difficulty and complexity in defining 'a common economy' should not be underestimated. Does he refer to a common economy limited to the territorial boundaries of the nation? Or, should it be understood as a common economy cutting across national boundaries, an economy over which the nation has little or no control? Besides, if the nation is, as Smith insists, 'a kind(s) of collective cultural identity' (Smith 2002: 15), why should it include a 'common economy' as a key feature?

(3) In my view, 'common legal rights and duties for all members' is not what one should expect from a cultural community, such as the nation. Rather, this is a function of the state, the political institution that regulates the lives of people within its territory. In modern societies, only the state has constitutions and written laws and embodies sufficient power to define citizenship rights and duties within its territory. By suggesting that the members of the nation ought to share 'common legal rights and duties', Smith was simply attributing to the nation one of the fundamental characteristics of the state.

In his latest definition, Smith has replaced 'common legal rights and duties' by 'common laws and custom', a much more vague and open requirement which avoids his previous *de facto* inclusion of citizenship as a feature of the nation. But, in spite of such a significant change, Smith does not explain the reasons behind his unprecedented move. In what follows, I examine some of the flaws of Smith's classical definition of the nation, *National Identity* (1991), which in my view account for its recent modification.

A critique of Smith's classical definition of the nation

If we were to take Smith's classical definition of the nation in a literal sense, then the German Democratic Republic (GDR) and the German Federal Republic (GFR), which did not share 'common legal rights and duties for all members' and lacked a 'common economy', stopped forming a single German nation after 1945. Should we understand that they became a single nation again after German unification in 1992, when they began to share – or should we employ expressions such as 'recover' and 're-establish' – a common economy and legal rights? Or, had they always remained a 'single' nation? And...if so, for how long could they have maintained separate economies, a public mass culture and legal rights and duties while still being considered a single nation?

In a similar manner, should we assume that Cyprus, after the Turkish invasion of its northern part – and the creation of the Republic of Northern Cyprus in 1974 (only recognized by Turkey) – and the subsequent construction of a completely different political regime, economy and public culture from that of the primarily Greek-influenced southern part of the island, is formed by two nations? Or, is it still a single nation?

In *The Ethnic Origins of Nations* (1986), Smith wrote: 'The Catalans are undoubtedly a nation today, just as they were an *ethnie* in the pre-modern world. Not only do they inhabit their historic territory (more or less), they are now able to teach in their own language and fund a mass, public, standardized education system in Catalan and in Catalonia' (Smith 1986: 166). Smith did not even mention that the Catalans had only just recovered (1979) their autonomous political institutions, the right to teach in Catalan and fund a mass, public education. Would he have referred to them as a nation between 1936 and 1975 when Franco's dictatorship proscribed the Catalan language and culture from the public sphere?

Furthermore, when it comes to Catalonia's sharing of 'a common economy', Smith describes it as being 'closely linked to the wider Spanish economy' (Smith 1986: 166) and this is certainly true. But, does having a common economy imply full power to control taxation, interest rates, the stock exchange, control over money reserves and the nation's central bank? If so, then Catalonia has a quasi-common economy which is completely dependent on Spanish decisions and which does not have Catalonia's specific progress as its main objective. Catalonia is only a part of Spain and experience shows that the prosperity and well being of a part has often been sacrificed in favour of a much wider sense of prosperity. Would such a situation arise within a hypothetical environment within which Catalonia either had its own state or was considered as an equal and free partner within an eventual Spanish federation? I doubt it.

In addition, Smith argues that Catalans have rights and duties as Catalans plus legal Spanish citizenship, and, in his view, this description fulfils the condition that all nation's members should enjoy 'common legal rights and duties' (Smith 1986: 166). The problem is that Smith does not specify whether such rights and duties have to be democratically agreed and established or whether, on the contrary, they could be imposed upon a population. The Catalans shared 'legal rights and duties' during the 40 years of Franco's dictatorship, but these were not only imposed upon them but involved the proscription of the Catalan language, culture and autonomous political institutions. Moreover, Smith not only seems to imply that Spain is a 'nation of nations', an expression which is at least questionable, but he also neglects to point out that the Catalans' rights and duties are conditional on their status as Spanish citizens.

The Spanish constitution (1978) stresses the existence of a single sovereign *demos* in Spanish democracy, constituted by all Spaniards, including the Catalans, which on ratifying the Constitution made the autonomy of Catalonia possible. This interpretation considers the Catalan people to be a 'sub-group' of the *demos* formed by all the citizens of Spain. We could infer, in accordance with the arguments defended in the Constitution and in the Catalan Statute of Autonomy (1979), that access to political power (*kratos*) by the Catalan people is determined by a *demos* of which the Catalan people form a part, and not by the specific free will of this Catalan people constituted as a 'sovereign *demos*'.

A further question, untouched by Smith, concerns the status of those Catalans living in the historical territory of Catalonia, which is now a part of France. Are they to be considered as a part of the Catalan nation? This is an open and highly controversial question with numerous parallel cases around the world. If French Catalans were to be considered as members of the Catalan nation, then it would become obvious that not all Catalans share the same rights and duties. At present there are cultural and political movements in French areas, which promote their Catalan heritage.

The Catalan case reinforces the inability of Smith's classical theory to establish a clear-cut distinction between the concepts of nation and state. It is my contention that such a distinction is crucial to understand why, for example, a nation lacking or having lost its political institutions may survive for relatively long periods of time or why an occupied nation, having its economy, legal rights and mass public culture in the hands of the invader, can still be called a nation. The distinction between nation and state is fundamental to account for the continuity of some nations after having lost their political institutions. But, it is also very important to understand the processes of nation-building promoted by the state which are closely connected to the rise of modern nationalism.

At this point I wish to consider whether Smith's new definition of the nation (2002) is capable of redressing the flaws I have identified in his classical definition. In my view, in spite of acknowledging that to exist a nation does not require a 'mass' public culture, 'common economy' and 'common legal rights and duties' for all its members, Smith's latest definition still contains some fundamental limitations. For instance:

1 Does a nation cease to exist whenever its culture is proscribed from the 'public' sphere and confined to the private one? How should the term 'public culture' be understood?
2 A far more complicated issue concerns the meaning of the expression 'common laws'. In my view, its meaning could be subject to differing interpretations depending on whether we apply it to modern or pre-modern

societies. In the former, it refers to a set of rules enforceable by the courts regulating the relationship between the state and its subjects, and the conduct of subjects towards one another, a definition similar to that of citizenship, which once again ignores stateless nations, in particular those whose territory is included within more than one state. When applied to pre-modern societies, however, the source, the enforcers and the subjects of 'common laws' become much more complex and diversified. They may include religion as well as other types of written and unwritten laws as key regulators of social life.

3 I argue that Smith's definition continues to ignore the political significance of being recognized as a 'nation' in modern societies. For instance, he disregards the fact that the state seeks to base its legitimacy on the idea that it represents the nation.

The nation, a cultural community, and the state, a political institution, have been subject to constant transformations throughout time and they have taken up different forms in different parts of the world. In my view, the distinction between nations 'with' and 'without' states could contribute to resolving some of the key dilemmas arising from Smith's classical definition of the nation as well as locating two different arenas within which nationalism emerges and evolves in modern societies.

On nations without states

I argue that a clear-cut distinction needs to be drawn between three main concepts: 'nation', 'state' and 'nation-state'.

By 'state', taking Max Weber's definition, I refer to 'a human community that (successfully) claims *the monopoly of the legitimate use of physical force* within a given territory' (Weber 1991: 78), although not all states have successfully accomplished this, and some of them have not even aspired to accomplish it.

By 'nation', I refer to a human group conscious of forming a community, sharing a common culture, attached to a clearly demarcated territory, having a common past and a common project for the future and claiming the right to rule itself (Guibernau 1996: 47–48).

The nation-state is a modern institution, defined by the formation of a kind of state which has the monopoly of what it claims to be the legitimate use of force within a demarcated territory and seeks to unite the people subject to its rule by means of cultural homogenization.

But there is yet another term that needs to be defined and distinguished from the ones I have just mentioned: the nation without a state. By 'nations without states' I refer to those territorial communities with their own identity and a desire for self-determination included within the boundaries of one or more states, with which, by and large, they do not identify. In nations without states, the feeling of identity is generally based on their own common culture and history (which often goes back to a time prior to the foundation of the nation-state or, to employ Smith's theory, to its ethnic roots), the attachment to a particular territory and an explicit desire for self-determination.

A nation without state is defined by the lack of its own state and by an impossibility to act as a political institution on the international scene. It is based on the existence of a community with a stable but dynamic core containing a set of factors, which have generated the emergence of a specific identity. It should be added, however, that nations are not unique, eternal or unalterable, and that throughout history there are many examples both of the disintegration of some nations that have played an important role during a certain period, and of the rise of new nations. There are also several examples of nations that have had their own state in the past and which, for various reasons, have become nations without states; Catalonia and Scotland are cases in point.

Self-determination, sometimes defined as political autonomy, does not always involve the independence of the nation, although it often includes the right to secession. Catalonia, Quebec, Scotland, the Basque Country and Flanders represent only a few nations without states currently demanding the right to self-determination, although with different nuances in each case. It could be argued that some of these nations do have some kind of state of their own and could be considered as 'quasi-states', since a substantial number of powers have been devolved, or are in the process of being devolved, to their regional parliaments. In all these cases, however, the powers transferred exclude foreign and economic policy, defence and constitutional matters. The 'quasi-state' that these communities enjoy is, as the term indicates, incomplete. This explains why it is still meaningful to refer to them as nations without states.

On Smith's theory of national identity

The ethnosymbolist approach lays special emphasis on the subjective components of national identity, while simultaneously underlining the sociological bases of collective cultural identities, like *ethnies* and nations (Smith 2002: 15).

'National identity', according to Smith, 'involves some sense of political community, history, territory, patria, citizenship, common values and traditions' (Smith 1991: 9). He argues that 'nations must have a measure of common culture and a civic ideology, a set of common understandings and aspirations, sentiments and ideas, that bind the population together in their homeland' (Smith 1991: 11). Adding that, the agencies of popular socialization – primarily the public system of education and the mass media – have been handed the task of ensuring a common public mass culture (Smith 1991: 11), an idea central to Ernest Gellner's own theory of nationalism formulated in his seminal book *Nations and Nationalism* (1983).

Smith considers national identity as multi-dimensional and lists five fundamental attributes:

1 historic territory or homeland
2 common myths and historical memories
3 a common, mass public culture
4 common legal rights and duties for all members
5 common economy with territorial mobility for members (Smith 1991: 14)

Smith's definition of national identity has been left untouched since its early formulation in 1991. As I have argued earlier on, in my view, the substantial changes which he has introduced to his definition of the nation (Smith 2002) are motivated by the need to allow for the existence of some nations in pre-modern times, one of the main assertions of Smith's theory, and by the urgency to overcome the amalgamation of nation and state characteristic of his approach. In spite of this, however, he has not yet produced a modified definition of national identity. For Smith, national identity continues to involve citizenship understood as 'common legal rights and duties for all members' and I believe that this seriously hampers the consistency of his theory for the following reasons:

(a) If national identity is to be based upon a common mass public culture and is to include citizenship, then it could not be found in pre-modern times when citizenship was restricted to the few. This contradicts Smith's position as developed in his latest piece 'When is a nation?' where he writes: '...we saw cases of strongly expressed national sentiments and national identity in pre-modern epochs, at least among the educated elite' (Smith 2002: 16).

(b) By including citizenship as one of the features of national identity, he is assuming that this is exclusively associated with the modern nation-state. To consider this point further, we should examine what Smith refers to as the external and internal functions of national identity. For him the former comprise territorial, economic and political functions while the latter refer to the socialization of the members as 'nationals' and 'citizens' through media and education (Smith 1991: 17). Smith defines national identity as a quality shared by the citizens of the state and he completely ignores that, in many cases, nation and state are not coextensive. Are we then to assume that Catalan, Quebecker, Scottish, Basque, Flemish and Corsican national identities do not exist? Should we ignore the fact that citizens of a single state may have different national identities?

In my view, it is paramount to discern between nation-states and nations without states (Guibernau 1999), because having or not having a state makes a great difference in terms of the access to power and resources enjoyed by a nation and, even more crucially, in its international status. Effectively, nations without states are excluded from direct representation in the major international and transnational organizations and institutions such as the EU, NAFTA, NATO, the IMF, the UN, etc.

Moreover, the chances of a nation without a state to promote its own national identity depend on two main factors. First, the nature of the state within which the nation is included, in particular its attitude towards internal diversity. As I have showed elsewhere, nations without states find themselves in radically different scenarios throughout the world; these encompass cultural recognition, political autonomy, federation and denial and repression (Guibernau 1999: ch. 2). Second, the existence of an alternative elite ready to provide cultural, historical, political and economic arguments to foster and sustain the distinctive character of the stateless nation and to legitimize its will to decide upon its political future, whatever this might be. Such intellectuals tend to be subversive and construct a discourse that undermines the current order of things while offering an alternative, which lies at the heart of their nationalist discourse.

Part Two
National identity in the twenty-first century

I argue that national identity is a modern phenomenon of a fluid and dynamic nature, one by means of which a community sharing a particular set of characteristics is led to the subjective belief that its members are ancestrally related.

Belief in a shared culture, history, traditions, symbols, kinship, language, religion, territory, founding moment, and destiny have been invoked, with varying intensity at different times and places, by peoples claiming to share a particular national identity.

Generally, national identity is applied to citizens of a nation-state. There are other cases, however, where national identity is shared among individuals belonging to a nation without a state of their own. Memories of a time when the nation was independent, endured collective oppression, or attained international leadership, together with the current desire for self-determination, strengthen a sense of common identity among those who belong to the nation, even if it lacks a state. National identity reflects the sentiment of belonging to the nation regardless of whether it has or does not have a state of its own.

In my view, national identity has five dimensions: psychological, cultural, territorial, historical, and political.

Psychological dimension

The psychological dimension of national identity arises from the consciousness of forming a group based on the 'felt' closeness uniting those who belong to the nation. Such closeness can remain latent for years and suddenly come to the surface whenever the nation is confronted with an external or internal enemy – real, potential or constructed – threatening its people, its prosperity, its traditions and culture, its territory, its international standing or its sovereignty.

Smith insists on the subjective nature of national identity's components (e.g., Smith 2002). In my view, the most relevant quality of those components is not whether they are or not subjective, rather what matters is whether they are *felt* as real by those sharing a common identity. And, throughout time, they have proved to be felt with great intensity because people have been in the past, and still are, prepared to make sacrifices and ultimately die for their nations. But, why is this so? Sharing a national identity generates an emotional bond among fellow nationals, which, as Connor puts it, is fundamentally psychological and non-rational. It is not irrational, only 'beyond reason' (Connor 1994b). This is so because, basically, a nation is a group of people who *feel* that they are ancestrally related. In Connor's view, the nation 'is the largest group that can command a person's loyalty because of felt kinship ties; it is, from this perspective, the fully extended family'. However, 'the sense of unique descent, need not, and *in nearly all* cases *will not*, accord with factual history' (Connor 1994b: 202) since nearly all nations originate from the mixing of peoples from various ethnic origins. For this reason, what matters is not chronological or factual history but sentient or felt history.

The attributes sustaining the belief in common ancestry are key to national identity and foster a sense of belonging which generally engenders loyalty and social coherence among fellow-nationals, who often, but not always, are also fellow-citizens.

In certain circumstances, sentiments of love and hate are intensely felt and rapturously manifested by those who belong to the same nation. Political leaders and agitators are fully aware of this and it is not uncommon for them to seek an emotional response from fellow-nationals. Calls for action and sacrifice in the face of threats to the nation are accompanied by appeals to the 'unique character' and 'qualities' of those who belong. This has the capacity to elevate people beyond their daily lives and routines, to transport them to a higher level in which their actions gain meaning and are qualified as crucial for the survival and prosperity of the nation. The strength of emotions overrides reason, because it is through a sentimental identification with the nation that individuals transcend their finite and, at least for some, meaningless lives. Their efforts and sacrifices become worthwhile, even heroic, and the conviction of having contributed to a higher aim, that of preserving and enhancing the nation, increases the individuals' self-esteem.

Cultural dimension

Smith has produced the most comprehensive analysis of the cultural components of national identity to date. Values, beliefs, customs, conventions, habits, languages and practices are transmitted to the new members who receive the culture of a particular nation. The process of identification with a specific culture implies a strong emotional investment able to foster solidarity bonds among the members of a given community who come to recognize one another as fellow nationals (Gellner 1983). Furthermore, they imagine and feel their community as separate and distinct from others (Anderson 1983).

Communication among fellow-nationals requires the use of a shared language. To a great extent, vernacular languages are employed, though there are some exceptions. For instance, where the vernacular language has been lost, this is replaced by the state's language. In Scotland the practical disappearance of Gaelic was primarily due to the imposition of English. In France, the imposition of French involved the irreversible weakening of other languages spoken within the territorial boundaries of the French nation-state such as Basque, Breton, Catalan and Occitan. There are cases where more than one language is official within the nation and they are both employed. This is the case in Quebec (French and English) and Catalonia (Catalan and Spanish in post-Francoist Spain) (Guibernau 2004).

Historical dimension

How far back in time should members of a given nation be able to locate their origin as a community? A century? Five centuries? Fifty years? There is no written rule about this. In fact, while nations such as England or France can easily trace back their origins to medieval times, other peoples such as Jews, Armenians, Greeks, Persians, Japanese and Chinese go back to antiquity. In contrast, the USA, Australia or Canada can claim a mere 200–300 years of history.

But, why is antiquity relevant? Antiquity is employed as a source of legitimacy for a nation and its culture. It binds individuals to a past stretching over their life spans and those of their recent ancestors. Antiquity stresses one of the key elements of identity, that is continuity, and, in so doing, it contributes to the preservation of the collective self. Acknowledging and documenting cultural antiquity is a modern activity which also provides nations and their cultures with a distinguished pedigree, so that when individuals look back in time they are not confronted with a blank picture about their own collective origin, but reassured by the deeds of their ancestors. Antiquity feeds the subjective belief in a kinship relation right at the heart of the nation. Culture is perceived as the particular way of being in the world adopted by each nation.

Members of a nation tend to feel proud of their ancient roots and generally interpret them as a sign of resilience, strength and even superiority when compared with other nations unable to display a rich past during which the nation became prominent.

Nations remember admirable and awesome experiences, but they also recall dreadful moments of humiliation and suffering. Catalonia's national day commemorates the occupation of Barcelona by Spanish forces led by Felipe V (11 September 1714) and the subsequent proscription of its language and the abolition of its autonomous institutions. Jews observe key dates of the Holocaust and revere the victims of the concentration camps, such as Auschwitz, where millions lost their lives. Only two years have passed since 11

September 2001, when the World Trade Centre in New York and the Pentagon in Washington were victims of a terrorist attack, and this date has already acquired meaning for millions of citizens of the USA who unite in grief to remember those killed or injured.

The selective use of history provides nationals with a collective memory filled with transcendental moments in the life of the community, events and experiences that allow people to increase their self-esteem by feeling part of a community which proved capable of great things and that might also be ready to become again a beacon to the world. All nations possess or construct some features that make them special and in a certain way, 'superior' to the rest. They all excel in something, no matter what, that makes them and their members unique. History contributes to the construction of a certain image of the nation and represents the cradle where national character was forged.

Territorial dimension

For centuries, the rural community and the local village have represented the limits of the individual's universe. Traditionally, the life of individuals revolved around a small territory where family, work, religious and administrative structures were concentrated. In turn, the individual's identity was defined by the roles he or she played within that limited territory.

A great shift was required for people to conceive the nation as their home, since a large sector of the population had never travelled around their own nation's territory. Even today, a fair number of people only know of some parts of the nation they belong to through the media and education. In some countries, it is quite common to discover that a considerable proportion of the population who, at some point, have travelled abroad, mainly on holiday, are lacking a direct knowledge of their own nations.

Print and other forms of media have contributed to individuals being able to imagine their nations and regard them as homelands (Anderson 1983). Smith emphasizes that 'nations, for nationalists, are special kinds of spatial communities, those that can trace their origins or "roots" to specific ancestral landscapes' (Smith 2002: 22).

International media and communications have brought about greater awareness of the territorial limits of nations, peoples and cultures. It is widely accepted that globalization has increased interconnectedness, and that it has heightened interdependence. But, how do ordinary people react to events taking place outside the territorial boundaries of their nation? Do they feel with the same intensity about loss of life, natural disasters or great sports achievements, regardless of where they take place? Surely not. While it is true that events happening miles away can have an impact upon our daily lives – changes in the Tokyo stock exchange, ecological disasters...– we do not react in the same manner to famine, war, epidemics, terrorist attacks or sport world records if they occur beyond the boundaries of our nation and they have 'foreigners' as their subjects.

In addition, within the nation, we tend to feel more intensely about events happening closer to us; this is within our region, city or local village. Certainly it appears much more difficult to feel for 'strangers', yet not all 'strangers' are perceived in the same way. Thus, in Britain, a citizen of the USA may be perceived as 'less foreign' than an EU citizen, and be regarded as 'almost' a fellow-national when compared with Japanese, Peruvian or Algerian nationals.

Globalization conveys visibility and awareness of the 'other', but for the large majority of peoples, the territorial boundaries of the nation signal the limits of their homeland and fellow-nationals are usually portrayed as if they were more 'human' than outsiders, as deserving our support, concern and nurture. Filial sentiments toward fellow-nationals are not matched by feelings for 'foreigners', 'unknown peoples', 'strangers', maybe potential 'enemies'.

In spite of globalization and emerging cosmopolitanism, which so far is primarily an elite phenomenon, local and national attachments remain strong and I expect them to continue to be so in the foreseeable future. This is not a process opposed to cosmopolitanism, but a process parallel to it. So-called 'citizens of the world' are bound to be primarily concerned about their nations, and this should not prevent them from displaying greater awareness and increasing sensitivity toward 'strangers'.

The dichotomy between the 'national' and the 'cosmopolitan' could be partially solved by Durkheim's identification of what he calls the 'national ideal' with the 'human ideal'. He argues that each state becomes an organ of the 'human ideal' in so far as it assumes that its main task is not to expand by extending its borders, but to increase the level of its members' morality (Durkheim 1973: 101).

Political dimension

In what follows I seek to redress Smith's failure to address the political aspects of nations and national identity. In my view, the political dimension of national identity derives from its relation with the modern nation-state. As a political institution ruling over a diverse population, from its foundational moment the nation-state pursued the cultural and linguistic homogenization of an otherwise diverse citizenry. This is, the state selected and imposed the culture and language of the dominant group within its territory and sought to create a single nation out of the diverse nations or parts of nations forming it. Conquests, annexations and marriages brought together peoples who were foreign to each other and saw rulers who could not understand, nor be understood by, their subjects. For centuries, nobody objected to the legitimacy of such political arrangements. The distance between elites and the masses was epitomized in the 'foreign' character of some rulers who shared very little with their subjects.

In my view, it is essential to acknowledge that nations have an ethnic origin, as Smith has proved throughout his work. In contrast with his theory, though, I locate the rise of the nation-state, national identity and nationalism in late eighteenth-century Europe and I consider their emergence linked to the ideas which gave rise to the American Revolution in 1776 and the French Revolution in 1789.

I understand the rise of the nation-state as the product of a multidimensional process changing the relations of power in society. The main elements of this process included the consolidation of territorial units by bureaucratic absolutist states that for the first time were able to hold the monopoly of the means of violence inside their territory; the transformation of frontiers delimiting different states in clearly fixed borders; the emergence of the bourgeoisie as a new class especially receptive to the ideas of the Enlightenment; and the new role of monarchs and rulers which was characterized by a fundamental change in the relation between rulers and ruled.

Before the eighteenth century, the right to rule was legitimated by appealing to God's will, royal blood or superior physical strength and these reasons were premised upon the belief that legitimacy came from above, rather than from the ruled. A radical shift occurred as a consequence of the spread of the new ideas of the *philosophes* emphasizing the cult of liberty, equality and particularly the idea of state power rooted in popular consent.

The whole process of translating the ideas of popular sovereignty into universal adult suffrage required a long and hard struggle during which the ideas of 1789 began a slow but compelling process, and permeated to varying degrees first the educated classes and then the masses in the various European countries. Another relevant feature of the French Revolution was the emphasis it placed on education, creating as a result the first comprehensive system of national education to raise new generations of virtuous and patriotic citizens. Only a common education, it was felt, could realize the unity of the fatherland and the union of its citizens.

This framework made possible the rise of modern nationalism, a device which proved to be exceedingly useful for refocusing a people's loyalty away from the monarch. Monarchy by divine right was an elegantly simple device for evoking emotional attachment. But, an aggregate of sovereign citizens could hardly perform that function. Then the nation, personified through symbols and rituals which symbolically recreate a sense of 'people', became the focus of a new kind of attachment. It helped to implement nationalism, the division of Europe into nation-states which favoured the definition of citizenship by nationality as well as by legal, political and social rights. Thus, as Heater argues, the French Revolution politicized the cultural concept of nationality and subsequently, during much of the nineteenth century, the association of nationalism with popular sovereignty encouraged the liberals of central and southern Europe to plot and agitate for the realization of the ideal in their own lands (Heater 1990: 21).

National identity refers to the set of attributes and beliefs shared by those who belong to the same nation and, as shown above, not all nations have a state of their own. The political aspect of national identity, when applied to the nation-state, focuses upon those state's strategies – often referred to as 'nation-building' – destined to foster a cohesive, loyal and, up to a point, homogeneous citizenry (Guibernau 2001: 242–68). Among the main strategies generally employed by the state in its pursuit of a single national identity capable of uniting its citizens are:

1 The construction and dissemination of a certain *image* of the 'nation', often based upon the dominant nation or ethnic group living within the state's boundaries and comprising a common history, a shared culture and a demarcated territory.
2 The creation and spread of a set of symbols and rituals charged with the mission of reinforcing a sense of community among citizens.
3 The advancement of citizenship involving a well-defined set of civil and legal rights, political rights and duties as well as socio-economic rights. The state by conferring rights upon its members favours the rise of sentiments of loyalty towards itself. It also establishes a crucial distinction between those *included* and those *excluded* from the community of citizens.
4 The creation of common enemies, imminent, potential or invented.
5 The progressive consolidation of national education and media systems.

Some of the state's citizens, however, may have a national identity different from that promoted by it. People of immigrant origin, ethnic communities and those belonging to national minorities may stand in opposition to the national identity instilled by the state.

There are at least two different approaches to the compatibility or coexistence of different identities within a single political institution. Some argue that the solution lies in the generation of multiple identities, although hardly do they ever specifically refer to multiple 'national' identities. Often they allude to ethnic, regional, national and transnational identities implicitly assuming that different types of identities are compatible precisely because they operate at different levels.

In contrast, others argue that people who share a common citizenship may have different national identities, thus separating membership of the state from the sentiment of belonging to the nation. At first sight, this may appear as a plausible solution, however, in my view it is not straightforward to sustain such a separation in so far as the nation is being regarded as a source of legitimacy for state power.

Conclusion

This paper has unravelled a fundamental flaw in Smith's classical theory of nations and national identity, this is, his failure to offer a clear-cut distinction between the concepts of nation and state.

I have shown that the ethnosymbolist approach, despite offering a rich and path-breaking contribution to the study of the cultural aspects of nations and national identity, fails to consider the political consequences of its findings. In my view, the dissociation between the cultural and the political aspects of nations and national identity casts some doubts over the ability of ethnosymbolism to capture the full meaning of nations and national identity in modern societies. The political consequences of being a nation, with or without a state and the role of the state in the construction of national identity cannot be ignored.

References

Anderson, Benedict. 1983. *Imagined Communities: Reflections on the origins and spread of nationalism*. London: Verso.

Armstrong, John. 1982. *Nations before Nationalism*. Chapel Hill, NC: University of North Carolina Press.

Connor, Walker. 1994a. 'When is a nation?' in Anthony D. Smith and John Hutchinson (eds.), *Nationalism*. Oxford: Oxford University Press.

Connor, Walker. 1994b. *Ethno-Nationalism: the Quest for Understanding*. Princeton, NJ: Princeton University Press.

Durkheim, Émile. 1973. 'Pacifisme et Patriotisme' translated by N. Layne in, *Sociological Inquiry* 43(2): 99–103.

Geertz, Clifford. 1973. *The Interpretation of Cultures*. London: Fontana.

Gellner, Ernest. 1983. *Nations and Nationalism*. Oxford: Basil Blackwell.

Guibernau, Montserrat. 1996. *Nationalisms: the Nation-State and Nationalism in the Twenty-first Century*. Cambridge: Polity.

Guibernau, Montserrat. 1999. *Nations without States*. Cambridge: Polity.

Guibernau, Montserrat. 2001. 'Globalization and the nation-state' in Montserrat Guibernau and John Hutchinson (eds.), *Understanding Nationalism*. Cambridge: Polity.

Guibernau, Montserrat. 2004. *Catalan Nationalism: Francoism, Transition and Democracy*. London: Routledge.

Heater, David. 1990. *Citizenship: the Civil Ideal in World History, Politics and Education*. London: Longman.

Hobsbawm, Eric and Terence Ranger (eds.). 1983. *The Invention of Tradition*. Cambridge: Cambridge University Press.

Smith, Anthony D. 1986. *The Ethnic Origins of Nations*. Oxford: Blackwell.

Smith, Anthony D. 1991. *National Identity*. London: Penguin.

Smith, Anthony D. 1998. *Nationalism and Modernism*. London: Routledge.

Smith, Anthony D. 2002. 'When is a nation', *Geopolitics* 7(2): 5–32.

Van den Berghe, Pierre. 1978. 'Race and ethnicity: a sociobiological perspective', *Ethnic and Racial Studies* 1(4): 401–11.

Weber, Max 1991 [1948]. *From Max Weber: Essays in Sociology*, Gerth, H. and C.Wright Mills (eds.). London: Routledge.

10

The ethno-cultural roots of national art*

ATHENA S. LEOUSSI

Introduction

This essay considers the problem of the representation of the nation in the visual arts. It shows the heightening and realising of collective experience through the image. By examining the historical record, and especially the period from the late eighteenth to the twentieth centuries, I outline the development in European culture of a new artistic category, that of national art. The new artistic orientation was taken from the doctrine of nationalism, a philosophy which idealised the nation, the historical and cultural community (Smith 1986). The new philosophy was part of the first modern awakening of the European mind to self-consciousness, that impulse to re-define the individual and collective sources of human existence. It gave rise to a particular type of nationalism, cultural nationalism, which Anthony D. Smith and John Hutchinson have identified as analytically and historically distinct from political nationalism (Smith 1991; Hutchinson 1987).

This essay is a tribute to the distinguished work of Anthony D. Smith. It draws on his path-breaking theory of *ethno-symbolism*. This theory recognises, first, the importance of ethnic cultures and ethnic symbols in the formation of nations; and second, the role of the various arts, painting, sculpture, music and literature, in giving concrete and recurrent embodiment to ethnic cultures and ethnic symbols (Smith 2002: 30).

Based on Smith's work, I show, first, that the visual arts, and especially painting and sculpture, have been crucial vehicles of cultural nationalism, affirming the ethno-cultural roots of human existence; second, that works of art have been accepted as 'national' only to the extent to which they have managed to capture and symbolise the way of life of the so-called 'masses', the historico-cultural community; third, that the poetical and aesthetic transformation of the ethno-cultural experience into image has contributed, not only to

* This study has greatly benefited from the support of a generous research grant from the Irving Louis Horowitz Foundation for Social Policy. The author wishes to thank the Foundation for this support.

the *prise de conscience* of this experience by its participants, but also to its celebration as a positive and central socio-cultural experience; and fourth, that these very works of art have become, like the primitive totem, visual symbols of the nation: agents of national integration and regulation (Smith 1993; Marsland 2001: 222).

From a more general point of view, I address the debate regarding the artificiality and modernity versus the authenticity and historical continuity of nations. I show that national art is not an invention of elites bent on creating new forms of human association and orientation which they call 'national', in the sense of all-embracing, homogeneous and integrative of a whole society (Hobsbawm and Ranger 1983). Rather, national art is the work of cultural elites whose aim is to organise, unify, streamline and standardise and, in this way, 'modernise' pre-existing ethnic identities and solidarities. It is this kind of modernisation of the fluid and informal ethnic cultures, which turns 'high cultures', in the sense of core, urban and education-embedded cultures, into national cultures (Smith 1995). Max Weber's concept of 'rationalisation' may also apply here to describe this process (Weber 1930). Consequently, the aim of what we might call nationalising cultural elites, is not to invent, but to revive, express and develop. They are, in Hutchinson's apt phrase, moral regenerators and innovators of modern societies (Hutchinson 1987 and 1999). Indeed, over a period of two centuries, and at the dawn of the new, twenty-first century, the 'national' identities and solidarities which such elites have moulded from pre-existing cultural material, have come to constitute the fundamental socio-cultural bases of the political, economic and social organisation of both industrial and post-industrial societies. This essay examines the participation of artists in this ethno-cultural re-moralisation of modern societies and new states.

The *ex nihilo* invention of collective identities which have no roots in the history and cultural inclinations of the community has always met with failure. This is evident, first, in the failure of the neo-classical ideology of the eighteenth century to move the French masses into the modern world; and second, in the twentieth century, in the failure of Soviet ideology and iconography to mould the new kind of man, Soviet man. This failure is most evident in the massive revival, after the collapse of the USSR, of pre-Soviet ethnic identities, symbols and iconographies (Leoussi 2004).

The article considers a wide range of instances and forms of national art from both European and non-European countries and examines their ethno-cultural roots. Through a brief survey of artists' attachment to the historico-cultural community, the article attempts the development of a two-fold typology of national art. This is based, first, on the distinction between content (subject-matter) and form (style); and second, on the traditional academic and hierarchical classification of subject-matter in European art into history painting, Portraiture, *Genre*, i.e. images of everyday rural or urban life, Landscape and Still-life. Within this framework the essay examines the nationalisation of artistic subject-matter, its transformation into images of the nation.

National art

I shall here use the category 'national art' to refer to art made by artists consciously inspired by their own, ethno-cultural heritage of symbols, memories, myths, values, traditions and natural environment, either in the form of their art, or in its content, or in both aspects of their work. In what follows, I shall explore, first, the importance of ethno-cultural material in the development of national art, and second, the connection between modernity and tradition in the development of national iconographies and styles.

The varieties of national art

i. The development of national subject-matter. Under the impact of the national idea and the growth of national self-consciousness, the European academic classification and hierarchy of subject-matter was transformed and even reversed. I shall examine below each type of subject-matter and its transformations. I shall concentrate on the four main types of academic subject-matter, those which involve the painting of the human figure and the painting of landscapes. I shall thus exclude still-life painting, even though this too was transformed along with the general consciousness. Examples include, Picasso's Cubist *Spanish Still Life* (1912) in which he declared his Catalan roots by including the Catalan flag (Rosenblum 1996: 68–70); and Chagall's Cubist-cum-Suprematist *Collage* of 1921, whose ethnic component is a triangular shape, akin to Jewish tombstones, inside of which there is an inscription, in Hebrew, 'TSEDEK', meaning 'Justice' (Foray 2003: 107, 111).

The nationalisation of the whole range of subjects which European artists depicted in their works is compatible with the very nature of the new cultural focus, the new sympathy towards the historico-cultural community, as a complete universe of human experience, both physical and spiritual (Kohn 1961: 3–24; Smith 1993). Anthony D. Smith has defined the ethnic community most precisely: 'a named unit of population with common ancestry myths and shared historical memories, elements of shared culture, a link with a historic territory, and some measure of solidarity, at least among the elites' (Smith 1995: 57).

The modernisation and politicisation of *ethnies* into nation-states gave them additional features. First, the institutionalisation of their culture into a homogeneous, standardised and unified, mass, public culture transmitted via a state-sponsored education system; second, a common, industrial economy; and third, common legal rights and duties for all members as citizens of the nation-state. This type of state was to become, in the course of the twentieth century, a truly global type of state (Greenfeld 1992: 3–26; Smith 2001: 19–22).

Through its multi-dimensionality, the historico-cultural community permeated the entire artistic repertoire, to which it lent its local colour and specificity. It would be the task of another, longer study, to explore systematic variations, over time and space, in artists' emphases on this or that aspect of ethno-national life.

ii. History painting and the representation of national history. In fully developed academic theory, history painting consisted of the painting of subjects taken from Greek and Roman history and mythology, the deeds of kings and nobles, and themes from the Christian story. It was the noblest form of art, and thus stood at the top of the so-called 'hierarchy of the *genres*' (Murray and Murray 1979). Paintings such as Ingres' *Jupiter and Thetis* (1811) belong to this category.

The new cultural self-consciousness propelled artists towards a new historical sensitivity to the history of their own ethno-cultural community. It echoed, and, indeed, was part of the Romantic protest, forcefully expressed in France, as 'Qui nous délivrera des Grecs et des Romains?' (Leoussi 1998: 57; Margalit 2001: 151). At the same time, and as Smith has observed, neo-classicism was also a form of nationalism (Smith 1993). The neo-classical attachment to classical Greece and Rome had new and diffferent motives from those of the academy and the *ancien régime* (Honour 1991). It was motivated by an attachment to the 'national' virtues of the ancient Greek and Roman cities: their solidarity, their pride in their cultural distinctiveness and achievement, and their freedom, both individual and collective.

Like much of history painting, the representation of the history of the ethno-cultural community was patterned on the cycle of organic life. This structured events in terms of origins, growth, decline, death and re-birth. It provided an understanding of the history of peoples and societies which went back, through Winckelmann and Herder to Plato and Aristotle. The new historical sensitivity turned history painting into ethno-history painting. At the same time, the idea of the nation expanded history painting by defining the finest moment of ethno-national experience, the golden age, in its own terms: in terms of its peculiar ideals of national identity, unity and autonomy (Smith 1991: ch. 4).

The concern with ethno-history has involved more or less idealised and telescoped depictions of the ethnic origins, golden age, decline and re-generation of the artists' own community of birth (Miller 1996: 413). It gave rise to images of its victories and defeats in wars of resistance against foreign rule or in its wars of conquest; to images of its 'awakening' and liberation; to illustrations of its myths, legends and cultural achievements. It showed, to use Herder, not only how the community 'was ruled' or 'how it let itself be slaughtered', but also, how it 'thought, what it wished and craved for, how it took its pleasures, how it was led by its teachers or its inclinations' (Berlin 1998: 385; Smith 1993: 65); and with the rise of the idea of race in the middle of the nineteenth century, how it looked (Leoussi 1998).

Several artists would depict the whole cycle of the ancestry, golden age, decline and re-birth of their national community. This is what Alphonse Mucha did in his monumental series of 20 paintings entitled, *The Slav Epic*, conceived in 1900 and completed in 1928. For this work, Mucha steeped himself in historical study and consulted several historians. On the basis of this learning, Mucha constructed some of the most powerful icons and under-standings of Slav history.

The *Slav Epic* included such 'national' themes as *The Slavs in their Original Homeland: between the Turanian Whip and the Sword of the Goths* (1912); *The Introduction of the Slavonic Liturgy in Great Moravia: Praise the Lord in Your Native Tongue* (1912); *The Coronation of the Serbian Tsar Stepan Dusan as East Roman Emperor: the Slavic Code of Law* (1926); *Jan Hus Preaching at the Bethlehem Chapel, 1412* (1916); *The Hussite King, Jiříz Poděbrad* (1925); *The Abolition of Serfdom in Russia: Work in Freedom is the Foundation of a State* (1914); *and Apotheosis of the Slavs* (1926), the last painting in the series. The cycle embodies complex ideas on nationality and statehood with far-reaching practical implications.

First, it affirms the linguistic criterion of nationality. This had been a primary criterion of social classification since Herder (Berlin 1998: 382–383). Here, Mucha proclaims the Slav origins and identity of the Czechs. Second, the cycle is a manifesto of Pan-Slavism. Pan-Slavism was a national ideology which united into a brotherhood all speakers of Slavic languages. For some pan-Slavists, like Mucha, but unlike Tomas Masaryk, this ideology included the vision of a pan-Slav monarchy led by the Russian Czar. Mucha's Russian sympathies are further evident in photographs of himself, from the 1890s, in Russian costume. Third, the cycle includes important references to the Czech Reformation. These may be interpreted as symbolisations of Czech distinctiveness and opposition to the Habsburg Empire, a 'Gothic' and notoriously Catholic empire – synonymous with the Counter-Reformation – from which the Czechs became independent in 1918, following its collapse. And fourth and finally, the *Slav Epic* portrays several Slav kings, including an Emperor. These, too, echo the nineteenth-century struggles for national independence of several Slav peoples living in the Austrian and Ottoman Empires, but also in the Russian Empire, affirming as they do the idea and experience of independent statehood and power among the Slavs (Dvořák 2000: 147–153).

In France, the idea of the Gallic or Celtic ancestry of the mass of the French population, as opposed to the Frankish origins of the French aristocracy, came to dominate French official thought under Napoleon III. It gave rise to a number of works of art, many of them bought by the state and meant for public display, such as Millet's statue of *Vercingétorix*, purchased by Napoleon III in 1865 (Grand Palais, 1986: 50, 374).

In Germany, images of ancient Teutons showed in monumental sculpture the ancestors of modern Germans, such as the statue of Arminius, the *Hermannsdenkmal*, near Detmold. Arminius, the German warrior who led the Germans in the victorious 'Battle of the Teutoburg Forest', against the invading Roman regions under Varus in AD9, had entered the German national movement since the late eighteenth century. Then, Schlegel, Wieland, Klopstock and others, inspired by the national ideals, turned him into a central character of German history and culture. The statue of Arminius sculpted by Ernst von Bandel, was inaugurated in 1875, in the presence of Kaiser Wilhelm I. Arminius, 'without doubt Germany's liberator,…in war undefeated' as an inscription on the monument reads, also came to symbolise the idea of German solidarity and political unity as evinced in the unity of the

Germanic tribes against the Romans and the foundation of the German Empire (Kesting 1982).

In Sweden, the artist Karl Larsson created a cycle of the origins of the Swedes in his decoration of the walls of the new girls' school in Göteborg of 1890–91. Larsson represented Swedish women from prehistoric times to the present, including, to use Michelle Facos' description, 'a Viking widow [who] stands stoically with her two children before the rune stone commemorating her fallen husband; [and] an eighteenth-century woman [who] embroiders a cloth with three crowns, a symbol of the Swedish nation' (Facos 1998: 37–38). At a time of intense Swedish national development, Larsson's cycle belongs to the nationalisation of the Swedish population through state-sponsored education, made universal and compulsory as early as 1842 (Facos 1998: 36).

In the work of the Mexican artist Diego Rivera we find the same attempt to recount and celebrate ethnic origins. Rivera celebrates the mixed, pre-Colombian ethnic and civilisational origins and continuities of modern Mexico. His large fresco cycles decorating several public buildings of Mexico City belong to the national movement known as *indigenismo*: 'the official attitude of praising and fostering native values' and the idea of common roots for the nation in the Indian past (Ades 1989: 198; Smith 1993: 76). Rivera's decorations include subjects such as *Deer Dance* (1923–4) for the Ministry of Education, and *The Huastec Civilization* (1950) for the Palacio Nacional (Ades 1989: 158).

In more general terms, the representation of indigenous origins and ways of life implying a partial or total opposition to non-natives is typical of anti-imperial or anti-colonial situations throughout the world. Mucha's *Slav Epic* contains an unmistakeably anti-Habsburg spirit. The Swadeshi (indigenous-ness) movement which marked Indian art as a protest against the British division of Bengal in 1905 led to the rise of visual symbols of anti-British sentiment (Mitter 1994: 235).

Ethno-history painting enriched the artists' repertoire of myths and legends which had hitherto been confined to Greek and Roman mythology. From the late eighteenth century onwards, ethnic myths and legends began to appear, both old and newly invented myths. Akseli Gallen-Kallela's illustrations of the *Kalevala* in the 1890s exemplify the first type (Smith 1993: 78). Macpherson's fictional *Ossian*, a favourite subject among both British and French artists, together with Nicholas Roerich's *Rite of Spring*, premiered in Paris in 1913, exemplify the second. Indeed, in the *Rite* which he created with Stravinsky, Roerich rewrote mythology for there exists no record of such ritual human sacrifice in Slavic religious practice (McCannon 2000: 290). Nevertheless, *Ossian* and the *Rite*, although 'inauthentic', are still important, for they represent modern mythopoeic attempts to capture poetically and imaginatively the Celtic and Slav spirits, respectively.

Around the middle of the nineteenth century a new way of tracing ethnic origins and collective identities emerged, which was to become widespread: physical appearance, or race (Banton 1998). The idea of race emphasised physical appearance as a vital and, indeed, determining component of national identity, inherited at birth. It created a physical ideal which all nations claimed for themselves and tried to approximate: the ideal of physical strength and health. Its model embodiments were the statues of ancient Greek athletes from whom most, if not all European nations also claimed descent as 'Aryans' (Biddiss 1970; Mosse 1975).

The new way of measuring and classifying mankind was the product of the modern sciences of anatomy and physical anthropology. These seemed to supply a supposedly more objective, empirical criterion to claims of genealogical descent and civilisational ability. The new science also advocated the necessity to care for one's body in order to avoid physical degeneration. Physical degeneration, caused by modern, sedentary and unsanitary urban life, not only deformed the body, but also caused physical weakness and inability to defend the nation in battle against invaders or in the achievement of independence.

Care for the body implied, above all, regular physical exercise and exposure of the body to the sun and the open air, like the ancient Greek athletes. The nudist movement of the turn of the twentieth century was another of its implications (Facos 2002: 117). The strong and healthy athletic body was pursued *en masse*, as a national institution sponsored by the state, in schools and public gymnasia, swimming pools, bathhouses, athletic academies, and public holidays (Leoussi 1998; Anderson and Tabb 2002). It was thus that Western culture returned, yet again, as if abiding by some kind of law of return, to ancient Greece. Muscularity dominated ethno-national identifications until well into the twentieth century. It determined the path along which all other national ambitions had to be pursued.

Permeating the arts, the idea of race gave a new meaning to the traditional, academic and universalistic image of the naked human body, turning it into the national body (Clark 1980). The nude no longer needed the conventional context of Greek and Roman mythology and the stories of the loves of the pagan gods, for its appearance. Now, images of muscular bodies, both male and female, and of naked, lay figures in natural surroundings, bathing or sunning themselves, became commonplace in late-nineteenth-century European art. These nudes expressed the search for physical revitalisation, in an almost vegetative way, or as in the myth of Antaeus, from direct contact with nature and land, and especially the native land and water. Kirchner's rather awkward, angular nudes, such as *Two Pink Nudes by the Moritzburg Lake* (1909–20) and Anders Zorn's three female nudes preparing to bathe in *Out of Doors in Dalarö* (1888) are good examples (Royal Academy 2002; Facos 2002: 110).

It is interesting to note that the figure of Venus, herself a daughter of the sea, which had dominated European art since the Renaissance, persists – albeit with a more nationally-specific meaning – as the type of the female Mediterranean body. This body was claimed by the French, as a 'Southern' people, and most urgently, in the context of French anti-Prussian irredentism after 1871 (Moeller 2003: 25). Examples include Cezanne's reproduction, in his series of bathers, such as *The Large Bathers* (1898–1905), of the attitudes of classical statues of

Venus; Renoir's *Judgment of Paris* (1908) and his own series of robust, pink, classicising bathers, beginning in 1881 with *Baigneuse Blonde I*; and Maillol's *La Méditerranée* (1905) which reproduces the proportions of the Venus de Milo (Leoussi 1998:133–142; Cowling and Mundy 1990:150–152).

The same desire for muscularity, not only as an aesthetic ideal, but also as a means of gaining national pride and independence, we find in the work of the Berlin-based Jewish artist, Lesser Ury. Ury depicted his biblical characters, such as *Rebecca at the Well* (c.1908), with physically robust bodies (Bilski 1999: 112). In this he echoed Max Nordau's appeal to Jews to revive the 'muscle Jewry' which had once existed, in order to counteract the prevailing image of the Jew as physically weak: 'We must think of creating once again a Jewry of muscles… For history is our witness that such a Jewry had once existed' (Nordau quoted in Bilski 1999, note 42:143; Leoussi and Aberbach 2002). Ury also painted emaciated figures of Jews, as the product of exile, following the destruction of Jerusalem, in *Jerusalem* (1896).

In Victorian England, the President of the Royal Academy, Frederick Leighton, became an arch-exponent of muscular nationality. His sculpture, *Athlete Struggling with a Python* (1877) is a good example, as is G. F. Watts' equestrian statue, *Physical Energy* (1883) (Leoussi 1998). In the twentieth century, the more viciously aggressive pursuit of muscularity gave rise to the Nazi, Aryan warriors of Arno Breker (Mangan 1999).

iii. Portraiture and the portrayal of national heroes and personifications of the nation. Portraiture was transformed from the portrayal and celebration of particular individuals for their personal power or achievements, to the commemorative portrayal of individuals as either founders of the nation or as representative examples, and thus symbols of the nation and its virtues (Smith 1993: 70). As Kedourie has observed, albeit critically, this nationalisation of individuality is characteristic of the national idea (Kedourie 1971: introduction). However, it is a characteristic of every human society to celebrate those individuals who have realised its highest ideals.

The statue of Arminius discussed above, also belongs to this category of portraiture of national heroes. Other examples include the *Pantheon* in Paris (from 1791-onwards), the *Walhalla* (1842) in Regensburg, Bavaria, and *Mount Rushmore* (1941) in South Dakota, USA.

Mucha's designs for the Mayor's Hall in Prague, completed in 1910, as part of the decoration of its new Municipal House, a central, pre-independence, Czech institution, included several famous personalities of Bohemian history, symbolic of national virtues: *Justice – Jan Hus; Fidelity – Comenius,* and *Maternal Wisdom – Eliska Premyslovna*, she being the mother of Prince Wenceslas, the future 'Father of his Homeland', Charles IV (Wittlich 2000: 49).

In Zimbabwe, The Heroes Acre is an example of an African post-colonial monument to national heroes, here symbolised by means of two young men and one young woman, bearing generalised African and European features, dressed in military costume, and standing around a flag pole of the Zimbabwean national flag (Government of Zimbabwe 1986).

Allegorical portraits of the nation depicted as a person, usually with generalised and stereotyped ethnic features and national symbols, belong to this category. We find personifications of the nation in Britain's Britannia and France's Marianne. In Poland, in Jacek Malczewski's pre-independence *Polish Hamlet* (1903), 'two allegorical figures stand for the old, enslaved Poland tearing off its chains' (Ławniczakowa 1984, cat. no. 22: 64). In Fuseli's *The Oath of the Rütli* which was commissioned from him in 1778 by the Zurich council, the three original cantons of Switzerland, Schwyz, Uri and Unterwalden, who defended the independence of their valleys against Habsburg rule, are personified as three huge, Michelangelesque male figures (Smith 1993: 71). Outside Europe, in India, Abanindranath Tagore's Swadeshi *Bhārat Mātā* (c.1905) is a good example. Here, Tagore painted a haloed 'Mother India as a Bengali Lady' holding four symbolic objects in her four hands, in the conventional manner of a Hindu deity (Mitter 1994: 235, 295 and pl. XXI).

iv. The representation of peasants as images of the nation. The national movement incorporated peripheral, ethno-cultural values and forms of conduct, located in the countryside among the rural population, into the 'core', central values, institutions and symbols of the state (Shils 1975). It turned 'low culture' into 'high culture'. Under the influence of Herder, the folk, peasant community, was understood to be, not only a natural source of morality, but also the carrier and repository of the authentic character of a people. This was a character unadulterated by contact with other cultures and unaffected by the demoralising and rootless spirit of anomie which dominated the expanding, modern city (Kohn 1961). And as the city incorporated the countryside, the countryside embraced the city, modernising itself, turning peasants, gradually, into citizens in the long process of nation-building.

The artistic equivalent of this process was the massive rise of images of peasants in painting and sculpture as the new 'high art'. Scenes of rural life were transformed from picturesque anecdote and erotic scenes with shepherdesses, to ethnographic studies of the nation, and their status raised to that of history painting. Although the concern with peasant life had a variety of motives, the national motive was an important one.

As rural life acquired national significance, artists took their easels to the village to capture its communal ethos, religious faith, costumes, customs and habits as these were developed in direct contact with the land and nature. These images of the countryside were taken back to the city where they were incorporated into the national consciousness as sources and aspects of national life. Often, they formed the basis of the decoration of public buildings in the great cities or the contents of national art galleries.

Swedish art of the turn of the twentieth century is typical of this movement which in Sweden became known as National Romantic. It included works such as Carl Larsson's *Crayfishing* (c.1894), Nils Kreuger's *Seaweed Carters on the Halland Coast* (1898), and Anders Zorn's *Midsummer Dance* (1897) (Facos 1998). In Germany, the return to the German countryside and its *Volk* acquired a specifically organic, vital and integral meaning, as 'the only link between a new German 'spirit' and its past' (Facos 1998: 55). This is the spiritual context of Fritz Mackensen's *Church Service on the Moor* (1895).

In this category of national ethnographic art, we also find the idea of regional diversity as a component of the national character. This took various forms, including the French self-understanding as a microcosm, in which all climates, 'toutes les fleurs et toutes les couleurs', co-existed with a wide range of customs and mores (Thiesse 1991 and 1997). Gauguin's Breton and Provençal paintings from the 1880s exemplify French regional variety. In Mussolini's Italy, as Simonetta Fraquelli has observed, the grass-roots movement Strapaese 'called for a truly Fascist art that would highlight the rural and regional side of Italian life, with its inherent order, serenity and sobriety' (Fraquelli 1996: 131). The peasant acquired an additional meaning in Mexican paintings such as David Alfáro Siqueiros' *Peasant Mother* (1929). Set in a dark and barren landscape of cactuses, it showed to the urban elites the poverty of the Indian peasants, and the need to develop and incorporate them into the orbit of modern industrial prosperity (Ades 1989: 195).

The life of the periphery not only decorated the walls and ceilings of the great public buildings of the modern metropolis and national capitals; it also shaped its architecture. In this, the English Arts and Crafts Movement was a great inspiration (Greenhalgh 2000). Thus, the Museum of Applied Arts in Budapest, designed in 1896 by the pioneer of the 'Hungarian' style, Ödön Lechner, reproduced motifs from Magyar and Asian folk art, believed to be the 'common ancestors of the new Hungarian style' (Éri and Jobbágyi 1990: 73–74). These included oriental arches, the capping of its dome with a *baldachin*-shaped lantern, richly coloured tiles and evocations of the ancestral tent of the semi-nomadic Magyar tribes (Crowley 2000: 349). In fact, Lechner's buildings combined modernity with tradition in the principle of *Bekleidung*: the use of folk motifs as decorative cladding of basically modern constructions.

v. From landscape to ethnoscape. Man's need for a home is primordial. It found one of its fullest ideological expressions in the doctrine of nationalism (Grosby 1994; Margalit 2001). The idea of the homeland is central to the idea of the nation conceived as a spatial community (Smith 2002: 22). It had a profound influence on landscape painting. It transformed it from the representation of picturesque topography or classical landscapes, such as those by Valenciennes and Claude, to the painting of what Smith has called *ethno*scapes (Smith 2002: 22; Vaughan 1999: 205–223). Artists became interested in the representation of the national territory as the 'home' of both the rural and the urbanised population: as the common, national homeland.

We may discern at least five meanings of 'home' in landscape painting:

First, Rousseau's Romantic naturalism inspired among urban elites a return to and immersion in nature for physical and spiritual revival as man's natural home.

Second, nature was particularised into the local landscape. The local landscape was seen as the natural force that shaped the national character. This environmental determinism was associated with Winckelmann in his explanation of classical thought as arising from the unique qualities of the

Mediterranean environment. It was adopted by Herder in the concept of *Klima*, meaning primarily the natural environment, and grew into a popular notion (Mitchell 1993: 134–135). According to Herder, the physical diversity of nature had created the cultural diversity of mankind. Thus, localism and cultural relativism should be maintained as natural: 'Whom nature separated by language, customs, character, let no man artificially join together by chemistry' (Herder quoted in Berlin 1998: 374).

Third, the native land, as this became extended from the particular place of a person's birth to the national territory, acquired the primordial charisma and affection of the family home, precisely because it included one's own birthplace, the place where 'one's life and the life of one's family [was] propagated, sustained and transmitted' (Grosby 2001 and 1995).

Fourth, the land as sovereign territory was 'home' because, as in the privacy of one's home, the ethno-national community can freely translate its ideals into practice and create its habitat (Smith 1981; Miller 1996: 417). The nation-state thus becomes a 'home': the place which belongs to one, and to which one belongs because there one can behave naturally and spontaneously; and the place where, to quote the American poet Robert Frost, 'when you go there, they have to take you in' (Margalit 2001:151–152).

And fifth, the land was the home of the future not only for the exiles, but also for the founders, conquerors and settlers of new worlds.

These meanings can be found, often combined, in such ethnoscapes as Caspar David Friedrich's depictions of 'our German sun, moon and stars, our rocks, trees and plants, our plains, lakes and rivers' (Mitchell 1993: 145). In Constable's images of domesticated and fruitful nature, such as *The Haywain* (1821), and *The Cornfield* (1826), we find an idea of the English countryside as Arcadia and a self-sufficient, life-sustaining 'home'. Furthermore, Constable's landscapes are also literally 'home' for they are images of his native Suffolk (Vaughan 1999: 211–213). Here, as the American Romantic poets put it, 'going out,... was really going in'.

Early American landscape painting shows the creation of new homes. *Mount Ktaadn* (1853) in Maine, by Frederic Edwin Church, shows 'the founding fathers' American dream of small-scale agrarian communities hewn from the wilderness' (Barringer 2002: 126). Paintings like Ury's *Jerusalem* (1896), mentioned above, express the devastation caused by the loss of a sense of home, which the Jewish community has suffered from both the historic loss of Jerusalem and anti-Semitism (Margalit 2001; Horowitz 1980). In the same vein, Wilfredo Lam's *The Jungle* (1942–3) symbolises, in the words of another member of the young, international Negro elite of the 1930s and 1940s, the Martinican poet Aimé Césaire, the cruel situation of 'Black man exiled from his native soil' (Linsley 1988: 532).

Finally, Chagall's paintings figuring Vitebsk, his hometown, such as *Autoportrait aux sept doigts* (1912–3) with a view of Paris through the window and a vision of Vitebsk, also belong to the category of ethnoscape. First, they affirm the artist's ethno-territorial roots; and second they show the crucial dilemma of modernity: the choice between the 'pays natal' and the international metropolis of strangers (Foray 2003: 107, 111).

Modern art and the development of national art

The development of national art has been intimately associated with the development of modern art. Looked at from a purely formal, stylistic point of view, national art has taken many forms, both traditional, in the sense of academic, and modern, in the sense of avant-garde, international, experimental and innovative. It has not been a regressive phenomenon (Hutchinson 1987: 30–40). The national idea was an idea of national *development*, as well as ethnocultural *continuity* and *revival*. And both these processes were constitutively modern to the extent to which modernity involved innovation, a change in established patterns.

In art the national idea introduced new subjects into the established repertoire, and in this sense it bore already the mark of modernity. It also revived traditional, ethnic artistic styles and techniques. The revival was in itself innovative, while its 'primitivism' became constitutive of the art of the European avant-garde (Green 2000: 233–253). European primitivism in art encompassed both European and non-European ethnic subjects and styles. Gauguin's Tahitian subjects and forms, and Picasso's African sources are cases in point. I shall here consider the revival of European, pre-modern artistic styles and their role in the development of a modern, national art.

The relationship between national art and modern art has been complex. We can discern the following three 'pure' varieties of this relationship.

First, national art could be ethno-cultural in content and modernist in form. Chagall's Biblical subjects show the complexity of this link. They offer an ethnicised account of a universalistic and vital tradition shared by both Jews and Christians, and rendered in a radically modern style. For example, borrowing from Cubism, Expressionism, Suprematism and Surrealism, Chagall created in *La crucifixion blanche* (1938) an image of both universal and particular, Jewish suffering, in which Jesus' loin cloth is replaced by the *Tallit* –'le Christ est judaïsé' (Foray 2003: 230–241).

National subjects have been rendered in a variety of 'modern' styles as artists poured old wine into new bottles: Neo-classical, Romantic, Naturalist, Impressionist, Expressionist, Cubist, Surrealist. Monet's series of the Cathedral of Rouen, of 1892–4, show a French national symbol in a luminous, Impressionist *enveloppe*. Picasso in his *Guernica* (1937) rendered the modern nationalist struggle in a most inventive, radically modern and, indeed, personal style. Symbolism, the use of the objective world to communicate the 'inner' world, has been particularly suited to national subject-matter, given the national artist's need to give form to ideas such as the nation and its virtues. Such is Friedrich's use of the oak tree to symbolise the German nation in *The Solitary Tree* (1822) (Vaughan 1994: 210–211). Mucha's murals for the Prague Town Hall combined Symbolism with Art Nouveau.

Second, national art could be ethno-cultural in both content and form. Dante-Gabriel Rossetti's interest in Dante, such as *Dantis Amor* (1859), a subject inspired by his own, Italian roots, is painted in such a 'primitive', revivalist, Pre-Raphaelite manner (Hilton 1979: 96). Gauguin's *The Four Breton Women* (1886) is characterised by a flatness which suggests that Gauguin was looking to popular woodblock prints such as the *Images d' Épinal* (House 1981: 73). And Mucha's later posters for various Czech events after independence employed a hybrid Parisian/Bohemian peasant style (Arwas 1993: 23).

And third, national art could be modern in content and ethno-cultural in form. Here, the revival by Kirchner and his group Brücke, founded in 1905, of the mediaeval woodcut as a specifically German artistic tradition, is a good example. Kirchner understood the expressive power of the woodcut which, as Magdalena M. Moeller has observed, 'had always been a characteristic of German art from Dürer, via Matthias Grünewald and Lucas Cranach the Elder' (Moeller 2003: 24). Kirchner was inspired in many ways by these German Old Masters, thereby 'revitalising German art' (Moeller 2003: 25). He treated such modern subjects as a nude woman in the studio wearing a black hat both as a woodcut and in oil, while the figure of the woman was modelled on *Venus* (1532), an oil painting by Lucas Cranach the Elder (Moeller 2003: 25). By positioning himself in this way within the tradition of German art Kirchner affirmed 'his German identity' while modernising it (Moeller 2003: 23).

We may conclude from the above that the divide has not been that great between modern art and national art. Many of the most cosmopolitan, avant-garde, anti-academic and innovative artists of the late nineteenth- and twentieth-centuries produced national art: art inspired by the national idea. They 'looked in', to use Victor Arwas' phrase, as well as 'out' (Arwas 1993: 23). Furthermore, the bridging of modernity and native tradition was the express aim of many artists, including, literally, the Brücke artists, and that most emphatically national*ist* art of the twentieth century, Fascist art (Fraquelli 1996: 130).

Much of Modernist propaganda advocated the total rejection of tradition. Nevertheless, many Modernist movements, not only Expressionism, but also Art Nouveau (despite its name) and Art Deco, were fired by a vision of Modernism which saw traditional styles in a 'modern way'. While borrowing from them, they modified and thereby modernised them (Hibou 2003: 91–98). In this way, they transformed historical and ethnic styles into modern, national styles. Thus, of most national art, as of most modern art, we can say, in the words of the Art Deco slogan, 'there is no modernity without tradition and there is no tradition without modernity'.

Conclusion

This article showed the emergence of a new category of art, national art. From the eighteenth century onwards, native, historical and ethno-cultural motifs became a dominant source of artistic subject-matter and aesthetic effect, both inside and outside Europe. It further showed the creative dynamism of this art, and its decisive role first, in modernising *ethnies* into nations, and second in modernising art.

Drawing on the work of Anthony D. Smith as well as John Hutchinson, this study indicated the participation of artists in the formulation, crystallisation and celebration of the ethno-cultural roots and identities of modern societies. These ethno-cultural identities transformed modern societies, made prosperous and free by the scientific, industrial and democratic revolutions, into nations.

So-called modern man refused to believe that he was made *ex nihilo*: that he was born without a navel (Smith and Gellner 1996). In the darkness of the Faustian night cast by the Enlightenment, it was as if he listened to the words of Isaiah's Watchman, made famous in sociological analysis by Max Weber: 'return, come' (Isaiah 21: 11,12). For as his reason freed him from the compulsion of inherited culture, it also enabled him to return to it as a lover.

Modern man realised that he could not live by bread alone, and that reason could not teach him how to live his life. Both reason and culture were vital (Gellner 1992). The return to and revival of the culture into which man was born before his 'Fall', before the revolutions, was embodied in the idea of the nation. It was a recognition of man's spirituality and spiritual achievement, where the idea of progress, as Weber has pointed out, does not apply (Weber 1957). The idea of the nation helped to stabilise and integrate modern personalities confronted by the cultural dilemmas of the age of reason.

As a carrier and generator of ethno-cultural symbols, national art has contributed first, to the ethno-cultural moralisation of the new, urban centres of modern life; and second, to the replacement of imperial ethno-national centres with native ones, following independence. By incorporating the native, ethno-cultural fund of the periphery into the subject-matter and styles of high, metropolitan and public art, artists transformed ethnicity into nationality – a state-sponsored status – and the nation into art.

References

Ades, Dawn. 1989. 'Indigenism and social realism' in Dawn Ades (ed.), *Art in Latin America: the Modern Era, 1820–1980*. New Haven, CT: Yale University Press, 195–213.

Anderson, Susan C. and Bruce H. Tabb (eds.). 2002. *Water, Leisure and Culture: European Historical Perspectives*. Oxford: Berg.

Arwas, Victor. 1993. 'Alphonse Mucha' in *Alphonse Mucha*. London: Barbican Art Gallery, 11–23.

Banton, Michael. 1998. *Racial Theories*. Cambridge: Cambridge University Press.

Barringer, Tim. 2002. Cat. Entry no. 24 'Mount Ktaadn' in Andrew Wilton and Tim Barringer. *American Sublime: Landscape Painting in the United States 1820–1880*. London: Tate Gallery.

Berlin, Isaiah. 1998. 'Herder and the Enlightenment' in Henry Hardy (ed.), *The Sense of Reality*. London: Pimlico, 359–435.

Biddiss, Michael. 1970. *Father of Racist Ideology: the Social and Political Thought of Count Gobineau*. London: Weidenfeld and Nicolson.

Bilski, Emily D. 1999. 'Images of identity and urban life: Jewish artists in turn-of-the-century Berlin' in Emily D. Bilski (ed.), *Berlin Metropolis: Jews and the New Culture 1890–1918*. Berkeley, CA: University of California Press, 103–45.

Clark, Kenneth. 1980. *The Nude*. Harmondsworth: Penguin.

Cowling, Elizabeth and Jennifer Mundy. 1990. *On Classic Ground: Picasso, Leger, de Chirico and the New Classicism 1910–1930*. London: Tate Gallery.

Crowley, David. 2000. 'Budapest: international metropolis and national capital' in Paul Greenhalgh (ed.), *Art Nouveau 1890–1914*, London: Victoria and Albert Museum, 346–59.

Dvořák, Anna. 2000. 'The Slav epic' in Sarah Mucha (ed.), *Alphonse Mucha*. Prague: Mucha Ltd and Malcolm Saunders, 147–53.

Éri, Gyöngyi and Zsuzsa Jobbágyi. (eds.). 1990. *A Golden Age: Art and Society in Hungary 1896–1914*. London: Barbican Art Gallery.

Facos, Michelle. 1998. *Nationalism and the Nordic Imagination: Swedish Art of the 1890s*. Berkeley, CA: University of California Press.

Facos, Michelle. 2002. 'A sound mind in a sound body: bathing in Sweden' in Susan C. Anderson and Bruce H. Tabb (eds.), *Water, Leisure and Culture: European Historical Perspectives*. London: Oxford: Berg, 105–17.

Foray, Jean-Michel. 2003. 'Autoportrait aux sept doigts' in *Chagall: Connu et Inconnu*. Paris: Grand Palais.

Fraquelli, Simonetta. 1996. 'All roads lead to Rome' in Dawn Ades et al. (eds.), *Art and Power:Europe under the Dictators 1930–45*. London: Thames and Hudson, 130–6.

Government of Zimbabwe. 1986. *A Guide to the Heroes Acre: Zimbabwe*. Harare: Government Printer.

Gellner, Ernest. 1992. *Reason and Culture*. Oxford: Blackwell.

Grand Palais. 1986. *La Sculpture Française au XIXe siècle*. Paris: Grand Palais.

Green, Christopher. 2000. *Art in France: 1900–1940*. New Haven, CT: Yale University Press.

Greenfeld, Liah. 1992. *Nationalism: Five Roads to Modernity*. Cambridge, MA: Harvard University Press.

Greenhalgh, Paul. 2000. '*Le style anglais*: English Roots of the new art' in Paul Greenhalgh (ed.), *Art Nouveau 1890-1914*. London: Victoria and Albert Museum, 126–45.

Grosby, Steven. 1994. 'The verdict of history: the inexpungeable tie of primordiality', *Ethnic and Racial Studies* 17: 164–71.

Grosby, Steven. 1995. 'Territoriality: the transcendental, primordial feature of modern societies', *Nations and Nationalism* 1(2): 143–62.

Grosby, Steven. 2001. 'Homeland' in Athena S. Leoussi (ed.), *Encyclopaedia of Nationalism*. New Brunswick, NJ: Transaction.

Hibou, J. 2003. 'National traditions' in Charlotte Benton and Tim Benton (eds.), *Art Deco 1910–1939*. London: Victoria and Albert Museum, 91–9.

Hilton, Timothy. 1979. *The Pre-Raphaelites*. London: Thames and Hudson.

Hobsbawm, Eric and Terence Ranger (eds.). 1983. *The Invention of Tradition*. Cambridge: Cambridge University Press.

Honour, Hugh. 1991 [1968]. *Neo-classicism*. London: Penguin.

Horowitz, Irving Louis. 1980. *Taking Lives: Genocide and State Power*. New Brunswick, NJ: Transaction.

House, John. 1981. Cat. Entry 82: 'The four Breton women' in *Post-Impresssionism*. London: Royal Academy of Arts.

Hutchinson, John. 1987. *The Dynamics of Cultural Nationalism: the Gaelic Revival and the Creation of the Irish Nation State*. London: Allen and Unwin.

Hutchinson, John. 1999. 'Re-interpreting cultural nationalism', *Australian Journal of Politics and History* 45(3): 392–407.

Kedourie, Elie. 1971. 'Introduction' in Elie Kedourie (ed.), *Nationalism in Asia and Africa*. London: Weidenfeld and Nicolson.

Kesting, Hermann 1982 [1965]. *Arminius: Biography of the Liberator, History of the Monument*. Detmold: Buchdruckerei und Verlag Hermann Bösmann GmbH.

Kohn, Hans. 1961 [1944]. *The Idea of Nationalism: a Study in its Origins and Background*. New York: Macmillan.

Ławniczakowa, Agnieszka. 1984. 'Jacek Malczewski' in *Symbolism in Polish Painting 1890–1914*. Detroit, MI: Detroit Institute of Arts, 56–75.

Leoussi, Athena S. 1998. *Nationalism and Classicism: the Classical Body as National Symbol in Nineteenth-Century England and France*. Houndmills: Macmillan.

Leoussi, Athena S. 2004. 'Text and image: dominant nations and state symbols in post-Soviet constitutions' in Athena S. Leoussi and Steven Grosby (eds.), *Nationality and Nationalism*. London: I.B.Tauris.

Leoussi, Athena S. and David Aberbach. 2002. 'Hellenism and Jewish nationalism: ambivalence and its ancient roots', *Ethnic and Racial Studies* 25(5): 755–77.

Linsley, Robert. 1988. 'Wilfredo Lam: painter of negritude', *Art History* 11(4): 527–44.

McCannon, John. 2000. 'In search of primeval Russia: stylistic evolution in the landscapes of Nicholas Roerich, 1897–1914', *Ecumene* 7(3): 271–97.

Mangan, J. A. 1999. 'Icon of monumental brutality: art and the Aryan man' in J. A. Mangan (ed.), *Shaping the Superman: Fascist Body as Political Icon–Aryan Fascism*. London: Frank Cass.

Margalit, Avishai. 2001. 'The crooked timber of nationalism' in Mark Lilla et al. (eds.), *The Legacy of Isaiah Berlin*. New York: New York Review of Books, 147–59.

Marsland, David. 2001. 'National symbols' in Athena S. Leoussi (ed.), *Encyclopaedia of Nationalism*. New Brunswick, NJ: Transaction, 220–22.

Miller, David. 1996. 'On nationality', *Nations and Nationalism* 2(3): 409–35.

Mitchell, Timothy F. 1993. *Art and Science in German Landscape Painting, 1770–1840*. Oxford: Clarendon.

Mitter, Partha. 1994. *Art and Nationalism in Colonial India, 1850–1922*. Cambridge: Cambridge University Press.

Moeller, Magdalena M. 2003. 'Kirchner as a German artist' in Jill Lloyd and Magdalena M. Moeller (eds.), *Ernst Ludwig Kirchner: the Dresden and Berlin Years*. London: Royal Academy of Arts, 23–5.

Mosse, George L. 1975. *The Nationalization of the Masses: Political Symbolism and Mass Movements in Germany from the Napoleonic Wars through the Third Reich*. New York: Cornell University Press.

Murray, Peter and Linda Murray. 1979. *The Penguin Dictionary of Art and Artists*. Harmondsworth: Penguin.

Rosenblum, Robert. 1996. 'The Spanishness of Picasso's still lifes' in Jonathan Brown (ed.), *Picasso and the Spanish Tradition*. New Haven, CT: Yale University Press, 61–93.

Royal Academy of Arts. 2000. *Masters of Colour*. London: Royal Academy of Arts.

Shils, Edward. 1975. *Center and Periphery: Essays in Macrosociology*. Chicago, IL: University of Chicago Press.

Smith, Anthony D. 1981. 'States and Homelands', *Millennium* 10(3): 187–202.

Smith, Anthony D. 1986. *The Ethnic Origins of Nations*. Oxford: Blackwell.

Smith, Anthony D. 1991. *National Identity*. Harmondsworth: Penguin.

Smith, Anthony D. 1993. 'Art and national identity in Europe,' in J. C. H. Blom et al. (eds.), *De onmacht van het grote: cultuur in Europa*. Amsterdam: Amsterdam University Press.

Smith, Anthony D. 1995. *Nations and Nationalism in a Global Era*. Cambridge: Polity.

Smith, Anthony D. and Ernest Gellner. 1996. 'The nation: real or imagined?', *Nations and Nationalism* 2(3): 357–70.

Smith, Anthony D. 2001. 'Nations and history' in Montserrat Guibernau and John Hutchinson (eds.), *Understanding Nationalism*. Cambridge: Polity, 9–31.

Smith, Anthony D. 2002. 'When is a nation?', *Geopolitics* 7(2): 5–32.

Thiesse, Anne-Marie. 1991. *Écrire la France, le mouvement littéraire régionaliste de la Belle Époque à la Libération*. Paris: Presses Universitaires de France.

Thiesse, Anne-Marie. 1997. *Ils apprenaient la France, l'exaltation des régions dans le discours patriotique*. Paris: Éditions de la Maison des Sciences de l'Homme.

Vaughan, William. 1994. 'Romanticism' in Keith Hartley et al. (eds.), *The Romantic Spirit in German Art 1790–1990*. Edinburgh: Scottish National Gallery of Modern Art and London: Hayward Gallery, South Bank Centre, 210–11.

Vaughan, William. 1999. *British Painting: the Golden Age from Hogarth to Turner*. London: Thames and Hudson.

Weber, Max. 1930. *The Protestant Ethic and the Spirit of Capitalism*, trans. T. Parsons, London: Unwin.

Weber, Max. 1957. 'Science as a vocation' in *From Max Weber: Essays in Sociology*, H. H. Gerth and C. Wright Mills (eds.), London: Routledge & Kegan Paul.

Wittlich, Petr. 2000. *Alfons Mucha in the Municipal House*. Prague: Municipal House.

11

Nationalism and globalisation

MARY KALDOR

Eric Hobsbawm argues that the current wave of nationalism will be short-lived. Nationalism, he suggests, is an anachronism best suited to an earlier historical period dominated by industrialisation and print technology. In a much quoted passage, he wrote: 'The owl of Minerva, which brings wisdom, says Hegel, flies out at dusk. It is a good sign that it is now circling round nations and nationalism' (Hobsbawm 1990: 181).

Anthony Smith takes the opposite view. He does not think that nations have been transcended in the global era. On the contrary, the current wave of nationalism to be observed in various parts of the world testifies to the enduring nature of the national idea, the way in which it responds to some deep-felt human need.

'It would be folly to predict an early supersession of nationalism and an imminent transcendence of the nation. Both remain indispensable elements of an interdependent world and a mass-communications culture. For a global culture seems unable to offer the qualities of collective faith, dignity, and hope that only a "religious surrogate" with its promise of a territorial culture-community across the generations, can provide. Over and beyond any political and economic benefits that ethnic nationalism can confer, it is the promise of collective and territorial immortality, outfacing death and oblivion, that has helped to sustain so many nations and nation-states in an era of unprecedented social change and to renew so many ethnic minorities that seemed to be doomed in an era of technological uniformity and corporate efficiency' (Smith, 1995: 160).

In addressing this debate, I want to emphasise the political character of nationalism. I do not agree that nationalism necessarily possesses the kind of transcendent character attributed to it by Anthony Smith. Like Renan, I consider nationalism to be a political process, a 'daily plebiscite', a subjective affirmation and re-affirmation; nationalism will only persist to the extent that individuals, movements, and groups choose to be nationalists. On the other hand, I do not think that nationalism will necessarily go away in an era of globalisation. We are in the midst of a period of political experimentation, as earlier political ideas and institutions have been eroded by dramatic socio-economic and cultural change. Various political ideologies are currently in competition, including market fundamentalism, global Islam, cosmopolitanism, Europeanism, and, of course, nationalism. Some of these ideologies are forward-looking or reformist, that is to say, they offer a policy prescription for coming to terms with underlying structural change, ways in which individuals are expected to be able to benefit from globalisation. Others are backward-looking or regressive, appealing to an imagined past, and proposing to reverse at least some aspects of the current changes. Future developments will be determined by the outcome of this competition; unfortunately, there is no a priori reason to suggest that the more forward-looking ideologies will triumph over the backward-looking ideologies.

One of these ideologies is nationalism. What I call the 'new nationalism' is both shaped by, and shapes, the various phenomena we bunch together under the rubric of globalisation. I would argue that the 'new nationalism' is regressive, and, in so far as it persists, will contribute to a wild, anarchic form of globalisation, characterised by violence and inequality. I do not exclude the possibility of forward-looking small nationalisms, as suggested by Guibernau (1996), but I would argue that they have to be situated within a broader cosmopolitan perspective.

In developing this argument, I will start with some preliminary remarks about the theoretical debate on nationalism and how the changing global context alters the parameters of this debate. I will then describe some of the key features of the 'new nationalism', with particular attention to global Islam, which is a new phenomenon, sharing some but not all of the characteristics of the new nationalism. Finally, I will discuss the potential for cosmopolitan and/ or European ideologies. In the conclusion, I will sketch out the possible scenarios that might follow from different ideological combinations.

In defence of the modernist paradigm

What Smith has dubbed the modernist paradigm, argues that nationalism is a modern phenomenon, inextricably linked to the rise of the modern state and to industrialisation. Perennialists, primordialists, and ethno-symbolists criticise the modernist paradigm on several grounds (see, for example, Smith 2001; Özkirimli 2000).

First, they argue that the modernists, and in particular the work of Ernest Gellner, are too functionalist. Gellner suggests that the modern state and modern industry requires what he calls 'modular man'. The term 'modular' is taken from the idea of modular furniture in which components can be fitted together in different ways, while maintaining a harmonious whole. Modular man has certain basic skills including a shared language and can adapt himself to a variety of positions in modern society. Modular man is 'capable of performing highly diverse tasks in the same general cultural idiom, if necessary reading up manuals of specific jobs in the general standard style of the culture in question.' (Gellner 1994: 102) Nationalism, the principle that the cultural and political unit is congruent, is a collective ideology, ideally suited to the construction of modular man, making possible everyday encounters with the state and modern industry.

Gellner contrasts the vertical territorially based national cultures typical of modernity with the more differentiated cultures of traditional societies. Before the invention of printing and the spread of writing in vernacular languages, it was possible to distinguish between horizontal, i.e. non-territorial, 'high cultures' generally based on religion and a scholarly written language, e.g. Latin, Persian or Sanskrit, and a variety of local vertical low cultures (Gellner 1983). The emergence of national cultures is associated with the rise of the modern state and the spread of primary education. One of the many local cultures is elevated through printing and education and spread within a territorial area bounded by the state.

The functionalist critique, in my view, fails to take into account the complex relationship between agency and structure. Structural arguments, which are typical of the modernist paradigm are not necessarily determinist arguments. Rather they point to the importance of structural change and the ways in which different political initiatives or ideologies are helped or hindered by structural conditions. Politics is always about experiment; some policies succeed in the sense of increasing the legitimacy of political institutions and others fail. Success, at least to some extent, depends on underlying structural conditions. The validity of the modernist argument does not derive from a linear relationship between nationalism and industrialisation or the rise of the modern state. The modernist argument, for example, does not need to hold that nationalism arose in order to create the conditions for industrialisation nor that nationalism is an inevitable outcome of industrialisation, although I do think that one aspect of industrialisation, namely print technology, is a critical component in the rise of nationalism. The rise of the national idea may come about autonomously as a consequence of a variety of factors; the point is rather that as an ideology it fits the modern state and industrialisation. Nationalism, industrialisation and the modern state reinforce each other, although not always harmoniously.

A second related criticism is that the modernist paradigm is too instrumentalist. Modernists, like Gellner or Hobsbawm, suggest that nationalism is inculcated from above through the state's control of culture, particularly language policies and education. Hobsbawm talks about 'social engineering' and 'invention'. Even the variant of modernism put forward by Anderson that the nation is 'imagined' through the spread of secular literature in the vernacular like the newspaper or the novel, is criticised on the grounds of artificiality (Anderson 1983). Even though there are important elements of mobilisation from above, the critics would argue that nationalism only succeeds where it has some popular resonance, appealing to 'authentic' sentiments among ordinary people that derive from folk memories, traditions and customs. I share the view that the populist appeal of nationalism has to reflect populist sentiment. But that sentiment is not necessarily cultural or ethnic; indeed the view that ordinary people need ethnic or cultural symbols seems to me to be over paternalistic. Popular sentiment can also be based on political demands – for democracy, for example, or anti-colonialism. This difference between the political and cultural bases of nationalism mirrors the distinction between civic or ethnic nationalism or between Western and Eastern nationalism. According to Hans Kohn, the Western 'nations emerged as voluntary unions of citizens. Individuals expressed their will in contracts, covenants and plebiscites. Integration was achieved around a political idea and special emphasis was laid on the universal similarities of nations. In the non-Western world, the nation was regarded as a political unit centering around the irrational pre-civilized folk concept. Nationalism found its rallying point in the folk community, elevating it to the dignity of an ideal or a mystery. Here emphasis was placed on the diversity or self-sufficiency of nations' (Quoted in Özkirimli 2000: 42).

Anthony Smith argues that this distinction is overdrawn and that in both variants of nationalism, both political and cultural elements are to be found. This is probably true but I would argue the more open and democratic a society, the more likely it is that nationalism is a forward-looking political project, and the more authoritarian and closed the society, the more likely it is that popular mobilisation will build on cultural and religious traditions.

Related to the instrumentalist criticism is the charge of 'blocking presentism', that modernists focus exclusively on the present generation. Those who argue that nationalism has to have some ethnic popular resonance insist that the nation has to have some pre-history. Nationalism, they say, is not invented or engineered; rather it is reconstructed and reinvented out of the past. Smith strongly disagrees with Gellner that any old 'cultural shred or patch' will serve the nationalists purpose (quoted in Smith 2001: 65). He says:

We need to understand nationalism as a type of collective conduct, based on the collective will of a moral community and the shared emotions of a putatively ancestral community and this means that we need to grasp the nation as a political form of the sacred community of citizens. (Smith 2001: 82)

But I am concerned about 'blocking pastism'. The focus on the history or pre-history of the nation often obscures the everyday experiences and concerns of present generations, why, for example, people who have lived together for centuries as is the case in many less modernised and therefore culturally rich societies, should come into conflict with each other. It also carries with it a sort of determinism, that can be very oppressive, the notion that people cannot escape from their ethnic pasts.

A third and related argument is about passion. The modernists, says Smith, cannot account for the passion of nationalism. They cannot answer the question: why die for the nation? For Smith, the answer lies in the 'sacred community' of shared memories and ancestry. I would suggest another answer and that is war. Passion and, indeed, religious feelings, are closely connected with death, as Smith himself argues. Indeed, I would invert the argument and suggest that war constructs nationalism rather than the other way round. That is why military heroes and battles are such an important part of the nationalist narrative. Nationalism has to be understood, I would argue, as a nodal point in the intimate relation between the modern state and war. This is a point made by both Charles Tilly and Michael Mann. In the eighteenth and nineteenth centuries, the state's monopoly of violence was established through war, which led to increases in taxation, conscription, war loans and the increased reach and efficiency of public administration, as well as the consolidation of the idea of the 'nation'. This idea was reproduced through conscription and military drill in an imagined war. Both the idea of the 'nation' and the idea of the 'other' were given substance in war. Earlier wars were about religion or about a variety of overlapping and competing sovereignties (fiefdoms, city states, princely states, etc.) and created similarly differentiated loyalties. In the eighteenth and nineteenth centuries, national wars between states became, in Europe, the predominant form of warfare. Clausewitz well expounded the extremist logic that followed from popular mobilisation for war.

The sharp distinction between the internal and external functions of the state dates from this period. The internal functions had to do with the preservation of the rule of law, public services, cultural and socio-economic policies, and, at least in the west, respect for individual rights and citizenship. The external function of the state was defence of the nation as a whole.

The link between nationalism and war was well understood by contemporary thinkers. One of the earliest theorists of nationalism, Heinrich von Trietschke, argued that: 'It is only in the common performance of heroic deeds for the sake of the fatherland that a nation becomes truly and spiritually united.' Echoing Hegel, he insisted on the role of war and bravery in upholding the collective idea:

'The individual must forget his own ego and feel himself a member of the whole; he must recognise what a nothing his life is in comparison with the general welfare. The individual must sacrifice himself for a higher community of which he is a member; but the state is itself the highest in the external community of men' (quoted in Guibernau 1996: 8).

Of course, there were liberal nationalist thinkers like Mill, Hugo or Mazzini, who conceived of nationalism as a democratic project and who thought that the spread of nationalism would end wars. But these were modernist thinkers. For them, nationalism was about reason not passion and they entertained the possibility of the nation as a temporary historical phenomenon.

The argument of Hobsbawm and others that nationalism is a passing phenomenon no longer suited to current structural conditions is sometimes used by critics of the modernist paradigm as evidence for the weakness of the paradigm. Guibernau, for example, suggests that Gellner's argument about the way in which industrialism's demands for homogeneity leads to 'culturally unalloyed nations' is much too simple 'when applied to a world in which globalisation processes favour constant cultural interconnectedness. If Gellner is right, we should be witnessing a tendency towards a single uniform world nationalism. But in fact, the effect is exactly the opposite' (Guibernau 1996:

78). But this is an overly simple description of globalisation. The modernist paradigm is about the construction of ideology in the context of structural change. Globalisation processes do not only favour cultural interconnectedness, they favour cultural disconnectedness as well. Globalisation breaks down the homogeneity of the nation-state. Globalisation involves diversity as well as uniformity, the local as well as the global. I would like to point to three changes, in particular, that have implications for the future of nationalism.

First of all, the rise of the information-based economy reduces the importance of territorially based industrial production. The global economy is both more transnational and more local. Growing sectors of the economy like finance and research and development are increasingly global. At the same time, markets are increasingly specialised and local as profits are increasingly derived from catering to a differentiated market (economies of scope) rather than from low cost mass production (economies of scale). What we are witnessing is a profound change in the division of labour. On the one hand, there is a growing class of what Robert Reich calls 'symbolic analysts', people who work with abstract symbols in finance, technology, education, or welfare. These are the graduates of the explosion in tertiary education, who communicate across borders and generally speak a global language, usually English. On the other hand, there is a growing underclass of people who service the new symbolic analysts, who work in the informal sector and who trade in cultural diversity through a variety of menial tasks. The classic industrial worker who formed the backbone of the nationalist ideology is increasingly marginalised.

Secondly, the shift from print technology to electronic communications has momentous implications, which it is probably much too soon to describe. On the one hand, as many analysts of globalisation point out, Internet, satellite television, faxes and air travel make possible new global virtual communities (Kaldor-Robinson 2002). On the other hand, radio and television reach out to local communities that do not have the reading habit and make possible much more rapid and dramatic political mobilisation.

Thirdly, a crucial change is in the nature of war. War between states as in the eighteenth, nineteenth and early twentieth century is becoming increasingly rare. I agree with Smith when he says that globalisation does not mean a decline in the nation state but rather a change in its functions. 'What we have been witnessing is a shift in state functions and powers from the economic and the military to the social and cultural spheres, and from external sovereignty to internal domestic control' (Smith 2001: 125). But I believe he underestimates the extent to which the loss of external sovereignty and the decline of the military function weakens the potential for reproducing the national idea. Instead of war, we are experiencing new kinds of political violence that are both local and transnational – terrorism, 'new wars', and American high tech wars. And these new forms of violence are constructing new ideologies as I shall discuss below.

One of the developments often neglected by theorists of nationalism is blocism, which, for 50 years, supplanted nationalism, at least in Europe. Writing in 1945, E. H. Carr wrote that nationalism is under attack.

'On the plane of morality, it is under attack from those who denounce its inherently totalitarian nature and proclaim that any international authority worth the name must interest itself in the rights and well-being not of nations but of men and women. On the plane of power, it is being sapped by modern technological developments, which have made the nation obsolescent as the unit of military and economic organisation and are rapidly concentrating effective decision and control in the hands of great multi-national units' (quoted in Özkirimli 2000: 47). These 'great multi-national units' were held together through new non-nationalist ideologies constructed out of a great imaginary war far surpassing anything nations had ever achieved. The west was bound together in an imagined struggle of democracy against totalitarianism, while the Eastern bloc cast the struggle as one between socialism and capitalism (Kaldor 1990). Blocism, I would argue, was a transitional phenomenon, combining both the new 'post-modern' elements of horizontal transnational association with a traditional emphasis on territory. Blocism was ideally suited to the Fordist large-scale model of mass production. Blocism failed, I would argue, both because new communications made it impossible to sustain ideologies within closed territorial units and because it was not possible to sustain the imminent idea of war. The collapse of blocism created an ideological vacuum into which rushed a range of new ideologies, including the revival of nationalism.

Contemporary nationalisms

A friend from Nagorno Karabakh was visiting England at the time of the Jubilee celebrations. He had been one of the founders of the Karabakh Committee, established in the last years of Soviet rule, to demand that Karabakh, a predominantly Armenian enclave inside Azerbaijan, should become part of Armenia. A bloody war followed after the break-up of the Soviet Union – some 150,000 people were killed and over a million people were forced to flee their homes from Armenia and Azerbaijan as well as Nagorno Karabakh. My friend joined the crowds in the Mall, waving flags as the Queen and the royal family passed by. 'So what do you think of British nationalism?' I asked him afterwards. 'That's not nationalism' he replied, 'that was a Soviet crowd. Nationalism is about passion.'

The jubilee celebrations, like the May Day parades in the Soviet Union or the images of Bush on an aircraft carrier at the moment of supposed victory in Iraq, are one form of contemporary nationalism, what I would call 'spectacle nationalism'. Spectacle nationalism is an evolution from the more militant nationalism of the first half of the twentieth century. It is official ideology, that is to say, the ideology that serves to legitimise existing states. It requires passive participation, watching television or joining a crowd but its capacity to mobilise active participation such as paying taxes or risking one's life in wars is greatly weakened. It has something in common with 'banal nationalism' although it involves consciously mediated construction, spectacular events like the Jubilee celebrations.

What I call the new nationalism is to be found in places like Nagorno Karabakh or Bosnia-Herzegovina and is bred in conditions of insecurity and violence. The new nationalism is exclusive, that is to say, it excludes others of a different nationality, and has much in common with religious fundamentalism, the insistence that religious doctrines be followed rigidly and imposed on others. Indeed, there is a considerable overlap between militant nationalist and religious movements (see Kaldor and Muro, 2003). This is not only because of the religious character of nationalism but also because many nations are defined in religious terms – Bosnian Muslims, for example, or Hindu nationalists – and many religions are described in national terms – Judaism, for example, or Islam.

In the last two decades, we have seen an increased political presence of these groups both in electoral terms and through their involvement in violent episodes, both terrorism and war. These movements have to be understood, not as throwbacks to the past, but as phenomena closely connected to contemporary structural conditions. Just as earlier nationalisms have to be explained in terms of the first phase of modernity, so the new nationalism is both shaped by and shapes what is variously described as globalisation, post-modernity, or late modernity. It is often claimed that the new nationalism was repressed or frozen during the Cold War years only to burst forth when the Cold War was over. I would argue that, on the contrary, the new nationalism has been constructed or invented in the post-Cold War period. Both the electronic media and new forms of violence have been important tools of construction.

Like earlier nationalisms, the new militancy was constructed both 'from above' and 'from below'. Political leaders have tended to use nationalist and religious appeals when other tools of political mobilisation have failed. Often it was secular leaders who opened the space for these ideologies. Thus the Congress Party in India began to use Hindu rhetoric long before the rise of the BJP. In the former Yugoslavia and Soviet Union, nationalism grew within the administrative confines of the centrally planned system because other forms of ideological competition were excluded. In Africa, patrimonial leaders used tribal networks as a way of rationing out scarce governmental resources. And in the Middle East, the failures of Arab nationalism led many leaders to emphasise a religious identity and the conflict with Israel.

Smith would argue that these efforts at political mobilisation only succeed if they appeal to some popular sentiments derived from memory and tradition. It is undoubtedly true that memories of violence, especially not too long ago, facilitate mobilisation. Today's Hindu–Muslim clashes reproduce the clashes of previous generations, while in former Yugoslavia, living memories of atrocities during World War II provide a fertile source for contemporary nationalism. All the same, it is insecurity and frustration resulting from dramatic structural change that provides a more convincing explanation for why today's generation, often brought up in multi-cultural environments, are so vulnerable to exclusive ideologies. The last two decades have witnessed, in many regions, substantial decline in state provision and public employment, rapid urbanisation, the growth of an informal criminalised economy and large-scale migration from countryside to town and from poor countries to the industrialised West. Typical recruits to these movements are the restless young men, often educated for roles that no longer exist because of the decline of the state or of the industrial sector, often unable to marry because they lack income, and sometimes needing to legitimate semi-criminal activities in which they can find their only source of income. Membership in nationalist or religious groups offers meaning, a sense of historical relevance, and also adventure.

Related to the sense of insecurity is the encounter with globalisation and the sense of impotence that arises when crucial decisions that affect everyday life are taken further and further away. The young men that committed suicide on September 11 were all educated in the West. This is typical of many nationalist and religious militants. Seselj, the leader of the extreme nationalist Serb party, had written his PhD at the University of Michigan. Many of those who are mobilised are migrants, either from countryside to town or from South to West, who have experienced the loss of ties to their places of origin and yet do not feel integrated in their new homes.

The ideologies of these movements can be described as both modern and anti-modern. Most new nationalists believe in territorially based sovereignty and their goal is to control existing states or to create new states, in the name of the nation or the religion. But their ideology is anti-modern in its rejection of the doubt and questioning that characterises modern society; in its vision of a pure and unpolluted past, on nostalgia for a golden age when the aspirations of the nation or religion were fulfilled; and, above all, in the idea of a cosmic struggle between good and evil that is the most common shared characteristic of these movements. These ideologies are backward-looking in that they want to revert to a modern, e.g. pre-globalisation, conception of the nation-state.

The organisation and strategies of these movements, on the other hand, are typical of 'late modernity' and make use of the various phenomena that are known as globalisation. In organisational terms, the new nationalism tends to be transnational. Although the goals are often local, the organisation depends on the construction of a horizontal network of supporters, involving migrant communities in other countries – Diasporas often play a critical role. In many cases, these movements create parallel structures – religious schools for example or humanitarian NGOs – that fill the vacuum left by the decline in state provision. Funding comes from wealthy supporters in the Diaspora or else through a range of criminal and informal activities.

All of these groups make use of the 'new media' – television, Internet, video cassettes – both for linking the network and for political mobilisation.

Many groups have their own TV or Radio Channels. Hindu nationalists benefit from the new Satellite Channel, Star TV. Serbian television paid a critical role in the years leading up to the Yugoslav wars in promoting nationalist propaganda, interchanging contemporary events with the Second World War and the 1389 Battle of Kosovo. Bin Laden's speeches are circulated through video cassettes world-wide. In Africa, the radio is literally magic, and it was Milles Collines Hate Radio that incited the genocide in Rwanda.

For many of these movements, violence is a central strategy for political mobilisation. In earlier wars or guerrilla struggles, violence was directed against strategic targets such as the capture of territory or attacks on radio stations or important officials as part of a clear strategy; political mobilisation was needed to implement the strategy. Nowadays, violence is directed against symbolic targets and against civilians. Symbolic violence is a form of message, a way of making a statement. Terrorist attacks against civilians are typical of 'symbolic violence'. Violence is 'deliberately exaggerated' and often macabre. The Lord's Resistance Army in Uganda cuts off ears and lips. Hamas suicide bombers put nails in their bombs so as to kill as many people as possible. Juergensmayer likens 'symbolic violence' to theatre – these are what he calls 'performance acts' – 'stunning, abnormal and outrageous murders carried out in a way that graphically displays the power of violence – set within grand scenarios of conflict and proclamation' (Juergensmayer 2000: 222). The targets of such attacks are often important symbols – the World Trade Towers, the Federal Building in Oklahoma that symbolised welfare and gun control, the Mosque in Ayodha. These 'rituals of violence' carry with them an other-worldly significance and produce the sense of struggle, of Armageddon or Jihad, or of cosmic war.

The theatrical character of much violence is illustrated by the way many of the perpetrators dress up for killing as though it is not they themselves who perform the acts. The notorious Frenki's Boys, who were responsible for atrocities in Bosnia and Kosovo, wore cowboy hats over ski masks and painted Indian stripes on their faces. Their trademark was the sign of the Serbian Chetniks and a silhouette of a destroyed city with the words 'City Breakers' in English. Joseph Kony, the leader of the Lord's Resistance Army, wears aviator sunglasses and dresses his hair in beaded braids hanging to his neck; sometimes he wears women's clothes.

But violence is not merely symbolic, not just 'letters to Israel' as one Hamas activist described the suicide bombers. In many of the recent armed conflicts, the aim has been deliberate elimination or indeed extermination of the 'other'. The Hutus in Rwanda wanted to get rid of the Tutsis, just as Hitler wanted to get rid of the Jews. The goal of the wars in the former Yugoslavia or the South Caucasus was to create ethnically pure territories. In these cases, exaggerated violence was aimed at making people hate their homes. Systematic rape, for example, was widespread in the former Yugoslavia. This was rape, not as a side effect of war, but as a deliberate weapon of war with the aim of making women, particularly Muslim women, feel ashamed and defiled so that they would not want to return to their homes. Likewise violence against symbolic targets was aimed at removing any trace of the culture of the 'other'. In Banja Luka, during the Bosnian war, two unique sixteenth century Ottoman mosques were razed to the ground. They were blown up on a Friday and a Monday, the bulldozers came and grassed over the site so that you would never know they ever existed.

These new forms of violence can be understood the way that the extremist groups succeed in mobilising extremist sentiment. It is in situations of pervasive insecurity that fear and hatred, passion and prejudice, are more likely to come to dominate political choices. For example, it is difficult to explain the suicide bombers in Palestine as a way of achieving a Palestinian state, just as it is difficult to explain the brutal Israeli responses as a way of improving security. But if the goal is to strengthen extremist sentiment – support for Hamas or the extreme Zionist groups, what is happening is much easier to explain.

In the former Yugoslavia, the killings and displacement in the various conflicts generated the very ideologies that were supposed to have been the cause of the conflict. They left a legacy of fear and hatred, of memories of lost relatives, which provide the fuel for a grass roots nationalist passion that is much more pervasive than before the wars. Indeed this may be the point of the violence. People in Bosnia will tell you that 'the war had to be so bloody because we did not hate each other'. Something similar happened in Nagorno Karabakh. The idea that political control depends on the expulsion of those with a different nationality, says one commentator, 'spread as the scale and intensity of the conflict increased' and was 'converted into a deadly ideology by fears of pre-emption and memories of past blood shed' (Melander 2001: 65).

In the late 1990s, a new variant of the new nationalism emerged with wholly novel features. This was the ideology of global Islam promulgated by Osama Bin Laden and Al Qaeda. Of course, this is a religious movement but the ideologists of the movement talk about the 'Islamic nation' and the basic idea of uniting around a common culture, Islam and a religious language, Arabic, is a nationalist idea. It is a network, typical of the global era. It is built up through new forms of communication (Internet, the circulation of video cassettes, the use of satellite television, i.e. Al Jazeera, as well as air travel) and new forms of violent struggle.

The ideology seems to have emerged sometime in the mid-1990s when Bin Laden spent time in Sudan and made contacts with a range of Islamic groups, including those who had fought in Southeast Asia and in Bosnia and Chechnya. The elements that mark this ideology out as a new phenomenon are:

- First, the global character of the discourse. There are huge differences among Islamic groups both in doctrine and in goals; most political groups are oriented towards local institutions. Bin Laden's hero was Saladin, the Kurdish commander who united Islamic groups against the Crusaders in the twelfth century. Bin Laden's aim was to copy Saladin and to unite these disparate Islamic groups in a global struggle. In August 1996, he issued his 'World Declaration against the Americans occupying the lands of the two holy places', which was the first time the focus of political Islam had been directed towards the USA. 'It should not be hidden from you' says the Declaration that 'the people of Islam have suffered from aggression, iniquity, and injustice imposed on them by the Zionist-Crusaders Alliance and their collaborators…[Muslim] blood was spilled in Palestine and Iraq. The horrifying pictures of the massacre of Qana in Lebanon are still fresh in our memory. Massacres in Tadjikistan, Burma, Kashmir, Azzam, the Philippines…Ogaden, Somalia, Eritrea, Chechnya, and Bosnia-Herzegovina…send shivers in the body and shake the conscience' (quoted in Burke 2003: 147).[1]

- A second novel element is the focus on spectacular violence, using 'martyrs' (suicide bombers) in 'raids'.[2] The targets are no longer local but global and the 'raid' is designed for maximum media impact – hence both the symbolic character of the targets and the high level of civilian casualties. The raids are viewed as 'jihad as testament', demonstrating to spectators an incredible self-sacrifice for the faith or the nation.

- Thirdly, global Islam is much more 'anti-political' than earlier variants of political Islam, which were directed at winning power in local contexts. In part, the rise of Al Qaeda reflects the marginalisation of political Islam – many commentators have argued that political Islam had passed its peak by the late 1980s. The current version of global Islam is much more preoccupied with political mobilisation than with specific goals. Of course, Bin Laden and others do express specific demands – for the withdrawal of Americans from Saudi Arabia, or for a Muslim caliphate in the Middle East. But as Bin Laden put it in 1999: 'We seek to instigate the [Islamic] nation to get up and liberate its land' (Burke 2003: 35). The attack on the World Trade Towers succeeded probably beyond the wildest dreams of the perpetrators, in publicising the global Islamic idea. In December 2001, in a videotaped message to Al Jazeera, he said : 'Regardless if Osama is killed or survives, the awakening has started, praise be to God' (Burke 2003: 238). A parallel can be drawn with revolutionary terror. The discourse legitimises nihilistic acts of anger and frustration. And where the idea is millenarian, i.e. conceived around some future utopia of liberation, what matters is mobilisation not the achievement of specific goals.

Al Qaeda as an organisation had its heyday in the period 1996–2001, when its infrastructure in Afghanistan was able to provide a focal point for training, funding and expert advice on what appear to have been relatively autonomous operations by different local groups (see Glasius and Kaldor 2002). This infrastructure was destroyed in 2001. Nevertheless, the ideology appears to be more powerful than ever. The American 'war on terror' has fed the idea of cosmic struggle and elevated the movement to a worthy enemy of America. The apparent swarming of Islamic militants into Iraq bears testimony to its continuing appeal. As Burke puts it:

The legitimising discourse, the critical element that converts an angry young man into a human bomb, is now everywhere. You will hear it in a mosque, on the Internet, from friends, in a newspaper. You do not have to travel to Afghanistan to complete the radicalising process; you can do it in your front room, in an Islamic centre, in a park (Burke 2003: 248).

Cosmopolitan or European politics

There is, of course, another type of contemporary nationalism and this is the small nationalism of ethnic minorities who survive in states where national homogenisation was incomplete but which, unlike the new nationalism described above, are non-violent, open and inclusive. I am thinking of Scotland, Catalonia, or Transylvania. Some would say that the distinction between these nationalisms and the new nationalism is artificial just as Kohn's distinction between Eastern and Western nationalism is overdrawn. But the distinction is important because it is about cultural diversity as opposed to cultural homogeneity. The new nationalism favours cultural homogeneity both large (i.e. Hindu nationalism or global Islam or anti-immigrationism in Europe) and small (i.e. Croats, Abkhazians, Chechens) and is therefore closed and exclusive. But small nationalism can also be about enhancing democracy at local levels, and the defence of cultural diversity. There are, of course, both camps in places like Scotland or Transylvania, though in these two cases, the democratic process has tended to override ethnic division (see Gruber 1999). It is important to stress the distinction between the two types because it illustrates what is meant by cosmopolitanism.

Critics of the modernist paradigm also tend to be critics of the cosmopolitan idea. This is because modernists argue that the nation is a temporary phenomenon. 'The nations are not something eternal. They had their beginnings and they will end' (Renan, 1990: 20). Modernists, therefore, tend to favour what they see as more forward-looking ideologies better suited to the structural conditions associated with globalisation.

Two kinds of criticism are levelled by the critics of the modernist paradigm against the cosmopolitan, and by implication European, idea. One is that there is no such thing as a global culture or if there were, it would be a grey, technological uniform culture, incapable of generating passionate loyalties. This is a misunderstanding of the meaning of the term 'cosmopolitanism'. Culturally, cosmopolitanism means openness to different cultures. According to Urry, cosmopolitanism is 'a cultural disposition involving an intellectual and aesthetic stance of 'openness' towards peoples, places and experiences from different cultures, especially those from different 'nations'. Cosmopolitanism should involve the search for, and delight in, the contrasts between societies rather than a longing for superiority or for uniformity' (Urry 2000). Politically, cosmopolitanism must be distinguished from humanism. Humanism is about universal human values, what we now call human rights. Cosmopolitanism combines humanism with a celebration of human diversity. In *Perpetual Peace* from which the political meaning is derived, Kant describes a world of nation-states in which cosmopolitan right overrides sovereignty. Kant says that, the condition for perpetual peace, is that cosmopolitan right be confined to the right of hospitality. What he means by this is treating strangers with dignity. Kant, writing at the end of the eighteenth century, was opposed to colonialism but he also criticised those natives who maltreated their European visitors. The right of hospitality means both respect for human rights and respect for difference (Kant 1991).

A similar point is made by Anthony Appiah (1996) in his article on 'Cosmopolitan patriots'. Appiah talks about the importance of the notion of a 'rooted cosmopolitan', someone who loves his or her homeland and culture and feels a responsibility towards making that homeland a better place. But a cosmopolitan is also free to choose the place where he or she lives and the practises in which they take part; you can migrate out of choice not through pressure and choose to respect some traditions and not others. Patriotism can mean freedom not exclusion. A cosmopolitan politics would be one which insisted both on global guarantees for human rights and on a global strategy for promoting the survival of cultures. What makes Sarajevo, for example, such a vibrant place, is precisely the fact that different cultures have survived side by side for so long – the mosque, the orthodox church, the catholic church and the synagogue are all within a few hundred yards of each other. A cosmopolitan is proud of such diversity. A cosmopolitan respects these different practises and rejoices at the fact that they can co-exist.

The second criticism is that a cosmopolitan or European culture has no memory. According to Smith:

[A] timeless global culture answers no living needs and conjures no memories. If memory is central to identity, we can discern no global identity in the making, nor aspirations for one, nor any collective amnesia to replace existing 'deep' cultures with a cosmopolitan 'flat' culture. The latter remains a dream confined to some intellectuals. It strikes no chord among the vast masses of people divided into their habitual communities of class, gender, region, religion and culture (Smith 1995: 24).

Indeed, Smith goes even further and suggests that a European culture would need to forget all the bad things that have happened – wars, imperialism, and the holocaust. This astonishing claim illustrates the way in which the critics of modernism tend to neglect the political character of ideology. Just as national ideologies in Western Europe arose out of demands for democracy, so a European ideology is being built out of demands for human rights and an end to wars. The two main waves of Europeanism were after 1945, when the European movement was founded in the Hague in reaction to the horror of war, and, after 1989 and the end of the Cold War with the coming together of peace and human rights movements.

Far from forgetting the horrible experiences of European history, these form the basis of a new cosmopolitan memory. Both Robertson and Shaw argue that the Holocaust and Hiroshima have become global memories that underpin our conception of ourselves as part of a global community. Levy and Sznaider show how memories of the holocaust are being reproduced through museums, education and scholarly conferences and the ways in which this memory construction influenced the humanitarian thinking that led to interventions in Bosnia and Kosovo (Levy and Sznaider 2002).

People in the West are no longer willing to die for the spectacle brand of nationalism. Despite's Smith's assertions, I see no reason why people should not be willing to risk their life for human rights as human rights activists and humanitarian agencies already do. Policemen and fire fighters, after all, risk their lives to save other people, whatever their nationality. Defending human rights is, of course, different from national wars in which people are willing not only to risk their lives but to kill for their nations and to destroy their enemies. Surely, we are better off without that kind of passion.

Conclusion

I have defended the modernist argument that nationalism is a constructed or imagined idea and that its success is derived from the fact that the idea suited the structural conditions associated with modernity. It provided the glue that made possible the modern state and modern industry. I have also argued that the strength of the idea depends on politics as well as culture and that politics is more important than culture in open democratic societies. I explain the passion associated with nationalism not in terms of the strength of culture but as a consequence of war and the role of war in constructing nationalism.

The structural conditions that gave rise to modern nationalism have changed. The information economy is supplanting industrialism and requires a much more differentiated workforce. Electronic communications are now much more important than print technology making possible new horizontal or transborder cultural communities. Wars between states are becoming an anachronism and new forms of violence are constructing new militant nationalist and religious ideologies.

The vertical homogeneous cultures of the nation-state survive as a sort of spectacle. This form of nationalism is supplemented by new horizontal ideologies. On the one hand, we are witnessing new exclusive and fundamentalist political networks including nationalism (that is nowadays both local and global because of Diasporas) and global Islam. On the other hand, cosmopolitan and European ideologies that include small open nationalisms, are being mobilised not only from above but also from below by human rights and peace movements.

So will nationalism be transcended? This is a political question. A world in which spectacle nationalism, as in the USA, depends on the idea of a struggle against new nationalism or global Islam, is at odds with underlying socio-economic developments. This is why they are backward-looking. It is extremely difficult to sustain closed national societies in a global era and this can only be done through violence and terror. But if spectacle and small nationalisms could be harnessed to a cosmopolitan politics that reflected the complexity of contemporary conditions, then this would allow for global standards combined with cultural and democratic devolution. A cosmopolitan world would prioritise reason and deliberation as opposed to passion. Violence unfortunately squeezes the space for reason and deliberation. The fact that a good case can be made as to why cosmopolitanism is more likely to contribute to progress does not mean that such a world will come about.

The choice between these two ideal-type worlds depends on the actions of individuals, groups and movements. It depends on debates like this one. I do not agree with the critics of the modernist paradigm, which I believe does explain earlier nationalisms, but as a late or reflexive modernist, I am much more doubtful about the future than some of the earlier proponents of the modernist paradigm.

Notes

1   Nationalist parties captured power in the Balkans, for example, or in India. Islamic parties are ruling in Iran and Turkey and have done well in elections in Pakistan and Algeria, where electoral victory led to a military coup. In Western Europe, right-wing anti-immigrant parties have increased their share of the vote and in the USA Christian fundamentalist and Zionist groups are increasingly influential in the Republican Party.

2   In the last ten years before his death, the Prophet redefined the notion of a 'raid', which had been characteristic of pre-Islamic nomad groups, as part of Jihad, to mean a raid aimed at the benefit of the whole community and not individual gain. Al Qaeda have resurrected the term and it is used to describe their form of action, for example the attacks on the World Trade Centre and other operations (Mneimneh and Makiya 2002).

References

Anderson, Benedict. 1983. *Imagined Communities: Reflections on the Origins and Spread of Nationalism*. Verso, London.

Appiah, Kwame Anthony. 1996. 'Cosmopolitan patriots' in Joshua Cohen (ed.), *For Love of Country: Debating the Limits of Patriotism: Martha C. Nussbaum and Respondents*. Cambridge, MA: Beacon.

Burke, Jason. 2003. *Al Qaeda: Casting a Shadow of Terror*. London: Taurus.

Gellner, Ernest. 1994. *Conditions of Liberty: Civil Society and its Rivals*. London: Hamish Hamilton.

Gellner, Ernest. 1983. *Nations and Nationalism*. Oxford: Blackwell.

Glasius, Marlies and Mary Kaldor. 2002. 'Global civil society before and after September 11' in M. Glasius, M. Kaldor and H. Anheier (eds.), *Global Civil Society 2002*. Oxford: Oxford University Press.

Gruber, Karoly. 1999. *From the Beginning of Reason to the End of History: the Politics of Postmodernism and Ethno-nationalist Renaissances of Pre-post modern Natures*. D Phil Thesis, University of Sussex.

Guibernau, Montserrat. 1996. *Nationalisms: the Nation-State and Nationalism in the Twentieth Century*. Cambridge: Polity.

Hobsbawm, Eric J. 1990. *Nations and Nationalism since 1870: Programme, Myth, Reality*. Cambridge: Cambridge University Press.

Juergensmayer, Mark. 2000. *Terror in the Mind of God*. Berkeley, CA: University of California Press.

Kaldor, Mary. 1990. *The Imaginary War: Understanding the East-West Conflict*. Oxford: Blackwell.

Kaldor, Mary and Diego Muro. 2003. 'Religious and nationalist militant networks' in M. Kaldor, H. Anheier and M. Glasius (eds.), *Global Civil Society 2003*. Oxford: Oxford University Press.

Kaldor-Robinson, Joshua. 2002. 'The virtual and the imaginary: the role of diasphoric new media in the construction of a national identity during the break-up of Yugoslavia', *Oxford Development Studies* 30(2): 177–87.

Kant, Immanuel. 1991 [1795]. 'Perpetual Peace: A Philosophical Sketch' in *Kant: Political Writings*. Cambridge: Cambridge University Press.

Levy, Daniel and Natan Sznaider. 2002. 'Memory unbound: the holocaust and the formation of cosmopolitan memory', *European Journal of Social Theory* 5(1): 87–106.

Melander, Erik. 2001. 'The Nagorno-Karabakh conflict revisited: was the war inevitable?', *Journal of Cold War Studies* 3(2), spring.

Mneimneh, Hassan and Kanan Makiya. 2002. 'Manual for a "raid"', *New York Review of Books* 17 January.

Özkirimli, Umut. 2000. *Theories of Nationalism: a Critical Introduction*. London: Macmillan.

Renan, Ernest. 1990 [1882]. 'What is a nation?' in Homi K. Bhabha (ed.), *Nation and Narration*. London and New York: Routledge.

Robertson, Roland. 1992. *Globalisation: Social Theory and Global Culture*. London: Sage.

Shaw, Martin. 2000. *The Global State*. Cambridge: Cambridge University Press.

Smith, Anthony D. 1995. *Nations and Nationalism in a Global Era*. Cambridge: Polity.

Smith, Anthony D. 2001. *Nationalism: Theory, Ideology, History*. Cambridge: Polity.

Urry, John. 2000. 'The global media and cosmopolitanism', Department of Sociology, Lancaster , http://www.comp.lancs.ac.uk/sociology/soc056ju.html

12

Globalising national states

STEIN TØNNESSON

The challenge of globalisation

Globalisation is understood here in a broad sense of rapidly expanding trade, investments, financial flows, travel, information and other forms of worldwide communication. These trends received a boost from the demise of real socialism during the 1980s–90s, when formerly secluded continents were opened up to penetration to global economic and cultural forces. Within the globalised world, the role of the state is changing. The distinction between internal and external policies is being increasingly blurred. It becomes more and more important for states to influence not only the regional but the global environment, and more and more impossible to determine developments inside one's borders without engaging in supra-national decision making. Foreign ministries and diplomatic services are being transformed. While they mainly used to manage bilateral diplomatic relations with other states, they now seek to promote and co-ordinate all kinds of trans-national interaction, and must spend considerable time on preparing and advocating their own policies in multilateral forums. Every government finds it increasingly problematic to define the division of labour between its Ministry of Foreign Affairs and the other ministries. Politics is often hampered by the fact that its subject matter is trans- or international whereas the electorate, its consciousness and concerns remain focused on so-called domestic affairs.

The success of states in today's world is not so much measured in terms of capacity for defending borders or creating uniquely national institutions, but in terms of ability to adapt to regional and global trends, promote exports, attract investments and skilled labour, provide a beneficial environment for trans-national companies, build attractive institutions of research and higher learning, wield political influence on the regional and global scene, and also 'brand the nation' culturally in the international market-place. A book epitomising the market-oriented approach to national planning is *The Marketing of Nations*, published by a Thai-American team in 1997. It applies the concepts, theories, and tools of strategic market management to guide nations in their pursuit of economic wealth building, and the main audiences targeted are government and political leaders who are involved in 'planning for a nation's prosperity', and economic ministries and development officials within governments (Kotler et al. 1997: x). States compete with each other for various kinds of ratings. With exception for the biggest ones, states are no longer primarily a regulatory body above the market, but an agent on the trans-national market, operating on the same level as corporations (the intimate cooperation between the Finnish state and the trans-national company Nokia is an interesting case of mutually beneficial cooperation). The main difference between states and companies is that the former have territories and citizens whereas the latter have only assets, shareholders and employees. Loyalty to companies is also normally less emotional, more temporary, and more closely linked to a reward system than loyalty to a state. States and companies need each other but do not control each other. No single state or regional organisation can manage the market. They all depend on it.

Theories of nationalism have normally been about the reasons for its strength, its relationship to modernisation, and about the state-nation nexus (i.e., Smith 1983). Only more recently have scholars started to discuss what is happening to national identity and national states under the pressure of globalisation. There are three schools of thought (Guibernau 2001: 245–248). The first argues that the national state is being undermined or superseded, and that other institutions such as trans-national companies, supra-national and multi-national government and non-government organisations (NGOs) are taking over their role. The second rejects this thesis, arguing that globalisation does not weaken the nation or the national state. On the contrary, the pressures of globalisation provoke new waves of nationalism and cultural mobilisation. States also retain or even expand their role in controlling populations, and remain crucial as building blocks of international society. The third school, to which the present author belongs, holds that globalisation *transforms* the state. The priorities of state policies change, and it becomes at the same time more important and more difficult for a state to be genuinely national, i.e., having a citizenry who identifies emotionally with it. The point is not just that government institutions have to shift attention from internal to regional and global affairs. Citizens are also subjected to persistent trans-national influences. It was far easier to foster cultural cohesion within one's national borders at the time of national broadcasting monopolies and a strictly national education system (such as in the 1950s–70s), than it is today when satellite television, the internet and student migration provide pervasive trans-national impulses.[1] However, this does not mean that states and nationalists have stopped trying, or that the general advantage of having emotional affinity between population and state has diminished. With international mass communication it is also now easier than before to link ethnic diasporas together globally. It surely seems that a fundamental change is occurring to the role of the state, which probably warrants the use of new terms to characterise the national state of the twenty-first century. Guibernau (2001: 243) speaks about 'the post-traditional nation-state' when referring to the globalised national state. As we shall soon see, another proposal is 'market-state'.

Out of respect for Anthony D. Smith, the term 'nation-state' is avoided in this essay. Smith (1995: 86; 2001: 123) defines 'nation-state' as requiring an almost complete match between ethnicity and political borders, a condition that barely exists anywhere, although Portugal, Norway, Japan and a few other countries may be close. Instead, Smith speaks of 'national states' when the ethno-political match is somewhat looser, allowing for sizable minorities. To Smith, however, the national state needs to be built around a majority ethnic group (or 'ethnie') in order to be national at all.[2] If taken seriously, this means that a great many states which are normally referred to as national or 'nations', can neither be considered 'nation-states' nor 'national states', but must be identified as 'plural', 'hybrid' or 'multi-cultural' (a few 'monarchic states' also remain, such as Bhutan, Brunei, Kuwait and Saudi-Arabia). Smith's terminology will not be fully respected in this essay. To the extent that 'plural states' (such as the federations India and the USA) have managed to create a strong national sentiment among their citizens, including an emotional attachment to national symbols and institutions, they should also be considered as national, albeit of a different type.[3]

On the basis of his own terminology, Smith has more recently discussed the impact of globalisation on the national state, and declared his allegiance to the school of the sceptics. He sees no supersession or fundamental change in the strength and role of nationalism and national states. Smith concedes that globalisation has in some ways transformed the state, but not that the state has been weakened. States were never fully sovereign, and economic globalisation has only brought 'a shift of state functions and powers from the economic and military to the social and cultural spheres, and from external sovereignty to internal, domestic control' (2001: 124–125). It is hard to agree that this is but a minor change, and that it does not weaken the state. What determines a state's capacity for spending money on welfare and culture, is the gross national product and the level of taxation that the government can impose on its citizens. If there has been a shift in state functions from the economic to the social and cultural spheres, then there are other institutions than the state itself who decide how much each state can use on welfare and culture. Hence the state's power in its own national domain has been weakened. In another area, though, the state is expanding its importance. This is the field of 'foreign policy', which is more and more becoming 'global policy'. There has been a significant shift in the function and power of the state from internal economic management to external marketing and multilateral policy-making.

This is grasped by Philip Bobbitt in his 922 page volume *The Shield of Achilles*, where he offers a historical timetable for fundamental changes in state strategy and constitutional orders. Based on his combination of insights into security strategy and the history of international law (but scant knowledge of nationalism and national identity) he defines a series of specific state forms, or 'constitutional orders', in European and global history (Bobbitt 2002: 346–347). Whereas the renaissance was characterised by 'the princely state', the sixteenth - seventeenth century period was first dominated by the 'kingly state' and then, from 1648, by the 'territorial state'. Most of the nineteenth century was dominated by 'imperial state-nations', but it also saw the emergence of the 'nation-state' which dominated the period from the late nineteenth century to around 1990. Now we are in a period of transition to the 'market-state'.

Since changes in the attribution and form of the dominant states have often been cumulative, and have differed widely in the various parts of the world, Bobbitt's scheme is much too rigid to accurately reflect historical change. Still, it does show trends in a way that theories operating with simple dichotomies between monarchic and national states, or empires and nation-states, do not. Bobbitt holds that whereas the 'nation-state' – be it parliamentary, communist or fascist – was predominantly preoccupied with enhancing the *material welfare* of its citizens, the market-state seeks to maximise the *opportunity* of its people. The state is no longer the principal actor on behalf of the nation since all kinds of corporations, organisations and other private institutions are active internationally. Instead the state has become a facilitator of practical affairs, an enabler and umpire more than a provider or judge (Bobbitt 2002: xxvi, 229, 235). Bobbitt sees the emergence of a (US-led) society of market-states, which will be 'good at setting up markets' but not at assuring political representation. Governments will assume more centralised authority. Citizens will change from participants to spectators, and the state apparatus will have to concentrate on infrastructure surveillance, epidemiological surveillance, and environmental protection rather than provision of welfare (Bobbitt 2002: 234). What he describes is a divorce between nation and state, with the state becoming less dependent on the active participation of its citizens through democratic institutions, but at the same time relying heavily on its performance in the global market. In the process of transition from national states to market-states there will inevitably be conflicts between the most powerful market-states and various alienated and disenfranchised populations.

Now, Bobbitt and Smith approach the challenge of globalisation from different angles. While Bobbitt is primarily interested in the state as such, Smith looks at the nation, or the historical *ethnie* that constitutes its core. While Bobbitt expects the national state to be superseded by the market-state, Smith does not expect any weakening of nationalism and national identity. Bobbitt and Smith's ideas are not necessarily incompatible. If Bobbitt's cynical description of the market-state as good at setting up markets, but bad at organising political representation is accurate, then there is every reason to expect groups getting in its way to mobilise against this type of state on ethno-national and religious grounds.

Bobbitt claims that some states are pioneers in becoming 'market-states'. These succeed better than others in the global market place. They are active globalisers while other states are stagnating or being marginalised. The question to be discussed in the following is whether or not the historical character of a state, the route it originally took to a status as national, and the degree to which it achieved such status – 'the *uneven* distribution of ethno-history across the globe' as Smith (2001: 140) calls it – have a bearing on each state's capacity for coping with globalisation. In order to discuss this we need to revisit the basic typologies of nations and states.

Routes to the national state

As A.D. Smith has remarked (2001: 39), the most celebrated and influential typology of nationalism is the distinction made by Hans Kohn in *The Idea of Nationalism* from 1944 between a benign Western form and a more virulent Eastern (in fact, East European) version. Despite its influence, Kohn's typology is of little use today, so we will instead revisit the more sophisticated typologies offered by the three most influential scholars of nationalism and national identity in the last two decades: Ernest Gellner, Benedict Anderson and Anthony D. Smith.

Gellner (1983) suggests a typology built on distribution of power, access to education, and ethnic division. In agrarian societies only the powerful used to have access to education, thus ethnic division did not present a problem. But when the cultural homogenisation required by industry set in, Gellner argues, uneven access to power and education between ethnic groups gave rise to nationalism and determined its form. If a group had little access to both power and education, it would form its own nationalism in opposition to the nationalism of the rulers. This is Gellner's first type of nation or 'route' to nationhood. He called it 'Habsburg' or 'Balkan', and claimed it had been emulated in twentieth-century sub-Saharan Africa. The second type had its origin in a situation where the powerless were given access to education and hence acquired an ability to coalesce into an ethnic majority within a culturally divided society. This provided for the 'classical liberal Western nationalism' of the Italian or German kind. The third type arose when the powerless had better education than the powerful, but represented a minority without a specific homeland. This gave rise to 'diaspora nationalism' of the Jewish kind. Gellner's typology is attractive, but since it was presented in conjunction with a controversial theory on the role of industry and modern education in the formation of nationalism as purely modern, his particular typology has not been adopted by many others.

In his celebrated *Imagined Communities* (1991), Benedict Anderson also operates with three types of nationalism, and his distinction between *creole, linguistic* and *official* nationalism (exemplified in the Americas, Germany and France) has been quite influential, not least because it converges with distinctions made by other scholars. In Anderson's view, America played the pioneering role in forging modern nationalism, and all three types of nationalism were created in America and Europe, whereafter they became available to people on other continents for 'piracy' or emulation.

After having dedicated two chapters in his *Theories of Nationalism* to various kinds of sophisticated typologies, Smith decided to just include two – or three – categories in his introductory texts of the 1990s (Smith 1983: 192–229). His typology is similar to Anderson's, but starts in Europe, not America. Smith derives his typology from the 'route' that each nation followed to statehood. There were basically two routes: one *civic*, from above, where agents of the state incorporated the population, such as in France (Smith 1995: 41; 1991: 123); and one *ethnic*, from below, where an ethnie formed a new state through separation, such as in Ireland, or through unification, such as in Italy. Smith (1991) only reluctantly added a third *plural* type to cover the USA, India and a number of other states. This third type (which corresponds to Anderson's first pioneering one), did not quite satisfy Smith's basic criterion for being a national state since it did not evidently have an ethnic core. To fit the third route into his scheme, Smith argued that the USA had been built around an ethnic core of English emigrants, that a 'Hindu community' formed the core of India, and that Islamic communities formed core ethnies in several Muslim states (1991: 149–150; 1995: 41). He would later qualify his characterisation of the USA by saying that it was originally built on a protestant, English core, but had later become a 'truly polyethnic and plural nation' (Smith 2001: 42). Smith however tends to see 'plural nations' as not quite nations at all. Thus he mainly discusses the distinction between 'ethnic' and 'civil'. Smith has also become quite critical of any typology. Since many states and ethnies have moved along different routes at various times, the true picture is far too complex to be grasped by a simple typology. This general point shall not affect the discussion here. Smith's warnings against typologies, and his reluctance to recognise the 'plural nation' as a nation will be disregarded. Anderson's three types are thus accepted, although with Smith's nametags on them, 'ethnic', 'civic' and 'plural' (Smith 1995: 108).

A fourth route to nationhood is also added, in accordance with a suggestion by two scholars specialising in Asian studies (Tønnesson and Antlöv 1996). When looking into national forms in Asia, they found it difficult to fit the communist national states into models derived from the American and European experience. In China, an armed revolutionary movement led by a party under Han (ethnic majority) Chinese leadership had been able to forge alliances with several ethnic minorities, then waged a class war against a rival Han Chinese nationalist movement, leading to the establishment of a radical People's Republic within the former borders of the Qing dynastic realm. This provoked the creation of a counter-republic in Taiwan, and a growing Han Chinese diaspora who, for more than three decades, cut their ties with the homeland. Mao Zedong, Ho Chi Minh, Kim Il Sung, Pol Pot, their parties and their movements were all nationalist, but they were not primarily 'ethnic' since their main enemies – apart from the colonial powers – were members of the same ethnic group as themselves. They were also not 'civic' since they were revolutionary and thus did not build on an existing state. Finally, they were not 'plural' since they built on a majority ethnie and made frequent use of nationally distinctive historical myths linked to ancient heroes and battles.

Tønnesson and Antlöv suggested that these nations had followed a fourth route to the national state, based on the idea of *class*. Because the communist nationalists directed their struggle against the social elite of their own ethnie, they could behave tolerantly towards those minority ethnic groups who sided with them in the struggle, and award them a recognised minority status, while they sought to eradicate or extinguish the propertied and educated classes of their own ethnie, whom they accused of being traitors to the nation. The victories of the Asian revolutions created briskly nationalist regimes combining respect for ethnic minority cultures with a hostile relationship to a diaspora of refugees belonging to their own ethnie. The communist states in Asia, say Tønnesson and Antlöv, constitute a fourth national type. If not entirely convincing, this is a tempting proposition, and we may ask if the 'class route to nationhood' has also played a role in shaping some national states outside of Asia. The Russian example does not perhaps quite fit, since the result of the Russian revolution was not primarily the Russian Federation, but a Union of Soviet Socialist Republics that allowed minority groups to manifest themselves culturally if not politically, but downplayed Russia's own distinct culture and ethnicity in favour of a cosmopolitan vision of a future Soviet man (Rowley 2000). By contrast to their Asian comrades, the Russian communists more or less abstained from developing their own national identity. This may partly explain why Chinese and Vietnamese communism turned out to be more resilient than the Russian. The successful Asian leaders combined communism and nationalism.

The concept of the 'class nation' could perhaps also provide a clue to understanding the peculiar version of nationalism that exists in Sweden. After the lower and middle classes peacefully seized control of the Swedish state in the beginning of the twentieth century, they created a future-oriented modernist national ideology rejecting the most auspicious periods of the Swedish monarchy's past. The 'golden ages' were denounced instead of admired. The King remained on the throne, the nobility kept their titles and properties, and the bourgeoisie was allowed to play a leading role in finance and industry, but they were politically and culturally marginalised. Swedish schoolchildren were systematically taught how badly Sweden had behaved in the seventeenth century, and how military campaigns had represented an unbearable burden on the Swedish peasants. Under the aegis of its many popular movements *(folkrörelser)*, the nation had escaped from an oppressive and violent past and created a People's Home *(folkhemmet)*.

Now, which of these four types, the *ethnic, civic, plural* and *class*, are best suited to survive and make the best out of the age of globalisation?

Routes to the globalised state

It may be generally assumed that states who are able to both actively engage with the outside world and keep up a national community built on trust and participation stand the greatest chance of coping successfully with the ambiguous effects of globalisation. This means that they need well-informed foreign policy debates, a widely connected multi-cultural diplomatic service, corporations with at once a national base and global networks, openness to immigration, a clear profile on the global cultural scene (including sports) as well as in international affairs, and an ability to instil loyalty and active interest in national decision-making among new generations as well as immigrants. For some nations, the greatest challenge will be to open up, for others to retain or shape a national community. Attempts to achieve both at the same time will necessarily lead to tension, but if governments and political leaders ignore one to the benefit of the other, there is likely to be a backlash.

The historical baggage of each nation, its myths and memories will doubtlessly influence the way it copes with globalisation, but this does not mean that any of the four main types of nations has an impossible task. It should also be emphasised, as Smith does, that the various routes to nationhood have often overlapped within the same nation, and that some have followed one route in one period, and another in the next. Thus there is a complex roadmap behind each nation, and today's leaders may choose which of the available historical narratives they want to promote and build upon.

Generally three kinds of states are probably at a disadvantage. The first are those with a well-established, but self-sufficient, inflexible and unaccommodating national system. Some of those states that displayed the most impressive economic performance in the 1950s–70s (Japan, Korea) have difficulties today. The second are those who never managed to build a national community during the period of the national state, but have populations identifying more with clans and sub-national ethnic groups than with the nation (Nigeria, Iraq, the states of Central Asia). To these weak states, the post-modernist ideology of superseding nationalism is thoroughly unhelpful, since the age of globalisation requires a certain degree of national cohesion within a state in order for it to be able to make the best out of its opportunities. Although intellectually discredited, *nation-building* actually remains essential in many parts of the world. The third kind of disadvantaged states are those who have failed to resolve basic national questions concerning borders, constitutions and symbols, and who have recently or are still engaged in violent internal conflicts (D. R. Congo, Sudan, Colombia, Sri Lanka, the Philippines, the Balkan states, Indonesia).

When nationhood is primarily based on a strictly defined ethnicity, be it linguistic, religious or custom-based a significant part of the citizenry is excluded. It is commonplace that this will hamper the capacity of the state to cope with globalisation. The establishment in 1979 of an orthodox Shiite Islamic state in Iran, for instance, severely damaged Iran's ability to realise national interests in a globalising world. If, however, a state resolved its ethnic question long ago, and perhaps did it peacefully, and the majority ethnie has grown able to accommodate minority groups either by negotiating arrangements to ensure their cultural survival and political representation, or through individual integration in a de-ethnicised but still national political system, then ethnic nations may well be capable of adapting to a globalised world.

As Smith has emphasised, there is not necessarily a great difference between the ability of a typical *civic* national state, such as the French unitary Republic, and a typical *ethnic* national state, such as the German Federal Republic, to accommodate immigrants (Smith 2001: 41). For European states the national question is today further complicated by the fact that they have to define both their own internal policies, and common regional policies within the European Union. In Europe there are now multiple tensions between nationalism and local minorities, nationalism and immigrant groups, nationalism and regionalisation, nationalism and globalisation, and regionalism and globalisation. From an anti-globalist viewpoint integration and globalisation may look like two sides of the same coin, since both threaten the national community. However, the European integrative project has become so ambitious that it not always enhances globalisation, but also in some ways could hamper European engagement with the wider world, partly because of tension with the USA, Turkey, and Russia, and partly because government bureaucracies are forced to spend most of their energy on regional decision-making instead of promoting national interests globally.

Some of the major European nations (Britain, France, Spain, Portugal, the Netherlands) and also Japan, have an imperial past established during Bobbitt's 'state-nation' period in the late nineteenth and early twentieth century. In the years 1945–75 these civic nations were all forced to accept the dissolution of their empires. Some tried to resist, but the retention of formal empires proved to have little political support domestically, and all these nations were able to strongly improve their economic performance once they had been deprived of their empires. To some extent their imperial past remains a barrier to these countries' international diplomacy. This is notably the case for Japan's diplomacy towards Korea and China. On the other hand, the networks and knowledge established in the imperial period continue to play a role in generating investments as well as cultural and political interaction.

The question now is if the plural and the class-based national states stand a better or worse chance than the ethnic and civil ones in coping with globalisation.

Philip Bobbitt (2002: 283–291) distinguishes between three kinds of 'market-states', the mercantile (Japan, China), the entrepreneurial (USA, Singapore), and the managerial (Germany, France). The mercantile state seeks market shares above all, in order to gain relative dominance in the international market. The entrepreneurial state seeks leadership through innovation, technological leadership and production of goods and services for global consumption. The managerial state seeks power through hegemony within a regional economic zone. This is Bobbitt's way of understanding the European Union. Germany and France seek to manage globalisation through the Union.

European countries are also, however, advocating management through global institutions, but find it increasingly difficult to enlist US support for this endeavour. Future co-ordination of the European Union's global policies may make this even more difficult, and also prevent the European nation-states from developing independent national profiles on the global political scene. This will deprive these nations of a chance to engage themselves independently in the world's most fundamental affairs, and therefore possibly leave the stage to the plural and class-based states.

Bobbitt thinks that the USA could well become a successful mercantile state if it wanted to, and it might also become managerial if it established a virtual region that included countries such as the United Kingdom, Singapore, India, the Philippines, and Canada. Managing Asia Pacific Economic Cooperation (APEC), or the whole world through the United Nations, Group of Eight, the International Monetary Fund and the World Bank might also be possible, but this is not what the US wants to do at the moment. Bobbitt sees the USA as already well advanced on its way to becoming an entrepreneurial market-state. He holds that 'the USA is remarkably well situated to become a market-state' (Bobbitt 2000: 242) because it is multiculturalist, has a free market, and is religiously diverse. Its habit of tolerance for diversity gives it an advantage over other countries in adapting to the new constitutional order. President William J. Clinton moved the USA far in the direction of a market-state, and President George W. Bush appears equally committed to this new constitutional order, says Bobbitt. The fact that American society has invested so little in its 'identity as an ethnic group' makes it 'well placed to make the transition from nation-state to market-state' (Bobbitt 2000: 290). Bobbitt also personally recommends that the USA follow this route, although he recognises the market-state's inherent weaknesses: 'its lack of community, its extreme meritocracy, its essential materialism and indifference to heroism, spirituality, and tradition', and also a lack of ability to show 'responsibility toward the unborn' (Bobbitt 2000: 285). Thus he sees a risk that the aggressive entrepreneurial market-state will disintegrate into 'regional, quasi-racial, and religious enclaves, devoid of any sense of overarching identity' (Bobbitt 2000: 290).

Against the background of this warning, it is striking to note that in parallel with the appearance of Bobbitt's massive treatise, another groundbreaking book was published by the American political scientist Walter Russell Mead entitled *Special Providence*, with the explicit purpose of establishing a distinctly American national foreign policy tradition. This would be in opposition to the hegemony of the 'European balance-of-power' school (represented in the USA, e.g., by Henry Kissinger), and its misleading distinction between 'realism' and 'idealism'. Thus, precisely at the time when the USA was stepping into its entrepreneurial market-state shoes, and just as the terrorist attacks against New York and Washington on 11 September 2001 provoked an upsurge of patriotism and intense preoccupation with national security and international politics among the American population, a leading scholar made an attempt to provide a genuinely national American vocabulary of foreign relations. Mead (2002) singles out four main foreign policy 'schools' in the USA, all with deep resonance in its national history, and named after a leading American statesman. It is Mead's thesis that the USA owes its many foreign policy successes not to luck or to God's mercy (as Bismarck would have it) or to its protected status behind the world's two major oceans, but to a counter-balancing interplay between four schools of thought within the American Republic's political institutions.

Mead's first school played a dominant role in the Clinton presidency. This is the market-oriented *Hamiltonian* school that always seeks to promote free markets, and US business interests abroad. The second school was last in power during the time of President Jimmy Carter. This is the *Wilsonian* school, with its basis in the US missionary movements, and with the ambition of exporting American-style freedom to the rest of the world. The third, the *Jeffersonian* school, is directly opposed to the previous one although it also celebrates America's unique brand of freedom. It wants to protect the American society's singular qualities by constraining the federal state and refraining from adventurous foreign policies. There is a strong element of this school in the warnings issued by Samuel Huntington (1996: 310, 316) against interfering in the affairs of other civilisations, and in 2003, Jeffersonians were virtually alone in warning against the US war against Iraq. Mead (2002: 333–334) claims that the 'strategic elegance' of the Jeffersonian tradition is the 'single-most-needed quality now in American foreign policy'. The Republic needs 'Jeffersonian caution, Jeffersonian conservation of such precious resources as liberty and lives, and the Jeffersonian passion for limits'. Mead's fourth school is the one that President George W. Bush thrives on, and which took centre stage after 11 September 2001: *Jacksonianism*. Jacksonians are preoccupied with honour and valour, favour the swift use of overwhelming military power, but are prepared to show magnanimity towards a repentant defeated enemy. It is not perhaps unthinkable that foreign policy debates between proponents of these four schools may lead to new changes in US global policies, and that pluralist American public opinion will become more than mere spectators, and assume a more active and responsive role in determining the global policies of the Republic.

Within the same league of 'entrepreneurial market-states', Bobbitt has a mini-state at the other side of the globe: Singapore. He has little to say about it, except that Singapore is 'more authoritarian' than the USA. Singapore holds that sovereignty lies in the State who grants rights to the people, whereas Americans derive government power directly from a portion of the sovereignty of the people (Bobbitt 2002: 799). The comparison between the superpower USA and the mini-power Singapore is alluring. Both are multi-cultural immigrant states with communities representing at least three of the world's major civilisations. Hence, their foreign policies are reflected in contradictions between the various immigrant groups (Caucasian, Black and Asian in the USA; Chinese, Malay and Indian in Singapore). The USA is dominated by

Caucasians and Singapore by Chinese, and these majority groups take care to accommodate the minorities so as to keep them loyal. The Caucasian president of the USA has a black national security advisor and secretary of state. The Chinese Prime Minister of Singapore has an Indian national security advisor and president.[4] Both the USA and Singapore are obsessed with vulnerability and national security and spend a very high proportion of their government budgets on the military. The USA spends billions on a National Missile Defence while Singapore diverts enormous resources to constructing water reservoirs to secure national survival in case Malaysia should stop the flow of water. Both Singapore and the USA are proponents of free market policies (although Singapore depends much more on them than the USA), and both are opposed to excessive treaty-based multilateralism. Both are extremely meritocratic. The main difference, apart from the size, is that Singapore does not share the American preoccupation with individual freedom. Singapore also lacks the Wilsonian foreign policy tradition. It is dominated by hard core Hamiltonian Social Darwinist Confucians. Only an elitist, disciplined, hard-working state can survive when placed in such a vulnerable situation, claims Singapore's strong-willed Senior Minister Lee Kuan Yew. Singaporean spokesmen have often compared their city-state to Israel (Barr 2000).

The most captivating aspect of 'the Singapore story' (Lee 1998, 2000) is the country's tremendous success. Since Singapore was forced to leave the Federation of Malaysia in 1965, and become an independent state, it has enjoyed stupendous economic growth, and has acquired an influential position not only in the Association of Southeast Asian Nations (ASEAN), but also in East Asia more generally, and in the world. Singapore sides with the USA in all major international disputes that are not motivated in Wilsonianism, and Singapore has done its best to retain a US military presence in East Asia so as to retain a balance of power preventing the regional powers from becoming hegemonic, either separately or in condominium.

During the heyday of the national state in the 1950s–60s, Singapore was an anomaly. Lee Kuan Yew, its pre-eminent political leader already then, was a captive of the period's general wisdom. He held in 1957 that a city-state like Singapore had no chance to survive without a hinterland: 'Island-nations are political jokes', he said (Leifer 2000: 27–28). His plan was to secure a position for Singapore within the Malaysian Federation, and it was despite himself that he declared Singapore's independence in August 1965, when he had fallen out with Malaysia's leader, Tunku Abdul Rahman. From then on, Lee made a virtue out of necessity and sought to construct Singapore as a trade and financial centre and industrial powerhouse, linking the world's three economic growth engines of Asia, Europe and the Americas together (Lee 2000: 49–69). Singapore's foreign minister Sinnathamby Rajaratnam held a famous 'Global City' speech in February 1972, depicting Singapore as the child of a modern technology which had allowed it to overcome the lack of a natural hinterland. Its hinterland would be the international economic system as such 'to which we as a Global City belong and which will be the final arbiter of whether we prosper or decline' (Leifer 2000: 36). Efforts were also made to construct Singapore as a civic nation with all the necessary paraphernalia, including (from 1978) a 'Singaporean Asian culture' (Barr 2000: 157–9), and also a narrative of national emancipation (just go through Singapore's historical museum and the dioramas at Sentosa Island). However, the problem of defining an 'Asian' culture, without making it too Chinese, would prove almost insurmountable. Singaporean nation-building met the same problems as Canada, the USA and Australia did when they organised national festivals to celebrate their centenaries and bicentenaries in 1967, 1976 and 1988. There was an in-built contradiction between the desire of official elites to impose a national definition and the needs of the state to legitimate itself to its citizenry and to the international order by claiming to represent all ethnic groups (Hutchinson 1994: 193). In their historical narratives, all four states emphasised their liberation from British colonial status. For Australia the defining moment was Gallipoli 1916, when Britain proved unworthy of Australian trust. For Singapore it was 1942, when Britain failed to protect its colony. These two British military catastrophes provided exemplary myths for an inclusive national narrative, but it was extremely difficult for such multi-cultural nations to construct more elaborate national mythologies. These would always one way or another favour some ethnic groups over others. By 1999 Singapore's Prime Minister Goh Chok Tong admitted that Singapore 'was still a fragile society and not yet a nation' (Leifer 2000: 2). Singapore has compensated for its small size and fragile society by realising, at a very early stage, the global ambitions of today's market-states. Thus in Bobbitt's conceptualisation of the market-state, Singapore serves as a model along with the USA.

What then about the Asian class-states, notably China and Vietnam? During the 1990s, both Beijing and Hanoi sought the advice of Lee Kuan Yew, as an elderly Asian statesman (Lee 2000: 645–660). After the fall of communism in Eastern Europe, the communist parties retained power in these two countries, and also in Laos and North Korea, but they gradually abandoned their class-based philosophy. Hence they could re-establish ties with their capitalist diasporas, adopt meritocratic Confucian values of the Singaporean kind, and define as their overriding national goal to achieve rapid economic growth. Just like Singapore had done, they applied highly pragmatic foreign policies with emphasis on friendly relations with as many other countries as possible, and they focused on the one overriding goal of obtaining economic growth through foreign direct investments and access to the world's richest markets. They did not democratise, but then Singapore also has maintained something close to a one-party system. What happened was that China and Vietnam actively sought to emulate Singapore. This ongoing process of emulation—which one could almost call 'Singaporisation'—has a potential for securing China and Vietnam a place among the most successful developing national market-states.

Conclusion

States need to strike a balance between excessive nationalism and social fragmentation. On the one hand they cannot have an exclusive national culture preventing engagement with the wider world. On the other hand they need active support from their population of a kind that only people identifying with their state can provide. It is no less important than before for a state to be national, but it is much more difficult than just a few decades ago. In today's world, with highly uneven economic and social developments both within and between nations, reactions against the effects of globalisation may reinforce national and religious sentiments. If governments and business leaders are too eager to embrace globalisation they may provoke serious tension with groups within their own populations.

Philip Bobbitt's model of the market-state is excessively non-national. If states engage only with the market, and fail to uphold the kind of national we-feeling that allow populations to identify with their national political institutions, then these states will get into trouble. They will find it difficult to maintain the kind of trust-based civic culture that makes people support each other and abide by the law. While an aging Japan may see as its main problem to overcome national parochialism, the main problem for a Singaporised China is rather to create a national culture and institutions with which its population can identify.

Guibernau (2001: 266) claims that European states need to construct a 'pluralist' national identity by which he means 'a type of identity grounded upon a renewed concept of the state as a democratic institution, efficient in solving its citizens' daily troubles, capable of opening new spaces for dialogue, and ready to accommodate national and ethnic diversity within its boundaries'. This resembles Bobbitt's 'market-state'. Hutchinson (1994: 135–163, 164) has argued that, for the foreseeable future, Europe is altogether a lost cause for those who wish to replace the traditional ethnie-based national identities with pluralist ones. The problem with a purely pluralist efficiency- and dialogue-based identity is that it easily becomes a non-identity, or at least a non-national identity. Political leaders worldwide are likely to continue to sense that social cohesion is more easily accomplished when citizens are not forced to globalise continuously, but also treated once in a while to Smith's favourite menu: community, territory, history and destiny, moderately spiced with special missions, 'golden ages', and 'glorious dead' (Smith 2001: 143–144).

A great challenge for national leaders is to rally their populations behind global political causes. Nations need national global policies. Ultimately the most successful national states may be those whose populations engage themselves not just individually, but nationally, in global issues. Nations need broadly based foreign policy debates, with a basis in shared national ideals. Such ideals may help create a national profile in the global 'market-place', and allow nations to become collective constituents of an emerging global society.

Notes

1 Smith (1995: 92–95; 2001: 139) argues that access to the most recent technology of mass communication makes it *easier* for national states to inculcate a national culture through the state-run national education system. This seems more true for the situation in the 1950s–70s than it is today. State-run national education systems have not been pioneers in the use of the newest electronic facilities. National education systems are increasingly being standardised to allow grades to be comparable internationally, and the English language is gaining ground as a global language of education and research. Students increasingly study abroad, and poorly funded universities find it impossible to attract the most talented students even from their own national pool. There is also now strong pressure to prevent government-funded schools from inculcating ethnic- or religiously based national cultures in order not to alienate minority groups.

2 Smith makes a subtle distinction between a modern nation and the pre-modern *ethnie*, which is more than just an ethnic group, but less than a nation. *Ethnies* are 'named units of population with common ancestry myths and historical memories, elements of shared culture, some link with a historic territory and some measure of solidarity, at least among their elites'. A *nation*, by contrast, is 'a named human population which shares myths and memories, a mass public culture, a designated homeland, economic unity and equal rights and duties for all members' (Smith 1995: 56–57; 1991: 14; 1986: 97).

3 A national state may be broadly defined as a state which the great majority of the citizens identify with to the extent of seeing it as their own. Nationalism is an ideological movement for attaining or maintaining a national state.

4 In order to make sure that the designated Indian candidate was elected, none of the ethnic Chinese candidates were allowed to participate in Singapore's presidential elections in 1998.

References

Anderson, Benedict. 1991 [1983]. *Imagined Communities: Reflections on the Origins and Spread of Nationalism*. London: Verso.

Barr, Michael D. 2000. *Lee Kuan Yew: the Beliefs Behind the Man*. Richmond, Surrey: Curzon.

Bobbitt, Philip. 2002. *The Shield of Achilles: War, Peace and the Course of History*. London: Allen Lane.

Gellner, Ernest. 1983. *Nations and Nationalism*. Oxford: Blackwell.

Guibernau, Montserrat. 2001. 'Globalization and the nation-state,' in Montserrat Guibernau and John Hutchinson (eds.), *Understanding Nationalism*. Cambridge: Polity.

Huntington, Samuel. 1996. *The Clash of Civilisations and the Remaking of World Order*. New York: Simon & Schuster.

Hutchinson, John. 1994. *Modern Nationalism*. London: Fontana.

Kotler, Philip, Somkid Jatusripitak and Suvit Maesincee. 1997. *The Marketing of Nations. A Strategic Approach to Building National Wealth*. New York: Free.

Lee, Kuan Yew. 1998. *The Singapore Story: Memoirs of Lee Kuan Yew*. Singapore: Times.

Lee, Kuan Yew. 2000. *From Third World to First: The Singapore Story: 1965–2000*. New York: Harper Collins.

Leifer, Michael. 2000. *Singapore's Foreign Policy: Coping with Vulnerability*. London: Routledge.

Mead, Walter Russell. 2002. *Special Providence: American Foreign Policy and How it Changed the World*. New York: Routledge.

Rowley, David. 2000. 'Imperial versus national discourse: the case of Russia', *Nations and Nationalism* 6(1): 23–42.

Smith, Anthony D. 1983 [1971]. *Theories of Nationalism*. New York: Holmes & Meier.

Smith, Anthony D. 1986. *The Ethnic Origins of Nations*. Oxford: Basil Blackwell.

Smith, Anthony D. 1991. *National Identity*. London: Penguin.

Smith, Anthony D. 1995. *Nations and Nationalism in a Global Era*. Cambridge: Polity.

Smith, Anthony D. 1998. *Nationalism and Modernism*. London: Routledge.
Smith, Anthony D. 2001. *Nationalism: Theory, Ideology, History*. Cambridge: Polity.
Tønnesson, Stein and Hans Antlöv (eds.). 1996. *Asian Forms of the Nation*. Richmond, Surrey:
    Curzon.

13

History and national destiny: responses and clarifications

ANTHONY D. SMITH

I am conscious of the singular honour, not to mention pleasure, of receiving these stimulating and thoughtful contributions which, in their various ways, address some of the main problems with which I have been concerned in my studies of ethnicity and nationalism. Their depth and diversity has in turn set me rethinking and clarifying some of the problems that I encountered when I began my studies nearly forty years ago.

Broadly speaking, the 1960s saw the high watermark of the modernist paradigm of 'nation-building'. This model appeared to offer so much in an era of decolonisation and new states. Such an activist, sociological approach contrasted with the previously dominant paradigms of primordial and/or perennial nations, in which human intervention played a very limited role. But, as the path-breaking studies of Carlton Hayes, Hans Kohn, Elie Kedourie and Ernest Gellner demonstrated, the latter were so often infused with a misplaced retrospective nationalism. Modernism appeared to offer a radical, sceptical assessment, not just of nationalism, the ideology and movement, but of the nature and role of nations; for it tied these phenomena firmly to the new sociological and cultural conditions of modernity since the French and American revolutions. In the 1970s and 1980s, the modernist paradigm was further developed and refined, particularly in the influential works of Tom Nairn, John Breuilly, Eric Hobsbawm and Benedict Anderson.

But the optimism of the 'nation-building' era did not last, and critics like Walker Connor and Michael Hechter were not slow to point to some of its obvious weaknesses, even when they broadly accepted modernist historical periodisation. At the same time, some radically dissenting voices like Edward Shils, Clifford Geertz and Joshua Fishman were revealing the limitations of modernism's underlying rationalism and (in many cases) instrumentalism. These doubts were reinforced by the growing interest in the relatively new field of 'ethnicity' and its relationship to nationalism, notably in the work of John Armstrong, Pierre van den Berghe, and Donald Horowitz, and more recently in the sociological studies of Steven Grosby. There has also been a 'neo-perennialist' revival among some historians, for example, in the work of John Gillingham and the late Adrian Hastings, which traces the roots of at least some nations to the Middle Ages.

My own doubts about modernism crystallised at the end of the 1970s, when I began writing *The Ethnic Revival*. While I remain convinced that the ideology of nationalism was modern and novel, the revival (or was it survival?) of ethnicity in many parts of the modern world, and its use by nationalists, suggested the need to explore the pre-modern bases of nationhood in the earlier manifestations of ethnic community. This entailed a break with what John Peel termed the 'blocking presentism' of so many modernist and constructivist approaches focused on the agendas and activities of recent political elites, which had resulted in a certain historical foreshortening; as if to say, that nothing before the eighteenth century mattered, and therefore no account need to be taken, and no enquiry made, of conditions before that time. Not only did such a restricted view preclude the study of relations between present activities and past legacies and traditions; it also tended to obscure the vital popular dimension, namely, the relationship between elites and the pre-existing social and cultural traditions of 'the people' in whose name they entered the political fray.[1]

Increasingly, it appeared that the 'people' in question constituted, not only 'the people', i.e. the non-elites, but equally 'a people', a culturally and historically distinct population. Of such cultural collectivities, the most common was the type known as the *ethnie* or ethnic community. This led me to posit, in *The Ethnic Origins of Nations*, a strong relationship (but not an invariant one) between *ethnies* and nations, arguing that the latter are modelled on, and often develop from, earlier ethnic communities. Given the many economic and political ruptures between pre-modern and modern collective cultural identities in the same area, any continuity between *ethnie* and nation had to be located in the cultural and symbolic spheres. This in turn led to the adoption of the term 'ethno-symbolism' for an approach that sought to establish relations between the different kinds of collective cultural identity by focusing on elements of myth, memory, value, symbol and tradition that tended to change more slowly, and were more flexible in meaning, than the processes in other domains.

As I began to work out the implications of this shift in focus as a general approach and research programme for the study of ethnicity, nations and nationalism, it became clear that it involved a distinctive set of assumptions and hypotheses about the origins and development of nations. These can be summarised as follows:

1. *La longue durée*. The study of nations and nationalism requires a long-term approach, one that seeks to trace patterns of development and change over *la longue durée* in collective cultural identities. While this clearly challenges the exclusive emphasis on the modern period characteristic of modernism, it also differs radically from the perennialist assumption that nations are immemorial and ubiquitous. Instead, it requires comparative empirical study of the patterns of nation-formation across periods without any preconceptions, with special emphasis on the recurrence of identical forms of community in different periods of history and across continents, continuity of specific communities across historical periods, and rediscovery of 'authentic' communal cultures by later generations.[2]

2. *Symbolic elements.* In such enquiries, symbolic elements such as myths, memories, values, symbols and traditions play a crucial role, because they a) differentiate and particularise individual collectivities of the same type, b) compose patterns of reproduction and transmission of distinctive cultures, as the bases of ethnic and national identities, c) sustain inter-generational continuity and recurrence in collective cultural identities, and d) can guide collective change through reinterpretation as a result of their in-built flexibility. Of these symbolic elements, the most important for ethnic and national formations and persistence are myths of ethnic origin and ethnic election, traditions of homeland attachment, myth-memories of golden ages, and myths of heroic sacrifice. In terms of ethnic survival and the persistence of national identities, myths of ethnic election, missionary and covenantal, have played a particularly vital energising role.

3. *Ethnie and nation.* Of the collective cultural identities whose symbolic patterns are most closely associated with those of nations, the ethnic community or *ethnie* is the most significant, because nations share with *ethnies* certain characteristics, notably named self-definitions, origin and other myths and symbols, as well as a link with particular territories. But in other respects the community of the nation differs from that of the *ethnie*, notably with regard to the occupation of a homeland, and the development of a distinctive public culture and standardised laws and customs with shared rights and duties for the members of a historic cultural community. However, the question of the historical relationship between *ethnies* and nations is an empirical one; we cannot, we should not, presume any one-to-one correspondence between anterior *ethnies* and subsequent nations, nor can we simply locate the former in pre-modern epochs, reserving the nation to the modern epoch.

4. *Dominant ethnies.* Nations have historically been formed mainly, but not invariably, around ethnic cores or dominant *ethnies*, which have provided the cultural and social basis of the nation, even when the nation has subsequently expanded to include individual members, or indeed whole fragments and parts, of other *ethnies*. The cultures of these dominant *ethnies* continue to provide the unifying elements (in terms of land, language, law and customs) of the modern nation, even after the addition of other ethnic and cultural elements; and they may be, and indeed often are, invoked in times of crisis, such as war and mass immigration, to reintegrate and purify contemporary polyethnic nations whose members experience the alienation of modernity.

5. *Routes of nation-formation.* There have been several routes in the creation of nations, which stem from differences in types of *ethnie*. Just as we can distinguish lateral-aristocratic from vertical-demotic and immigrant *ethnies*, so we can chart the development of nations through processes of a) bureaucratic incorporation of other classes and regions by an upper class ethnic state, b) vernacular mobilisation by a returning intelligentsia intent on rediscovering its communal roots, c) pioneering settlement by an ethnic

fragment wedded to a providentialist destiny. In each of these routes, we can trace the linkages and changes through analyses of the cultural and symbolic elements, notably in such modes of representation as art and architecture, literature and music, law and ceremonies, and in the responses of intellectuals – neo-traditionalist, assimilationist and reformist-revivalist – to the crisis of legitimation posed by the 'scientific state'.

6. *Impact of nationalism*. These different kinds of representation and imagery become even more widespread and significant with the advent of nationalism, the ideology and movement. While elements of nationalism, as an ideological movement for attaining and maintaining autonomy, unity and identity on behalf of a human population deemed by some of its members to constitute an actual or potential 'nation', can be traced back to pre-modern religious and classical sources, its quest for authenticity and belief in popular sovereignty are products of modern Europe, whence they were spread to other parts of the world. As a movement that seeks a return to an idealised past in order to regenerate the community and assure its unique destiny, nationalism can be seen as a species of 'political archaeology' which helps to undermine tradition and ensure modernisation. As such it is particularly attractive to all kinds of intellectuals and professionals – artists and writers, educators and journalists, scholars and technicians, lawyers and doctors – and conversely, the movement and its ideal of the nation stands in need of the advocacy and dissemination skills of these strata.

7. *Types of nationalism*. Stemming from the different routes to nationhood, there have been systematic variations in the nationalism of modern nations. We can broadly distinguish a territorial version, focusing on residence, legal community, citizenship and civic culture; a more ethnic version, emphasizing genealogical ties, vernacular culture, nativist history and popular mobilisation; and a more plural version, a union of different immigrant *ethnies* under an overarching public culture of land, language, law and history. In practice, pure types are rare; in given cases, these types overlap considerably and often alternate over the course of nation-formation and subsequently.

8. *Supersession of nationalism*. Given the ethnic bases of nations, the various kinds of nationalism, the uneven distribution of ethno-history and the cultural and political pluralism of the inter-national order, the chances of an early supersession of nations and nationalisms appear to be slim. On the other hand, globalising trends of economic interdependence and mass communications are transforming, even as they reinforce, the various kinds of national community and nationalisms. The degree to which national identities have become 'hybridised' is debateable, but there is no doubt that globalising (and localising) trends have compelled the members of well-established national states to reexamine received national traditions and identities, especially in the light of large-scale immigration and the encounter of different cultures within each national state. On the other

hand, the movement to a genuinely cosmopolitan, global cultural identity remains the preserve of a small elite, as it was before the age of the national state.

Most of these 'ethno-symbolic' assumptions and arguments have been addressed by the gracious and thought-provoking contributions to this volume, and they have helped me to clarify, and in some cases amend, my own positions.

1. *La longue duree*. It was John Armstrong in his path-breaking *Nations before Nationalism* (1982) who introduced the significance of *la longue duree* for the study of nationalism, and who embedded it within a larger enquiry into the pre-modern bases of ethnicity. Here he has generously included my work in the long-term project of tracing linkages between collective identities, notably between *ethnies* and nations, over successive historical periods, while laying on me the daunting prospect of exploring distant cultures to enrich such enquiries. Certainly, this is the kind of work in comparative history and historical sociology over *la longue duree* that confronts the student of ethnicity and nationalism, with all its difficulties and pitfalls, not least the lack of adequate source materials and the thorny problems of definition.

2. *Symbolic elements*. Similarly, I owe to John Armstrong the concept of 'myth-symbol complex' to help account for the slowly changing cultural elements that form the boundaries between communities. In the present essay he underlines the need for deeper study of the relations between religious myths and symbols and nationalism – something that I and others have recently sought to explore in more depth. But, not only religious, also political, social and linguistic myths, memories and traditions require systematic exploration, if we are to grasp the individuality, as well as the continuity amid change, of ethnicity and nations.[3]

In this context, myths of ethnic election have played a vital role in both ethnic survival and national persistence. This is the subject of Bruce Cauthen's cogent analysis of my ethno-symbolic approach to the issue, and its application to the histories of a variety of peoples. His own contribution illuminates the role that myths of divine election have played throughout the history of the USA, and particularly in the later twentieth century. Far from receding with secularisation, as many predicted, such religiously based myths have experienced a revival, under Presidents Reagan and Bush and following the tragic events of 11 September 2001. He ends with the intriguing question of whether the present troubled Franco-American relationship may not also stem from a conflict of 'chosen peoples' and their respective missionary myths of election.

3. *Ethnie and nation*. The relationship between *ethnies* and nations is the nub of the challenge, and the problems, of Walker Connor's trenchant critique of my position. Of course, any such inquiry involves the problem of

definitions; and here I am taken to task for supplying too wide and supple a definition of the 'nation', one that confuses it with loyalty to the state – a criticism also made by Montserrat Guibernau, when she cogently identifies the flaws in what she terms my 'classic definition' of the concept of the nation. For Walker Connor, the term 'nationalism' (or ethno-nationalism) should be confined to the largest group of people sharing a conviction of common ancestry, while the term 'patriotism' should be reserved for civic or state loyalty.

Now, I have always been indebted to Walker Connor for his clear and strong insistence on the centrality of ethnic identity in the explanation of nations and nationalism, at a time when very few wished to acknowledge this, or even mention ethnicity in this context (1994, Ch. 8). Nevertheless, though his definition has a persuasive logic, it fails, in my opinion, to do full justice to the historical and sociological complexity of nations. In a short rejoinder, it is impossible to discuss so large a question. At the most general level, try as we must to be rigorous, in this field of study conceptual precision can be bought at too great a sociological cost. What we need are concepts that delimit boundaries, not ones that seek to capture often elusive 'essences'. Now, while there is a crucial analytic distinction between the concepts of state and nation (and my later revised definition of the 'nation' in *Geopolitics* (2002) and my paper for the 2004 ASEN Conference acknowledges this), in practice there is also a good deal of overlap in many cases; and given the connotations of 'patriotism' with kinship (e.g. 'fatherland'), I doubt that we can draw any hard-and-fast line between it and nationalism. For example, I find it impossible to distinguish the 'patriotism' from the nationalism of the Swiss, but they are quite different from, say, Rhaetian or Ticinese ethnic sentiment; yet such a distinction cannot easily be made in Connor's terms. As he asserts, what counts is sentient history, not actual history: the Swiss as a whole feel they have been a nation for many generations and possess a common foundation myth, even though the original 'Alemannic' forest cantons were later joined by others from different ethnic groups – as, after all, were the English, the French, the Greeks or the Italians, only rather earlier.[4]

What I am arguing is that, while most nations are formed and crystallise on the basis of a dominant *ethnie*, they may, and often do, expand and 'develop away' from that original base and to some extent from its ancestry myth. Myths of descent are vital defining characteristics of *ethnies*, but much less so of nations. Other myths, memories, symbols and traditions (many of them admittedly pertaining to the dominant *ethnie*) become important, along with novel processes like residence in and attachment to the homeland, the dissemination of a distinctive public culture and the elaboration of rights and duties in standardised laws and customs. Incidentally, with regard to the latter two processes, it is important to note that neither require a national state for their creation and dissemination: they can operate quite well in religious communities like the *millets* of the Ottoman empire.

The problem of the relationship between *ethnie* and nation is also taken up by Thomas Eriksen in his generous appreciation of my work. It appears that, at a general, theoretical level, we are in broad agreement, though I have come round to his view that no real distinction can be made between (ancestry) myths and historical memories – and often now I speak of myth-memories, for example, of the golden age. On the other hand, Eriksen adds two dimensions – interpersonal networks and negative stereotyping – to my list of elements that define *ethnies*. They are undoubtedly vital to all group relations, but I wonder whether they are specific to *ethnic* communities, and should they therefore be included among the necessary dimensions of ethnicity?

Eriksen's article is particularly rewarding in its testing of the nature and extent of linkages between *ethnies* and nations. For, though I have always denied a simple correspondence view of their relations, I have also argued for the centrality of *ethnies* and ethnic cultures in the genesis and development of many, if not most, nations. For Eriksen, metaphoric kinship and metaphoric place are the 'prime movers' in collective identification, but, though ethnicity is the most important, it is not the only basis for nations. Now, it may be that a minority of present-day nations, or should we say 'nations-in-formation', do not have ethnic bases – Eriksen cites Eritrea and South Africa; but can we legitimately term these and other ethnically heterogeneous African (and some Asian) states 'nations', even when they display a vibrant nationalism? Can we not have nationalism without nations, as we can have nations without nationalism, and is there not much more to the concept of 'nation', on which Eriksen is silent?

4. *Dominant ethnies.* Ethnicity, this time dominant ethnicity and its relationship to different forms of nationhood, is also the focus of the cogently
   argued analysis and appreciation by Eric Kaufmann and Oliver Zimmer.
   For Kaufmann, the issue is to take the idea of contemporary dominant
   ethnicity further than I have done, and less equivocally, by showing how
   such *ethnies* delimit national boundaries as well as national cultures, even in
   'civic' and 'plural' nationalisms like (respectively) the French and
   American. These points are well taken, though my main concern has been
   with the significance of dominant ethnicity for the development and
   persistence of nations and nationalism rather than as a topic in its own right
   (which it surely is). Oliver Zimmer, while agreeing with my strategy of
   detaching the civic-ethnic distinction from its normative moorings, is
   critical of a treatment of concepts of organic versus voluntarist nationalism
   in terms of ideas rather than as mechanisms or metaphors in the
   construction of nationalist arguments. This is a valid point, but there is
   also a danger here of sociological reductionism. Ideas, to paraphrase
   Durkheim, have a life of their own, and nationalists often operate with
   received conceptual traditions. I hope at some point in the future to return
   to these issues. (I return to the issues of globalisation and ethnic-civic
   conceptions, below.)

5. *Routes of nation-formation*. The articles by Joshua Fishman and Miroslav Hroch focus on aspects of the 'ethnic' route to nationhood. Fishman's elaborate taxonomy of language corpus planning highlights the tendencies for linguistic purity and uniqueness sought by many nationalist movements in their attempts to modernise and upgrade their linguistic heritage. Both are dimensions of the quest for national 'authenticity' which is such a central feature of modern nationalism. For Hroch, the shift from *ethnie* to nation, which he exemplifies by a detailed analysis of the Czech case, can be explained in terms of his well-known three-phase theory, especially the move from phase A of intellectual circles to phase B, that of the political agitation. Of course, nothing in this development was predetermined; its outcome, acceptance of the (ethno-) linguistic Czech nation, propounded by Josef Jungmann in 1806, was more an example of the influence of Enlightenment patriotism applied to the need for social and linguistic equality for the artisans and peasants of Bohemia by the intellectuals than of Herderian Romanticism (though Herder's arguments were influential and would become even more so as the century progressed).

John Hutchinson's rich and wide-ranging account of the ideas and strategies of national revivalism also builds on the idea of a returning intelligentsia imbued with revolutionary Romanticism to create 'ethnic' nations through a vernacular mobilisation of 'the people'. Pointing to the role of revivalists as moral innovators aiming to 'regenerate' their communities, Hutchinson provides many examples of the ways in which a revolutionary national Romanticism, through its new conceptions of history, homelands, vernacular culture and a political community of sacrifice, has offered a viable third way in place of neo-traditionalism and westernising assimilation for communities assailed by Western modernity. In fact, heroic sacrifice turns out to be the most potent of these conceptions, with the Easter Rebellion of 1916 in Dublin a vivid case in point. Yet, significantly, the new *national* myths of heroic sacrifice do not replace older ethno-religious myths; the national myth is an overlay of tradition, and is presented as a renovation when older myths fail.

6. *Impact of nationalism*. The ideas of the nationalists themselves have had a deep and lasting impact on all areas of society and culture. In her article on national art, Athena Leoussi focuses on their impact on the subjects and forms of painting over the last two centuries, and more especially on the nationalisation of each nation's ethno-symbolic repertoire. Her rich and comprehensive survey reveals how, in each of the traditional genres, nationalism expanded the existing subject-matter and introduced new kinds, notably of ethno-history, peasants and ethnoscapes. One could, of course, go back further, to the Dutch golden age, perhaps even to the Renaissance; and one could also trace many national artistic motifs back to their Christian and classical sources. But, as Leoussi demonstrates, just as the abstract nation stood in need of art and artists to make it accessible and palpable, so the artists readily responded to the historicist 'political

archaeology' of modern nationalism and the aesthetic forms and ethno-symbolic contents of the national ideal.

7. *Types of nationalism*. The various kinds of nationalism resulting, I would argue, from different routes of nation-formation, are often summarised in the 'civic-ethnic' distinction. Though it has considerable analytical use, as in Oliver Zimmer's work on Switzerland, this distinction is sometimes overdrawn.[5] Most examples of nations and nationalism contain elements of both in varying proportions; and a given example will often, over time, oscillate between these two conceptions. The reason is that both relate to a community, not to a state or territory *per se* – with history and culture as pivotal links between the versions of community that they emphasize. (France, often upheld as an example of civic nationalism, presumes a commonality of culture and history – and the history and culture are mainly those of a dominant *ethnie*.) What, then, of the 'plural' nations which for Walker Connor can only be states? Here, the importance of dominant ethnicity becomes apparent (and therefore it is as much a case of nationalism as of 'patriotism', in Connor's terms). In the USA and Australia, at least, there was a dominant settler *ethnie* (in Canada, two), whose history, culture, language and law became the basis of a subsequent nation with its own 'vernacular ancestralism'. This remained the case to a large degree even when the state began to admit great numbers of ethnically different migrants, which resulted in a union of *ethnies* under the hegemony of the British-originating *ethnie* and its culture (which remains in place even after the decline of the dominant *ethnie* itself). To this triple distinction, Tønnesson and Antlov (1996) added a fourth type, that of a 'class' route to nationhood. But I must confess that the Asian communist nationalisms which they cite appear remarkably close to the civic nationalism of France during the Revolution, which also directed its struggle against the social elite of its own *ethnie* (while denouncing it as alien 'Franks').[6]

8. *Supercession of nationalism*. Not surprisingly, my scepticism towards the modernist (and post-modern) approach to a 'post-national' globalisation has attracted some attention. The points made by Eric Kaufmann in this regard, notably the massive shift in middle-class values to a liberal non-ethnic individualism, are well taken, but they should be read in conjunction with the evidence of ethno-religious revival based on the Puritan traditions of the dominant *ethnie* in the USA presented by Bruce Cauthen (see above). (I should add that, since my earlier foray into this vexed territory, I have moved back in time to consider problems of ethnic and national periodisation and of the religious sources of national identity.) As far as I can see, the basic situation in the West has not changed that radically. Despite the impact of globalisation and its psychological concomitants on the 'hybridising' of national identities, we still see plenty of evidence of the resilience of dominant ethnicity at the helm of national states which were supposed to have become obsolete, even in the heart of Europe, notably in France. One only has to recall periodic ethnic backlashes against

immigration and asylum-seekers, or for that matter, against too close European integration, in several of the European states. Moreover, the inter-national system whose ideologues may seek the supersession of nationalism, has itself become one of the chief bulwarks of nations and catalysts of nationalisms in a multipolar world – in the West, and not just in Africa and Asia.

Is this largely a 'spectacle nationalism', as Mary Kaldor argues? Apart from the everyday, banal nationalism in the West proposed by Michael Billig (1995), the huge outlay in military hardware, the endless diplomatic conflicts, the majority backlash against immigration, often racist in character, the spirited defence of national culture and institutions, and the continuing controls exercised by national states in the West over their populations, can hardly be dismissed as 'spectacle nationalism'. Nor, in another, profounder sense, can the great national remembrance ceremonies, for all their undoubted 'spectacle'. But the main point of Kaldor's vigorous defence of the modernist cosmopolitan critique of nationalism against its critics (including myself), is to highlight the constructed, political nature of nationalism and the closed, violent, homogenising and exclusive character of the 'new nationalism' to be found from Bosnia and Croatia, Nagorno-Karabagh and Chechnya, to India and Pakistan, Algeria, Iran, Turkey and America (Christian fundamentalism and Zionism in the Republican Party), not to mention the Lord's Resistance Army in Uganda, and Bin Laden's ideology of global Islam. But, in the absence of a clear definition, it becomes impossible to relate all these disparate religious and political groups to 'nationalism', or indeed the latter to the consequences of the structural needs of the modern state and industrialism. Besides, every ideology is politically constructed; the point is to account for its wide appeal. The use of a simple, normative 'forward-looking/backward-looking' dichotomy centred on cultural diversity and homogeneity, with some small European nationalisms in Scotland, Catalonia and Transylvania in the cosmopolitan progressive camp, alongside Europeanism and globalism, while the rest are consigned to an extremist, closed and dark past, can hardly enlighten us on the nature and goals of such a wide array of religious and political groups and movements. Mary Kaldor sees nationalism's return to the past, to a 'golden age', as a case of 'blocking pastism'. But this is to misunderstand the aims of nationalists, which are not to recreate the past in the present, but to use its example as an inspiration and means for renewing decayed or fragmented societies, so as to make them viable and confident in the face of the pressures of modernity. Besides, can we be so sure that a world of purely future-oriented men and women would lack passion and violence?[7]

Surely, matters are not that black and white. As Stein Tønnesson argues, the effects of globalisation, understood as rapidly expanding trade, investments, financial flows, travel, information and other forms of worldwide communication, have been ambiguous, especially for the national quality of states. I would agree with him that the shift in the powers and functions of the state from the economic and military to the social and cultural spheres, represents a major transformation, but I cannot see it seriously weakening the national state; indeed, with every year the state's intrusive powers are more keenly felt by all sectors of society – not least in the universities!

In the foreign policy field, as recent international events demonstrate, and as Tønnesson rightly underlines, national states are proving to be quite independent-minded. His discussion of the relative chances of different kinds of national state to adapt to market-oriented globalisation is lucid and instructive, including his interesting defence of the 'nation-building' model in many areas of the world. His recipe of 'nationalist globalisation' (my term), i.e. open, flexible adaptation to the emerging global economy, *but* as a consciously *national* collectivity, one with a clear national identity and shared national ideals, has much to commend it.

Finally, I return to the vexed but crucial issue of the nature and dating of nations.

This is a subject of intense scholarly discussion. Montserrat Guibernau, concentrating on the case of nations without states, demonstrates the confusion between 'state' and 'nation' in my earlier ('classic') definition of the nation. This is aptly illustrated by the case of Catalonia, which reveals the ability of nations to survive without a state over long periods, even if its culture is repressed and hence no longer 'public' (though still shared and intensely prized). Yet, at the end of her incisive and stimulating contribution, Guibernau appears to bring the two concepts together again in a somewhat puzzling manner, when she discusses the 'political' dimension of national identity and its relationship to the concept of the 'nation-state' – a term I try to avoid using. (Incidentally, I *have* provided a revised ethno-symbolic definition of the concept of 'national identity'.[8])

Montserrat Guibernau's main point is close to Connor's; indeed, she appears to accept his psychological definition of the nation as a sociocultural community (namely, a collective belief in ancestral relatedness), and correctly analyses my own move away from my earlier more modernist ('classic') definition, and the reasons behind it. Yet, it is only fair to point out that the earlier definition was more 'political' in orientation, and more tied to my political definition of the modern ideology and movement of nationalism than the later and broader revised version, of which she seems to be somewhat more approving.

There is a more basic point here. The 'nation' is not an essence or fixed state that is either present or absent, or that one either possesses or lacks, as Guibernau and Connor appear at times to imply. It is a precipitate of a set of processes which are variable in extent and intensity, and which may combine to produce a type of community that approximates, more or less, to the ideal-type of the nation. Hence, we can trace the appearance and degree of the relevant processes of nation-formation; the fact that the extent or intensity of one or other of them is diminished (perhaps as a result of external *force majeure*, as with Catalonia under Franco) serves only to distance the community from approximating to the ideal-type to some (small or large) degree, not to extinguish it as a nation. For this reason, we can speak of cultural collectivity X or Y being closer to or more distant from the ideal-type in a given period – with the specific cultural content being relatively open and subject to revision, though always within the limits of a particular cultural tradition.

In its recent form, the issue of 'dating the nation' was initiated by Walker Connor.[9] His argument, which would regard with suspicion any date for the nation earlier than the late nineteenth century, hinges on his characterisation of the nation and nationalism as 'mass' phenomena. I share his view that the ideology and movement of nationalism are modern, including their mobilising appeal to 'the masses', as indeed are most present-day nations – though I think some of them emerged earlier than he allows. But this consensus conceals a hornet's nest of problems. For Walker Connor, the key to the question of dating the nation is evidence of national consciousness across a broad spectrum of the putative nation, since for Connor 'mass' signifies the whole population, including the elites, and not just the 'masses' or lower classes. But, how does one elucidate the sentiments and consciousness of the majority of any population, particularly in pre-modern periods? Connor is acutely aware of the problems here. He contends that, unless one has other evidence to support documentary statements which in pre-modern epochs are inevitably elite records, the peasants being largely isolated, illiterate and mute, one cannot make any claims about the existence of a given nation. For contemporary nations, this means that we cannot give credence to assertions of their existence prior to the late nineteenth century.

But, this is largely an argument from silence. For Connor sweepingly dismisses the sources used by ancient or medieval historians as simply 'assertions'. But I see no reason to do so. We, at this distance of time, cannot *know* whether the elites of that period (who by virtue of living in that earlier period surely knew more than we) had a clear notion of sentiments lower down the social scale. So why should we assume that the peasants and artisans did *not* possess any such sentiments? (They often did have them in the case of religion.) It would certainly help to have other supporting evidence – of mass mobilisation in war, or large-scale ethnic protests or riots or persecutions, or of great popular festivals – and in some cases this evidence is available. But to argue that, without such evidence, we cannot say anything at all about the possibility of nations existing before the late nineteenth century is to leap too far in the opposite direction.

Walker Connor twice avers that he never said that nations might not exist in pre-modern times. But, in point of fact, his test for the presence of nations appears to rule out this possibility. It is, after all, only from the late nineteenth century that evidence of the (mainly head-counting) kind that he would credit becomes sufficiently abundant to enable a judgment to be made one way or the other. This is surely too restrictive a criterion. For how can we, at this distance in time, *know* that '... very often the elites' conceptions of the nation did not even extend to the masses'?

I should add that the same criterion of evidence would have to be applied to ethnic identity which, Walker Connor tells us, has been a 'fixture' throughout history. For ethnic identity, too, is, presumably, a phenomenon of 'mass consciousness', and one where we are also reliant upon the records left us by ethnic elites.

All this, to my mind, conflicts with Walker Connor's repeated insistence on the evolutionary character of the nation ('nation-formation is a process'), whose stages in a long process cannot be easily dated. Notwithstanding, Connor goes on to assert that it is only almost at the end of the process, when the majority of the population are aware that they belong to the nation, that a nation can be said to exist. (This does not take into account the shifting/ expanding borders of the 'nation', and hence the nature and size of the population, the consciousness of the majority of whose members is being sought.) But, allowing for the teleology of this framework, why only at the end of the process? Why not at the beginning, or in the middle, of the trajectory of nation-formation? Because, for Walker Connor, it is only at that point when the nation mobilises large numbers of people that it becomes a 'major force in history' – and this is, after all, what really interests the students of nations and nationalism. (This, too, is a rather restrictive criterion of significance.) But we could just as well argue that the nation was a major force in history when elites led the populace to victory (or defeat) in sixteenth century Europe, at the time of the Armada or the Dutch revolt, or even earlier, with the Swiss peasants at Sempach, or Wallace's mass army at Stirling Bridge – or indeed with the Israelites under Saul and Jonathan on Mount Gilboa when the 'mighty were fallen in battle'! Whether all the peasants who fought in these armies possessed national consciousness, we may never know. We can only judge the actions and the results.

The nation, in Connor's words, implies a single group consciousness that transcends the appeal of all lesser divisions within the group – though not all the time, as recent history reminds us (the Russian Civil War or Vichy France, for example). Even in these cases, the nation continued to exist, though its nationalism was temporarily eclipsed or fragmented. My point is that we cannot know that such a single group consciousness did not exist in some states or *ethnies* in the sixteenth century or even earlier, simply because we don't have the right kind of evidence of mass activity or consciousness.

Secondly, I cannot agree that nations are only consequential when their appeal 'has extended to all major segments of the people bearing the nation's appellation'. It may be enough, as Adrian Hastings remarked, for a significant section of the population outside the ruling class to feel that they belong to the nation, for us to speak of this population as a 'nation', and for it to be an effective force in history – though I would add that other processes of nation-formation would have to be well-developed (Hastings 1997: 26). Of course, this is not the secular 'modern Western nation' with its clearcut borders, its status as a legal-political community, its mass consciousness and its nationalist legitimation (see Smith 2004). It is, if you like, an elite or a middle-class nation, with a distinct public culture, a sense of historic homeland, shared myths and memories, a clear self-definition, and standardised laws and customs (though not usually political rights). And even if we cannot know, as Walker Connor himself contends, exactly how many members of a people must internalise a national identity to make appeals to it an effective force, this earlier kind of nation is just as effective for mobilising large numbers of people as the 'mass nation' of modernity.

But it would take another book to support these claims.

Notes

1 See Peel (1989: 198–215). For the debate about 'navel-less' nations between Ernest Gellner and myself, see Ernest Gellner (1996, 366–70).

2 For a fuller statement of 'ethno-symbolism', see Smith (1999, Introduction).

3 See the work of Hastings (1997 and 2003), Van der Veer and Lehmann (1999), and Smith (2003).

4 For Swiss history and myth, see Im Hof (1991) and Kreis (1991). For my earlier ('classic') definition of the concept of the nation, see Smith (1991: ch. 1); for the revised definition, see Smith (2002).

5 For which, see Zimmer (2003). For popular usages, see Ignatieff (1993).

6 On these nationalisms, see Tønnesson and Antlov (1996).

7 Similar problems beset Mark Juergensmeyer's (1993) account of 'religious nationalisms', on which see Greenfeld (1996).

8 For my later ethno-symbolic definition of 'national identity', as 'the continuous reproduction and reinterpretation of the pattern of values, symbols, memories, myths and traditions that compose the distinctive heritage of nations, and the identification of individuals with that pattern and heritage and with its cultural elements', see Smith (2001: 18).

9 See Connor (1990). For recent discussion and applications, see the essays devoted to the issue in *Geopolitics* 7(2): 2002. As must be clear, I do not share Connor's emphasis on the 'mass' nature of nations. This is an attribute of the modern Western variant of the nation, but not necessarily of the 'nation' as such. Besides, other processes are more important for the formation of nations; on which, see Smith (2002) and (2004).

References

Armstrong, John. 1982. *Nations before Nationalism*. Chapel/Hill, NC: University of North Carolina Press.

Billig, Michael. 1995. *Banal Nationalism*. London: Sage.

Connor, Walker. 1990. 'When is a nation?', *Ethnic and Racial Studies* 13(1): 92–103.

Connor, Walker. 1994. *Ethno-nationalism: the Quest for Understanding*. Princeton, NJ: Princeton University Press.

Gellner, Ernest. 1996. 'Do nations have navels?', *Nations and Nationalism* 2(3): 366–70.

Greenfeld, Liah. 1996. 'The modern religion?', *Critical Review* 10(2): 169–91.

Hastings, Adrian. 1997. *The Construction of Nationhood*. Cambridge: Cambridge University Press.

Hastings, Adrian. 2003. 'Holy lands and their political consequences', *Nations and Nationalism* 9(1): 29–54.

Ignatieff, Michael. 1993. *Blood and Belonging: Journeys into the New Nationalism*. London: Chatto and Windus.

Im Hof, Ulrich. 1991. *Mythos Schweiz: Nation-Identität-Geschichte, 1291–1991*. Zurich: Neue Zurcher.

Juergensmeyer, Mark. 1993. *The New Cold War? Religious Nationalism Confronts the Secular State*. Berkeley CA: University of California Press.

Kreis, Georg. 1991. *Der Mythos von 1291: Zur Enstehung der Schweizerischen Nationalfeiertags*. Basel: Friedrich Reinhardt.

Peel, John. 1989. 'The cultural work of Yoruba ethno-genesis', in Elisabeth Tonkin, Maryon McDonald and Malcolm Chapman (eds.), *History and Ethnicity*. London: Routledge.

Smith, Anthony D. 1991. *National Identity*. Harmondsworth: Penguin.

Smith, Anthony D. 1999. *Myths and Memories of the Nation*. Oxford: Oxford University Press.

Smith, Anthony D. 2001. *Nationalism: Theory, Ideology, History*. Cambridge: Polity.

Smith, Anthony D. 2002. 'When is a nation?', *Geopolitics* 7(2): 5–32.

Smith, Anthony D. 2003. *Chosen Peoples: Sacred Sources of National Identity*. Oxford: Oxford University Press.

Smith, Anthony D. 2004. 'Genealogies of the nation', Paper presented to ASEN Conference, LSE, April 2004.

Tønnesson, Stein and Hans Antlov (eds.). 1996. *Asian Forms of the Nation*. Richmond, Surrey: Curzon.

Van der Veer, Peter and Hartmut Lehmann (eds.). 1999. *Nation and Religion*. Princeton, NJ: Princeton University Press.

Zimmer, Oliver. 2003. *A Contested Nation: History, Memory and Nationalism in Switzerland, 1761–1891*. Cambridge: Cambridge University Press.

INDEX